BECOMING A JOYFUL LAWYER

Contemplative Training in Non-Distraction, Empathy, and Emotional Wisdom

BY

DEBORAH CALLOWAY

BECOMING A JOYFUL LAWYER
Contemplative Training in Non-Distraction, Empathy, and Emotional Wisdom

In *Becoming a Joyful Lawyer,* law professor Deborah Calloway, presents a splendid guidebook to happiness in lawyering through contemplative practices. Grounded in her experience with contemplative practice and with lawyering and legal education, *Becoming a Joyful Lawyer* is comprehensive, clear, and practical, as well as inspirational. And it is suffused with good sense and good wishes. This is a major contribution.

Leonard L. Riskin,
Chesterfield Smith Professor of Law
University of Florida Levin College of Law

Visiting Professor
Northwestern University School of Law

Becoming a Joyful Lawyer presents a concise, highly readable guide to effectively integrating meditation into your law practice and day to day life. For me, the practice of law has oft been filled with aggression, acrimony and, above all things, stress. Deborah Calloway's primer on meditation provides the techniques to neutralize these negative emotions and instead attempt to calmly embody the present. Her strategies have helped me to become a better listener, to be less distracted and more productive, to better react to adverse interactions, and to develop a greater sense empathy both in my professional and personal relationships. Simply put, this book will completely change your perspective.

Jennifer Y. Montgomery
Staff Attorney
State Elections Enforcement Commission
Connecticut

Whether you are a law student sweating through your first summer job, or a seasoned attorney at the pinnacle of your career, the intrinsic joy of the legal profession is yours to discover by practicing the meditative exercises set forth in Professor Calloway's guidebook to cultivating mindfulness, *Becoming a Joyful Lawyer: Contemplative Training in Non-Distraction, Empathy and Emotional Wisdom.* I know this truth from first-hand experience, having had the good fortune of attending Professor Calloway's class, Contemplative Lawyering, while a second year student at the University of Connecticut School of Law. Over the course of a semester, for an hour each morning, we gradually learned the mindfulness techniques set forth in this book—techniques which have undoubtedly enriched my practice as a busy associate at a law firm in Hartford. These meditation and post-meditation practices, when followed with care and discipline, will allow you to become a better listener, a more efficient researcher, and a joyful practitioner of our honorable, precious craft. I am grateful that Professor Calloway has shared her beneficial instructions and insights in this volume and I join in her hope that you, too, may find joy in the legal profession—the joy of mindfulness.

Gavah Meehan, Esq.
Cowdery, Eckert & Murphy, L.L.C.
Hartford, Connecticut

With many years of experience both in the legal profession and in practicing and teaching meditation, Deborah Calloway is uniquely qualified to make traditional Buddhist mind-training techniques accessible and helpful to lawyers. She understands how stressful the practice of law can be. She understands why many lawyers experience alienation, depression, and burnout. And yet her message is that the practice of law may be experienced in a completely different way.

In *Becoming a Joyful Lawyer*, Deborah presents a complete path to transformational experiences of serenity, joy, and deep fulfillment in the practice of law. The clear and accessible language and style make this book timely and fresh. The graduated levels and types of practices she presents are traditional in essence, yet modern in form. The practice instructions are detailed and yet not too technical. They are suitable for beginners as well as those more experienced in traditional forms of meditation. The book provides a simplified, yet complete overview and practice manual, one which uses ordinary language and terms offering a fresh and pithy view of the essential points of Buddhist practice. The practice instructions themselves are accompanied by a wealth of first-hand stories, observations, and insights drawn from the author's and her students' deeply-lived personal experiences. These all work together synergistically to offer a depth and range of perspectives that is valuable for practitioners of all levels.

Andrew Schuler is a long-time practitioner of Tibetan Buddhism. He has studied with Chögyam Trungpa Rinpoche and, more recently , is a student of Jetsün Khandro Rinpoche.

SUMMARY OF CONTENTS

PART III
Working with Emotions & Conflict

CONTENTS

CHAPTER 11
Cultivating Loving Kindness & Compassion for Individuals Who Intentionally Harm Others

CHAPTER 12
Loving Kindness & Compassion in the Context of Legal Practice.

PART III
WORKING WITH EMOTIONS & CONFLICT.

CHAPTER 13
Patience in Small Matters

PREFACE

Many articles have been written and published that talk about the benefits of meditation practice for legal practitioners. This book takes the next step by providing instructions in contemplative practices and providing guidance for bringing the skills learned in those practices into your legal practice and your life beyond legal practice.

My experience in meditation practice made me aware of the potential benefits of contemplative practice for lawyers. With this knowledge in mind, I created and teach a course based on meditation practices called Contemplative Lawyering. I took what I learned in a spiritual context and applied it to the secular environment of lawyering. I have shared the materials I developed for this course with law professors and legal practitioners who have encouraged me to make them available as widely as possible. In answer to these requests I have written and published this book.

Buddhism has religious trappings, but what is presented in this book is not religion. Buddhist teachings provide methods, practices, and scholarly writings about working with our mind—getting to know our own mind to discover its nature and how it functions. Meditation practices help us work with our mind and discover that mind's basic nature or basic state is free from confusion and complexity—its basic nature is calm, peaceful, and full of joy, clarity, compassion, and wisdom. At the same time we discover the nature of our daily experience of aggression, desire, and other disturbing emotions and learn how to work skillfully with our confusion and emotions.

My aspiration is that lawyers and law students who read this book and engage in the meditation practices presented here will benefit on a personal level. Further, my aspiration is that by engaging in these practices, lawyers will realize their inherent wisdom and compassion and that this understanding will allow them to work more skillfully with clients, staff, colleagues, judges, legal opponents, family, friends, and other individuals they encounter in their world of work and beyond.

ACKNOWLEDGMENTS

There are many individuals who have contributed invaluably to making this book possible. First and foremost, this book would not have been possible without the guidance and training in contemplative practices that I have received over the past eighteen years from many Buddhist teachers, but especially from Dzogchen Ponlop Rinpoche. I am deeply grateful to Rinpoche for providing me with the skills necessary to benefit others in this way. This book also would not have been possible without the support I have received from the University of Connecticut School of Law. In 2005, long before mindfulness training in professional education became popular, the University of Connecticut School of Law approved my proposed course, *Contemplative Lawyering*, which uses contemplative practices to teach essential legal skills. It was in the context of teaching this course that I wrote the materials that now appear in this book, materials that use secular language to make practices I learned in my Buddhist practice accessible in a non-religious context.

With respect to the specific materials that appear in this book, I owe a debt of gratitude to the students, professors, and lawyers who have participated in my *Contemplative Lawyering* courses over the last seven years. Many of them have generously permitted me to use their journal entries to illustrate the material I am presenting here. In addition, their comments and questions helped me recognize and respond more accurately to the needs of practicing lawyers. For example, the participants in these classes alerted me to the need to present practices designed to help lawyers work with sadness and fear.

The material in this book also reflects the contributions of lawyers who engage in contemplative practice. Susan Busby, David Kulle, and Andrew Spurrier are Connecticut attorneys who shared their experiences with my students and also have permitted me to include their insights in this book. Attorneys Carmen Rumbaut from Madison, Wisconsin and Kris Shaw from Seattle, Washington also generously shared experiences with me that are reflected in the materials offered in this book.

Chapter 11, *Cultivating Kindness and Compassion for Individuals who Intentionally Harm Others*, would not have been possible without the generosity of a young female kidnapping and assault victim who not only shared her experience of generating compassion with the students in my class, but also agreed to have her remarks transcribed and included in this book.

Charles Halpern (Director of the Berkeley Initiative for Mindfulness in Law)[1] and Professor Leonard Riskin (University of Florida)[2] contributed by promoting my course, writings, and course materials; by providing me with opportunities to interact with other lawyer/meditators; and by offering me opportunities to publish articles based on the materials in this book.[3]

---

1   Charles Halpern also created the *Center for Contemplative Mind in Society* which began to infuse a contemplative dimension into law, journalism, and business.

2   Professor Riskin also serves as the Director of the Initiative on Mindfulness in Law and Dispute Resolution.

3   See Deborah Calloway, *Using Mindfulness Practice to Work with Emotions*, 10 NEV. L. JOURNAL 338 (2010).

Many other lawyers, professors, and meditators have used or read these materials in earlier drafts and provided not only helpful comments, but also strong support for sharing these materials as widely as possible. In this regard I would especially like to thank Professor Lofty Becker, Dean Jeremy Paul, Bryan Castater, Patrick Lee, and Andrew Schuler. It was this repeated and consistent encouragement that moved me to create the final version of this book.

Finally, I want to acknowledge and thank Emily Kagan for proofing, editing, and providing substantive suggestions while preparing the final manuscript as well as Christine Hwang who provided the layout, design, artistic, and publishing skills necessary to bring this book to press.

INTRODUCTION

"In my practice, I see a great deal of fear, cloaked by anger and sadness. Being familiar with my own habitual reactions and being able to sit with my own emotions enables me to watch and participate, but not get caught up in the emotional reactions of others. This ability to forbear without judgment can be taught to clients and helps them avoid being cast in a leading role in the dramas created by the opposing party or counsel. The simple mindfulness practice of observing what arises without judgment or labeling—bringing awareness to habitual tendencies to respond or react and then allowing some space before acting—can help clients stay present in the moment without getting caught up in overpowering emotions."

> *(Susan V. Busby, A Practice with Heart (Connecticut Lawyer, December 2007/January 2008))*

"When I am truly professional, I am truly practicing contemplatively, and I can facilitate the best result that my clients can access at that time. My clients do not always reach agreement. However, due to my contemplative practice, I define professional success as helping my clients understand what lies beneath their positions. If they need to litigate—and I deeply respect the fact that some do—my clients will know why they have that need, and can better articulate it to their attorney or the judge."

> *(Andrew Spurrier, Connecticut Family Court Mediator)*

THE LIFE OF A LAWYER

After law school, I was one of the fortunate ones, securing a "dream" position in a prestigious law firm earning a good salary.

Like most new attorneys my day was controlled by my supervising partner. He was a bright and affable attorney, very pleasant. On the other hand, he viewed me as a sex object. Naively, I thought he would back off when my swelling midsection (pregnant) transformed my body into something resembling a watermelon. I was wrong. He loved my pregnancy-enhanced cleavage and ignored evidence of my happy marriage. He regaled our secretary with wisecracks about my appearance and loudly boasted about fathering my baby. I worked hard on my legal assignments and tried my best to shrug off his remarks.

However, one afternoon I delivered some research results to him in his office. Without even acknowledging me, he said to the partner he was meeting with, "Don't you love how she looks in that tight sweater!?" Perhaps I shouldn't have been wearing a tight sweater. It was tight because I was pregnant not because I was trying to be alluring. I had not yet acquired a new wardrobe to accommodate my expanding frame. His comment made me regret this oversight. While his comment appeared to be sexual, its fundamental nature was an exercise of power. His tone was condescending, his demeanor jovial. Could he possibly have thought I would appreciate this remark? Maybe he would realize his mistake if he really thought about it. But he didn't think—he just spoke. He was amused. Aggression lurked beneath his jovial demeanor. He had the power to get away with it. He was a full partner and my supervisor. I was a lowly associate in my first year at the firm.

What could I say? His remark left me speechless. He didn't even ask me why I was there. I froze like a deer in the oncoming headlights of a car. I could think of no skillful response. I wanted nothing more at that moment than to be capable of generating a skillful response. I couldn't. Struggling to maintain my composure, I silently turned my back and walked away.

I said nothing, but my mind replayed this scene over and over experimenting with various responses, hoping to discover a response that would force him to recognize how wrong he was, a response that would put me in control of our relationship, a response that would relieve my distress, my sadness, and my fear that it would happen again. Like Bill Murray in *Groundhog Day*—reliving the experience over and over again - trying to get it right.

This experience with my supervising attorney was not unique to me or even to young female attorneys. Like most attorneys, young and old, I endured many power-based interactions that did not involve sexual overtones, experiences that resulted in anguished mental chatter—"Maybe what they are saying is true. Maybe I can't actually write my way out of a paper bag. Maybe I am over my head here. Everyone else is so smart and educated. Maybe I do not belong here. But—they don't know how to write either. Maybe they are nasty because they feel inadequate. I shouldn't be so sensitive and fearful. Perhaps I should be more aggressive and stand up for myself. But then maybe I would be nasty like them. No, I definitely do not want to be that way." Round and round.

This is what happens to lawyers over and over again—they find themselves on the receiving end of ego-centricity, self-inflated arrogance, and criticisms that are belittling and insulting rather than constructive. Many lawyers experience hostile and difficult encounters not only with supervisors and colleagues, but also with opposing lawyers and even with clients. They work in adversarial situations that seem to demand aggression and hostility. Many lawyers work with clients who are confused, conflicted, and suffering.[1] Difficult interpersonal interactions are one of the sources of stress that cause attorney's to experience high rates of depression or even leave law practice altogether.[2]

It does not have to be this way. It is possible to maintain a sense of equanimity even in the stressful world that lawyers inhabit. It is even possible to find satisfaction and inspiration. Because I did not know how to work with adversity in my environment, I suffered anguish and missed opportunities to appreciate the people I was working with and the work I was doing.

Not only were the personal interactions stressful, often the work itself was boring, repetitive, and tedious—endless document review or extensive research on picky procedural questions. This work, while mind-numbing, was tinged with fear because even

---

1   See e.g., *Why I Left the Law,* The Ethical Spectacle (July, 1997), http://www.spectacle.org/797/law.html (last visited 1/23/2012); "*Why I Don't Like Being a Lawyer*" The Verdict: The Outlaw Mom's Blawg (posted, March 14, 2011), http://lawyer-mom.com/2011/03/14/why-i-dont-like-being-a-lawyer/; MomGrind, *Being A Lawyer Sucked,* (posted July 25th, 2008) (includes multiple comments by other dissatisfied lawyers) http://momgrind.com/2008/07/25/being-a-lawyer-was-sucking-the-life-out-of-me/.

2   Tyger Latham, Psy. D., *The Depressed Lawyer,* PSYCHOLOGY TODAY, THERAPY MATTERS (MAY 2, 2011) http://www.psychologytoday.com/blog/therapy-matters/201105/the-depressed-lawyer; W.W. Eaton, J.C. Anthony, W. Mandel & R. Garrison, *Occupations and the Prevalence of Major Depressive Disorder,* 32 J. OCCUPATIONAL MED. 1079 (1990); *Depression Statistics in General & In Lawyers,* LAWYERS WITH DEPRESSION, http://www.lawyerswithdepression.com/depressionstatistics.asp; *Depression in the Legal Profession: Lawyers are the Most Likely to Be Depressed,* LAW VIBE, (Sept. 24, 2009), http://lawvibe.com/depression-in-the-legal-profession-lawyers-are-the-most-likely-to-be-depressed/.

small mistakes could be extremely costly. This attribute of attention to picky details with a potentially costly impact is shared by many legal work environments.[3]

While the situation is unavoidable, it does not have to be a source of boredom and stress. It is possible to appreciate and find satisfaction in work of this nature. Like most lawyers, I did not know this and therefore suffered a mixture of boredom and anxiety.

The money was good, but I did not attend law school with an aspiration to make a lot of money. I dreamed of protecting people from discrimination and mistreatment. Instead I found myself on the other side, working long hours to defeat discrimination claims.

One weekend, working at home, I struggling to generate the creative arguments required to destroy a class action discrimination lawsuit against one of our clients. I was interrupted by my young daughter. She asked what I was working on. I didn't want to tell her what I was doing. I didn't want to admit that I was trying to destroy what may have been a meritorious discrimination lawsuit. I suddenly felt that I had sold my brain power to the highest bidder. Working on the case made me feel like my mind was enslaved—forced to work for a cause I did not believe in.

My experiences are consistent with the experiences lawyers identify as making them unhappy with their work: unpleasant interactions, tedious but difficult work, and working on projects they do not believe in. Lawyers experience distractions, stress, and conflict

---

3   MomGrind, *Being A Lawyer Sucked*, (posted July 25th, 2008) (includes multiple comments by other dissatisfied lawyers) http://momgrind.com/2008/07/25/being-a-lawyer-was-sucking-the-life-out-of-me/ ; Sally Kane, *5 Myths Regarding the Practice of Law: Realities of Law Practice*, ABOUT.COM LEGAL CAREERS, http://legalcareers.about.com/od/practicetips/a/lawyermyths.htm (last visited 1/23/2012)

on a daily basis—phones ring, colleagues knock on the door, deadlines loom, emails bring more assignments, impatient clients (and colleagues) demand results, opposing lawyers hurl insults, clients cry, Judges threaten, computers crash, machines break, files are misplaced, the hours are long, mistakes are made, cases are lost and on and on and on. Research has established that many lawyers experience significant depression and stress.[4]

Some lawyers seek happiness by leaving law practice to do something else. But what if lawyers could find joy in law practice itself? What if lawyers could find a way to focus on tedious tasks, listen deeply to suffering clients, and interact skillfully with hostile supervisors, colleagues, and opposing lawyers? What if it is possible to be a zealous advocate and effective lawyer without abandoning personal ethics? As you will see in the materials that follow, lawyers who practice meditation report that it is indeed possible to find happiness even in the contentious and chaotic world of law practice.

How can meditation (mind training) possibly relate to lawyering? How can sitting on a cushion or a chair possibly make you a more skillful and effective lawyer, a happier lawyer, or a happier person? Lawyers who meditate have shared their stories with me. Consider what these stories reveal about the power of meditation in action in the legal workplace.

---

4 See, e.g., Joan E. Mounteer, *Depression Among Lawyers*, 3 (1) THE COLORADO LAWYER 35 (Jan. 2004). See also, material cited in note 2, infra.

HOW MEDITATION HELPS LAWYERS PRACTICE SKILLFULLY

David Kulle worked for many years as an associate and later as a partner at a large law firm litigating employment law disputes on behalf of defendants. Like any litigating attorney David has faced the daily stresses associated with a heavy workload. David meditates every day. He shared his experience of the overall impact of meditation on his life and legal practice:

> "Ultimately, for all of us, how great it would be if everything we do could be done with total mindfulness—whether it is brushing our teeth, driving to the school or work, having lunch, working on a paper, whatever we are doing. You have to be capable of freeing your intellect and focusing on the task at hand. Most of the time we know we have to work—read some cases, extract some holding, impress a colleague, whatever—and we proceed mindlessly going about our tasks, not really clear on where we are or what we are thinking about, losing that connection with the breath and with our center, not really present with what we are doing. We may be thinking about getting this project done so we can go on to the next one or we may be distracted by anxiety or boredom. There is a difference between this approach and being fully present and aware of what we are doing. This gets to the core of where meditation ultimately takes one."[5]

Susan Busby practices divorce law. Like many lawyers she encounters clients and opposing lawyers who are dealing with strong emotions. She points out that the clients who come into lawyer's offices often are people who used to have a very good relationship with someone, perhaps a spouse, a doctor, a patient,

---

5   Contemplative Lawerying Class Presentation (Unpublished Transcript)

a customer, or a vendor. That good relationship has fallen apart and the client is hurt and angry. In the divorce context, Susan sees clients who are experiencing grief, loss, fear, and feelings of worthlessness. In cases involving infidelity or theft of assets, clients may be deeply angry. In cases involving abuse, clients may be suffering from fear and psychological harm.[6]

As lawyers, we play a significant role in shaping the process of resolving disputes on behalf of the unhappy and angry people we represent. We can hurt or help the dispute resolution process.

Susan knows lawyers who actually *cause* problems by stirring people up more and identifying problems that do not really exist. She has encountered lawyers who file multiple motions seeking to enjoin behavior that really isn't worth the time and expense associated with filing motions—the father fixed food the child doesn't like, the mother failed to show up at the child's school play, the father sent dirty clothes back with the child, or the mother was late when she picked up the child from the father's house. Susan knows that these issues are important.

Divorcing parents need to work out a method of relating to each other now that they are no longer living together as a couple. However, Susan has observed that trying to resolve these issues by getting angry and filing motions simply fuels the fire of discontent and distrust without actually addressing the source of the problem which may simply be that these parents have not yet learned how to deal with parenting from separate households. This is a new situation for them. They need time to learn.

6　Contemplative Lawyering Class Presentation (Unpublished Transcript); See also, Susan V. Busby, *A Practice with Heart, Connecticut Lawyer* (Dec. 2007/Jan. 2008)

Susan's meditation practice has helped her cultivate the skills of patience and compassion that allow her to recognize the futility of filing multiple motions complaining about small matters. By encouraging her clients to be patient with respect to small matters like these, she helps them reach beneficial solutions to important financial and custody issues.

I have observed that many lawyers seem to equate advocacy with nastiness, irritability, obstruction, and lack of cooperation. They act as though they believe that digging in, refusing to cooperate and acting really tough is what it means to work as a zealous advocate for their client. In the family law context, Susan encounters lawyers who insult her clients, calling them names or falsely accusing them of inappropriate conduct such as sexually abusing their children. This kind of behavior is not excellent advocacy. Lawyers who are angry, uncooperative or untruthful end up alienating juries, judges, and opposing counsel. Cooperative and courteous lawyers who are ready to meet people half way are more effective. They accomplish more and get better results. Think about the lawyers you have known and worked with. Who do you respect the most? Which ones have the most success in terms of attracting clients and getting good results in litigation and negotiation? Are those respected lawyers pleasant, cooperative, and courteous or angry, irritable, and contentious?

Of course, the best lawyers make sure to identify and aggressively assert legal arguments on behalf of their clients. This is an essential characteristic of good lawyering. But anything that is important enough to fight about can be asserted with solid and creative arguments, diligent preparation, and well-written briefs. Aggressive and effective advocacy is completely different from being angry and insulting.

For many lawyers, the challenge is learning to maintain civility and calm when other lawyers are being aggressive, angry, insulting, uncooperative, and contentious. Meditation helps us become aware of the thoughts arising in our mind and provides us with the space to work skillfully with those thoughts. Susan Busby finds that these skills, learned through meditation practice, allow her to remain respectful and civil when she encounters aggressive and angry lawyers:

> "If I am confronted with a situation, if I don't have my fear and my anger clouding my judgment, then I can see the situation clearly. Someone may say something nasty and untrue about my client such as asserting that he is lazy or a liar or abusive. If I go into a rage about that, I have lost control. I am now just responding. I am reacting to something they have said and then we have all forgotten what were supposed to be discussing. Meditation helps me watch my thoughts arise and watch my emotions arise so I can say, 'Oh, I am getting angry at this person. Okay, I need to take a little time out.' I can then calm myself down and respond skillfully."[7]

Sometimes we get angry or defensive as a result of our own mistakes. Susan talks about dealing with the uncomfortable feelings that arise when she finds herself in a meeting with opposing attorneys and recognizes that she has overlooked an important issue:

> "I can say, 'Oh, they are raising a good point. I didn't think of that.' If my mind freezes because I am afraid, I won't be able to respond skillfully. I need to understand that I didn't think of that issue and take a break and maybe call my office to ask someone to pull up a research file. If I am in a constructive discussion

---

7   Contemplative Lawyering Class Presentation (Unpublished Transcript)

with someone I can say, 'Oh, I haven't thought of that. What are your ideas about that?' You can say this instead of completely freezing. Meditation has helped me gain the ability to watch my thoughts, recognize that I am experiencing fear, and then stop and work skillfully rather than respond automatically and defensively."[8]

HOW MEDITATION REDUCES STRESS & PROMOTES CONTENTMENT

Learning to be mindful and non-distracted can reduce stress, promote feelings of contentment, and help you work more effectively. Learning to work with conflict and emotion makes the practice of law more skillful. The contentment associated with being fully present includes a sense of appreciation and wonder. We can appreciate the amazing power of the law to support business development, protect and promote research and discovery, regulate commerce, compensate victims, protect health, welfare and the environment, and so much more. We can appreciate the amazing computers, smartphones, cars, and printers that make our work possible. We can appreciate the comfort of our office and the view out the window. We can appreciate the education we have received, the knowledge and skills we have developed, and the creativity of our arguments.

David Kulle talks about appreciating our adversary system even when litigation becomes contentious:

"I just finished a month-long jury case. I represented a company in a sexual harassment and retaliation suit. We got a judgment

---

8 Contemplative Lawyering Class Presentation (Unpublished Transcript)

for our client. It was a long, drawn-out process and there was some contentious argument and there were some nasty people involved. But I want to share with you that every time I go into a courtroom I am always struck by the great act of peace involved in partaking in a dispute resolution process in an environment like that. Hundreds of years ago and in some other countries today we would be fighting it out and killing each other in order to further our case. We don't have to do that. We don't have to resolve our disputes with guns in the street and with fighting. We are blessed that we are able to come into a pristine environment and have a judge presiding and have rules of law and protocols of the court and a sense of order that we can treasure and rely on to resolve our disputes. This makes me look at litigation in a different way."[9]

HOW MEDITATION BRINGS JOY & MEANING TO THE PRACTICE OF LAW

Meditation can promote skillful and effective lawyering, contentment and appreciation. But what takes law practice beyond contentment, appreciation, and effectiveness? What transforms representing clients into an experience of joy?

Joy comes from recognizing that practicing law provides us the opportunity to benefit others, including clients, opposing parties, partners, taxi drivers, cleaning crews, associates, secretaries, legal assistants, court personnel, family and friends—everyone we encounter. Generating an aspiration to benefit others through our legal practice brings deep meaning to our work. Seeing the positive result when we help someone resolve a complaint or when we

---

9   Contemplative Lawyering Class Presentation (Unpublished Transcript)

simply treat others with kindness brings feelings of warmth and joy.

The first thing we can do to benefit others in legal practice is simply listen. Susan Busby talks about listening in the context of representing clients who are seeking a divorce:

> "What I often tell clients is that it takes a lot of courage to come into my office and tell me their story. The stories I hear are very, very personal. Sometimes they haven't even told their therapist or their best friend or their parents or sister what is going on in their life and now they have to tell me, a stranger, what is going on. I try to create an environment that feels very safe for them, a place where they feel that they can tell me everything they need to tell me. You can create an environment that helps clients feel like they can tell you these things. One of the ways I do this is by trying to really listen, not only to what they are saying, but to what they are not saying.

> For example, recently someone came into my office. We send out a packet of information before clients come in. One item in the packet of information is a worksheet that they fill out to give us facts. When I walked into the conference room to meet this client, I had spoken with her on the phone but I had never met with her. She was sitting with her arms folded tightly against her chest. She had the worksheet carefully folded up into a very, very small package which she was holding very close to her body. I took note of that and of her body language. She started talking and I just let her talk. She mentioned that she had previously cancelled an appointment with me because she didn't want to fill out the worksheet. I knew then that there was something on the worksheet that perhaps she was embarrassed to tell me.

I let her talk until she said it. As soon as she said it, her arms opened up. She finally had the courage to get it out and then she actually slid the worksheet towards me. I think you can pick up a lot from people by watching their body language. But again it is important to really listen to what they are saying and try to keep your own agenda out of the way. If I had conducted this meeting the way I usually do, I would have said, 'Let me have the worksheet.' Then I would have gone through it. But I was really listening to what she was saying verbally and nonverbally. To me it felt like she was very hesitant to be there so I just let her determine the pace of the interview. If you can do that and get your own agenda out of the way, you can allow clients to speak to you and tell you everything that they need to tell you."[10]

Susan's approach to listening helped her get the information she needed to represent this client. But what happened in this client meeting went beyond simply gathering the information required for legal representation. Susan helped this client simply by providing her with an opportunity to be heard. When someone has lived through a traumatic experience they yearn for the opportunity to talk about it with someone who is truly listening—someone who is not lost in his or her own agenda.[11] Listening deeply to clients who are in distress provides us with information and at the same time provides clients with an opportunity to tell their story.

Listening in this way is a skill that many of us do not possess. When we listen we tend to be distracted by our own agenda and experience. Contemplative practice helps us develop the skill of

---

10   Contemplative Lawyering Class Presentation (Unpublished Transcript)

11   "Many survivors seek the resolution of their traumatic experience within the confines of their personal lives. But a significant minority, as a result of the trauma, feel called upon to engage in a wider world." Judith Herman, *Trauma and Recovery: The Aftermath of Violence—from Domestic Abuse to Political Terror* 207 (BasicBooks 1997).

being present and non-distracted. In this book, I provide a variety of formal and informal contemplative practices designed to cultivate deep listening skills.

Getting your own agenda and ego out of the way and really listening also can make it possible for you to help clients resolve their disputes. Deep undistracted listening allows you to see more clearly what clients and opponents actually want to gain in the process of resolving a dispute. These interests may not be stated explicitly, but they can be understood by listening deeply. Gaining insight into the needs and desires that are driving a dispute may make it possible for you to resolve the dispute.

I experienced the benefits of deep listening while supervising the mediation of a discrimination dispute. In this case, a middle-aged, gay male filed a discrimination complaint alleging that he was insulted and threatened by the manager of a restaurant. The plaintiff and the owners of the restaurant agreed to participate in a voluntary mediation process made available by the Mediation Clinic at the University of Connecticut School of Law.

At the first meeting, the complainant, Jack,[12] came alone. The young restaurant owner was represented by a lawyer.

Jack reported that while he and his friends were eating at the owner's restaurant, they were disturbed by the conduct of a patron at a nearby table who was visibly drunk and talking loudly. Ultimately, this patron created a mess by spilling wine on the table, the floor and neighboring diners, including Jack.

Frustrated by the situation, Jack approached the restaurant manager

---

12   Names have been changed in this account to protect privacy.

asking for the mess to be cleaned up and for the offending customer to be ejected from the restaurant. The manager, already distressed by the offending patron, shouted angrily at Jack, threatening him and using anti-gay epithets. Jack reacted with strong language of his own. The argument escalated and the manager ejected Jack and his friends from the restaurant. Even so, the shouting match continued on the sidewalk outside.

At the mediation, the restaurant owner apologized profusely. His genuine distress about what had happened was apparent. However, the owner was not the manager who offended Jack. That manager was not present at the mediation. As a result, Jack was unmoved. The owner's apology and offer to financially compensate him failed to address his concerns.

He wanted the restaurant manager in the room. The owner and his lawyer couldn't understand why this would be helpful. They couldn't understand why the owner's apology and offer of financial compensation wasn't sufficient. They were afraid to bring the offending manager to the mediation. They were afraid that Jack could use the mediation context as an opportunity to renew the confrontation. They knew that the manager, a volatile individual, would respond unskillfully and they hoped that they could avoid a blow up by keeping him away from the mediation.

However, by listening deeply I understood that the complainant was not angry. Rather, he was profoundly hurt. He had experienced terror during the altercation at the restaurant. The complainant was a middle-aged man of very small stature who suffered from a serious illness. The manager was a large, strong, and imposing young man. The complainant recognized that his own language had been out of line, but he was frightened by how easy it had been for the manager to hurl stereotyping and negative insults at him; how easy it had been for the manager to hate him. He wanted an apology and an opportunity to try to change the manager's view of gay men. He wanted to confront his own fear.

It required a second meeting to convince the owner and his lawyer that the complainant was sincere in his request. The offending manager showed up at the third mediation session. In the end, the manager apologized and both the manager *and his lawyer* agreed to attend a training program offered by a gay rights group and designed to help people develop tolerance for people from diverse groups.

Listening deeply made this result (enthusiastically embraced by all parties) possible. Even the lawyer recognized that he could benefit from diversity training. Skills learned in contemplative practice made it possible for me to engage in the deep listening that helped facilitate this result.

The State anti-discrimination provisions that applied to this dispute did not provide this remedy. In fact, arguably they provided no remedy at all. This often is the case when we listen deeply. The remedies provided by the law may not reach the suffering that is being experienced by our clients. One benefit to listening deeply is that hearing clearly what the client wants allows us to explain what the law can and cannot do. It also may be possible to refer the client to sources of assistance that address the client's needs that cannot be met by the law. At the same time, listening deeply may provide us with information that helps us secure legally available remedies.

The context of negotiation and mediation provides opportunities to help clients resolve disputes. In these contexts the calm, presence, clear seeing, compassion, egolessness, and deep listening skills that result from contemplative practice can combine to promote dispute resolution at a deep level.

Andrew Spurrier is a family court officer who provides mediation and negotiation services in family law-related civil matters. He negotiates restraining orders, mediates child custody disputes, makes alimony and child support recommendations, and conducts custody evaluations, divorce pre-trials and settlement conferences. Viewing the conflict resolution process from the perspective he has gained through contemplative practice, Andrew has come to see that the root of conflict is often fear. His clients frequently have trust that has been badly broken and fear has taken root. Andrew knows that both the limited time he has with his clients and his lack of qualifications as a counselor make it impossible for him to actually repair the damage they have experienced. Nonetheless, he has learned that he can be helpful:

> "I can help them see and define their fear, set boundaries for it, and maybe even give it a name. Some clients are able to give it a funny name, a pet name. However the clients define it, their fear then becomes limited and workable. Once this is done, fear can be respected, assuaged, or perhaps recognized as inappropriate because the object of fear is imagined. Agreements arise from defining and limiting fear. While I work in the family law context, fear often is the source of conflict in other contexts as well." [13]

In the following entry Andrew talks about a negotiation he presided over. In this negotiation, he used skills developed in contemplative

---

13   Contemplative Lawyering Class Presentation (Unpublished Transcript)

practice to help a divorcing couple move toward resolving their differences about custody arrangements for their children.

The couple's relationship had lasted a long time and they had two very young children. They had reached what appeared to be an impasse concerning the children's primary residence. Their lawyers believed the impasse could not be resolved without a custody evaluation. Both parents agreed that the mother should have physical custody. However, the mother wanted to move roughly 2000 miles away to where she would have family support, a lower cost of living, and better professional opportunities while the father insisted that the children would benefit from staying in their current community. Andrew describes the negotiation as follows:

> "During the negotiation, both parents characterized their positions as best for the children. Remaining in the community would leave the mother and children dependant on the father's support. The mother didn't trust the father to provide that support. The father didn't believe that moving would make it possible for the mother to support the children.
>
> I asked each parent what he or she would do if the court ruled in favor of the other parent. The mother indicated that she would not relocate without the children. The father indicated that he would not relocate if the children relocated.
>
> I asked each parent to tell me what he or she thought was best for their children. The positions I have already described in an oversimplified manner were laid out in detail, with the parents exchanging many allegations, expletives, insults, and a few threats. They were still living together--tensions were very high and wounds still fresh.

Following the verbal storm, which seemed interminable but probably only lasted twenty minutes, I told them that in order for me to hear them and provide any assistance, I needed them to avoid insulting each other and stop talking over each other. Pauses began to appear in the dialogue. I became part of their attention--quietly, calmly, but assertively present between them in the small room we occupied--and I allowed there to be quiet and space. And they began to contribute to it. What initially had appeared to be a matter of broken trust regarding each parent's financial insecurities transmuted into something else in the openness and space we had all begun to realize. With this space, defensive and reactive statements and thought processes slowed and became observable phenomena rather than overwhelming emotive states. I could see them starting to reflect, look at their thoughts and explore why they were arising. The number and severity of allegations and barbs decreased.

Contemplative practice allowed me to be comfortable in this space and, at the same time, to convey comfort. In this space, I was able to hear them clearly and formulate precise questions that would not incite fear. By asking precise questions in that space the clients had come to appreciate, they could hear me, hear each other, and gradually, really talk about how to address their true, and shared, fear. Their fear was a common one, one that I could not reveal to them. They had to realize it for themselves. It is a fear that I believe is shared by most divorcing parents but too often remains unknown to them. Both the father and the mother not only realized but also acknowledged to each other that they had never wanted their relationship to end the way it ended, and that they didn't want to lose their children or cause the children to lose the other parent, however flawed.

From start to finish, one hour passed by. Through the flexibility we all shared, what started as a referral interview for a custody study became a mediation session. The clients invited their attorneys back in and together they crafted mutually agreeable custody and visitation proposal."[14]

Andrew's view is that we should not think of contemplative practice as a means of controlling anything, including ourselves. He has learned that it is easy for us to think that because we are meditators we are not suffering in the same way our clients are suffering. It is easy for us to delude ourselves into thinking that because we are legal professionals we will not allow our own emotions to play into their conflict. His view is that to be truly professional, all effort based on hope and fear must cease. Clients in conflict sense professional artifice as readily as they sense unprofessional emotionality. Both artifice and emotionality will distract them and draw them away from the real work at hand. We all have the necessary legal knowledge and professional experience readily accessible if wanted and needed. Without effort, using the skills derived from contemplative practice, we can help clients recognize, appreciate, and work in a quiet space. In this space, spontaneous insights arise, solutions are found (not imposed), and valid, self-justifying change occurs. Andrew believes that this sort of change is the closest to what most clients consider "justice" that our legal system can provide. He sums up his approach in this way:

> "When I am truly professional, I am truly practicing contemplatively, and I can facilitate the best result that my clients can access at that time. My clients do not always reach agreement. However, due to my contemplative practice, I define professional success as helping my clients understand what lies

---

14   Contemplative Lawyering Class Presentation (Unpublished Transcript)

beneath their positions. If they need to litigate—and I deeply respect the fact that some do—my clients will know why they have that need, and can better articulate it to their attorney or the judge."[15]

Andrew's ability to work with clients in this way comes from many years of contemplative practice joined together with many years of helping people negotiate and mediate. I have shared his story with you because it provides an example of what contemplative practice can accomplish. It provides an example of working with disputing parties without ego-centricity and with a deep sense of trust in their ability to see themselves and each other clearly. Even though reading this account is unlikely to make any of us able to instantly conduct a negotiation or mediation from a contemplative perspective, this account helps us see the potential benefits of joining the lessons of contemplative practice with legal practice. While it may take some time to reach a level of understanding and skill that makes it possible to conduct a negotiation in this way, contemplative practice provides immediate benefits for both legal practice and life beyond legal practice.

BRINGING THE BENEFITS OF MEDITATION PRACTICE INTO YOUR WORLD

Many articles have been written and published that talk about the benefits of meditation practice for legal practitioners.[16] This book

---

15   Contemplative Lawyering Class Presentation (Unpublished Transcript)

16   John Strazynski, *Meditation Great Way to Ease Stress*, THE LAWYERS WEEKLY (JULY 30, 2009) , http://www.lawyersweekly.ca/index.php?section=article&volume=29 &number=9&article=5; W. Blake Wilson, *The Benefits of Meditation for Lawyers, Law Students*, KU LAW BLOG (SEPT, 14, 2010, 9:14 AM), http://kuschooloflaw.blogspot. com/2010/09/meditation-for-lawyers.html; Craig Cormack, *Lawyers Turn to Meditation to Fight Stress and Improve Performance*, (Mar. 23, 2009), http://barbarasymmons.

takes the next step by providing instructions in contemplative practices and providing guidance for bringing the skills learned in those practices into your legal practice and your life beyond legal practice.

My experience in meditation practice made me aware of the potential benefits of contemplative practice for lawyers. With this knowledge in mind, I created and teach a three-credit course based on meditation practices called *Contemplative Lawyering*. I took what I learned in a spiritual context and applied it to the secular environment of a lawyering. I have shared the materials I developed for this course with law professors and legal practitioners who have encouraged me to make them available as widely as possible to both law students and practicing lawyers. In answer to these requests I have written and published this book.

Buddhism has religious trappings, but what I present in this book is not religion. The essence of Buddhism is simply a genuine science of mind. Buddhist teachings provide methods, practices, and scholarly writings about working with our mind—getting to know our own mind to discover its nature and how it functions. Meditation practices help us work with our mind and discover that mind's basic nature or basic state is free from confusion and complexity—its basic nature is calm, peaceful and full of joy, clarity, compassion, and wisdom. At that same time we can discover the nature of our daily experience of aggression, desire, and other disturbing emotions and learn how to work skillfully with our confusion and emotions. The meditation practices taught in this book are drawn

---

com/2009/04/01/lawyers-turn-to-meditation-to-fight-stress-and-improve-performance/; Nancy A Werner, *Rest in Silence*, Michigan Bar J 52-53(July 2008) available at: http://www.michbar.org/journal/pdf/pdf4article1385.pdf; Amanda Enayati, *Seeking Serenity: When Lawyers Go Zen* (May 11, 2011, 11:15 am) http://thechart.blogs.cnn.com/2011/05/11/seeking-serenity-when-lawyers-go-zen/.

from my Buddhist training, but I avoid "religious" trappings and unusual terms as much as possible. Whenever I use terms that are likely to be unfamiliar to most readers, I define those terms.

My aspiration is that lawyers and law students who read this book and engage in the meditation practices presented here will benefit on a personal level. Further, my aspiration is that by engaging in these practices, lawyers will realize their inherent wisdom and compassion and that this understanding will allow them to work more skillfully with clients, colleagues, judges, legal opponents, family, friends, and other individuals they encounter in their work and beyond.

THE STRUCTURE OF THIS BOOK

This book presents three basic types of contemplative practice. Part I presents several *tranquility* or *mindfulness* practices. These practices are the foundation for all meditation and provide an excellent basis for developing listening skills, letting go of judgments, and beginning to work with negative emotions. Part II teaches *visualization* practices designed to help one cultivate genuine empathy. Finally, Part III presents *insight* or *analytical* practices that help meditators work with the negative aspects of emotions such as anger, pride, jealousy, and obsessive attachment.

Part III also teaches practices that help alleviate fear and sadness. These practices are helpful because research has revealed that many law students and practicing lawyers suffer from some degree of depression.[17] Learning to work with sadness and fear is, therefore, an important component of transforming a lawyer's outlook on life

---

17   See materials cited in footnote 2.

and law practice. These practices also are helpful because sadness and fear often trigger anger and other strong emotions. In addition, from the perspective of serving clients, these practices help lawyers work more skillfully with clients who are experiencing fear and sadness. The basic tranquility meditation practices presented in Part I are a necessary foundation for the practices presented in Parts II and III.

Every formal meditation practice taught in this book includes an associated post-meditation practice or exercise. The post-meditation practices and exercises bring the experiences of formal meditation practice into the everyday experience of relating to life at work, at home, and in the world at large. The wonderful thing about these practices is that because they can be used in multiple contexts, it is possible to practice and learn skills in your personal world that will help you in the practice of law. At the same time, the skills you develop through applying these practices at work can help you outside of work as well.

Throughout the book I have interspersed comments by people who have engaged in these practices and applied them to their lives. These comments provide insight into the practices from the perspective of individuals who, like you, are just beginning to experience the results of meditation practice. These comments can help you see the difficulties and challenges presented by these practices. They also demonstrate the profound impact meditation can have on one's outlook when practiced regularly and in combination with post meditation exercises.

In order to help you establish a meditation practice in your life, I have provided an appendix with practice schedules associated with each set of formal and post meditation practices.

Finally, throughout this book you will find suggested reading materials. The suggested readings include books and articles providing additional meditation instructions, material discussing the relationship between meditation practice and lawyering skills, and traditional material on developing client counseling skills. In addition, in the Resources Appendix you will find lists of reading materials and resources including information on meditation retreats for legal practitioners, and other sources of meditation instruction.

PART I: Tranquility Practice & Mindfulness in Daily Life	**FORMAL PRACTICE 1 HR/DAY**

	Six Weeks
	• Tranquility Meditation:
	    – Following the Breath
	    – Counting the Breath
	    – Meditation on Objects

	Three Weeks • Tranquility Meditation of Choice
	Two Weeks • Tranquility Meditation of Choice

PART II: Generating Compassion & Loving Kindness	**Five Weeks**
	• Sending & Taking Practice:
	    – Impartiality
	    – See Kindness
	    – Appreciate Kindness
	    – Repay Kindness
	    – Cultivate Love
	    – Generate Compassion

PART III: Working with Emotions & Conflict; Patience in Small Matters	**Six Weeks** • Contemplate the Negative Aspects of Emotions • Sitting With Emotions • Contemplate the Insubstantiality of Emotions

POST MEDITATION PRACTICE	POTENTIAL BENEFITS

Mindfulness Reminder:
  – Return to Breath
  – Look at Mind
  – Return to Present
  – Return to reading
	Non-Distraction
	Contentment
	Appreciating the Present
	Effective Reading

Listening Exercises:
  – Two People at once
  – Just Listen
  – Listen to Suffering
  – Prepare to Listen
  – Speak and Listen
	Listening w/o Distraction
	Genuine Listening
	Improved Relationships

Slow Reversal Practice	Patience Skillful Interactions Skillful Speech & Conduct Contentment
• Watching for Judgments • See Kindness • Appreciate Kindness • Aspire to Repay Kindness • Aspire for Happiness • Generate Compassion	Genuine Empathy Loving Kindness Compassion Joy Skillful Interactions
• Patience in Small Matters • Selective Watering • Write a Letter to Yourself	Patience Skillful Interactions Skillful Speech & Conduct Resolving Conflict Contentment

PART I

GETTING TO KNOW YOUR MIND:

Tranquility Practice & Mindfulness in Daily Life

CHAPTER 1

TRANQUILITY MEDITATION— FOLLOWING THE BREATH

The first meditation practice is tranquility meditation. This practice will help you learn to focus without distraction, a skill that is an essential pre-requisite to effective listening, communicating, reading, and analyzing. These skills, in turn, are necessary for effective interviewing, counseling, negotiating, mediating, and litigating.

In addition, this practice provides the foundation for cultivating genuine empathy and for working with conflicting emotions, ours and those we encounter in others.

Tranquility meditation is not a quick fix. Meditation practice requires repetition in order to be effective. Meditation practice is similar to a clinical approach to learning legal skills because you learn by actual practice. Meditation can help you become more focused and present, less distracted, and able to work more skillfully with clients, colleagues, and adversaries.

An additional benefit of tranquility meditation is that engaging in meditation provides you with a time when nothing else needs to happen—a time when you can let go; a time when you can simply be who you are, relaxed in the present with clarity and awareness.

A good source of information on the benefits of tranquility or mindfulness meditation for legal practitioners is Professor Leonard Riskin's article, *The Contemplative Lawyer*.[18]

TRANQUILITY MEDITATION INSTRUCTION: FOLLOWING THE BREATH

Throughout this book I use the words tranquility and mindfulness somewhat interchangeably. Tranquility meditation is primarily aimed at settling your mind. Mindfulness is a skill that becomes possible as a result of or on the basis of tranquility meditation. Mindfulness makes it possible to generate insights about our minds, including insights about our confused thoughts and emotions. Some meditation traditions (Tibetan Buddhism) emphasize tranquility in some practices and insight in others. Tranquility is developed separately as the foundation for mindfulness and for the insight that results from applying that mindfulness. Other meditation traditions (insight meditation) combine tranquility and insight into one practice of mindfulness meditation.

Separating tranquility and insight practices allows us to focus on one skill at a time. Teaching mindfulness meditation that includes both tranquility and insight recognizes the reality that the two are, in fact, inseparable.

---

18   7 Harv. Negot. L. Rev. 1 (2002).

The meditation practices in this book are drawn primarily from the Tibetan tradition that treats tranquility as a foundation for insight rather than mixing the two. At the same time, however, I am drawing on the teachings of Thich Nhat Han[19] who presents a mindfulness meditation that includes both tranquility and insight. I am approaching meditation in this way because I recognize the power of both approaches: using tranquility as a foundation for insight and mixing tranquility and insight in a "mindfulness" practice. Therefore, the tranquility meditation that I am teaching encourages you to cultivate mindfulness and insight. At that same time, these tranquility practices provide a foundation for the compassion and analytical meditation practices I teach later in the book.

I have clarified this distinction because some readers may have previous familiarity with one of these meditation traditions and also because readers may be inspired by this book to read other books on meditation instruction. Without an explanation, you could be confused.

---

19   See.e.g. Thich Nhat Han, *Miracle of Mindfulness* (Beacon Press,1987); Thich Nhat Han, *Anger* (Riverhead Books, 2001). In the materials ahead, I will be recommending that you read portions of both of these books.

The Posture of the Body

The first instruction relates to your physical body—how to position your body to engage in meditation. The primary point is to create a stable physical basis for your practice. You can practice sitting in a chair or sitting on a cushion.

If you choose to use a cushion for meditation, select one that is not too firm and not too soft. Sit with your legs crossed. Place one foot immediately in front of the other or rest one foot on your thigh.

Another option is simply to cross your legs loosely; however, this posture can be somewhat unstable. In addition, it is important to place your knees below the level of your hips so that you don't slouch forward to keep from falling backward. Therefore, if you plan to sit with your legs loosely crossed, use a higher cushion.[20]

Finally, if you are very flexible in your hips, you can cross your legs in the lotus posture, which means that you place each foot on top of the opposite thigh. This is a very stable meditation posture if you are able to do it, but don't try it if it causes you pain. This position is not possible unless you have very loose hip joints.[21]

---

20 Meditation cushions are available from a number of sources. See Resource Appendix.

21 There are yoga postures that can help you increase the flexibility of your hip joints.

If you wish to meditate while sitting on a chair, one approach is to select a chair that allows you to place your feet flat on the floor with your knees in a ninety-degree angle. Alternatively, you can extend your legs in front of you and lightly cross your feet. The advantage of this approach is that you can relax the muscles in your legs. With your feet flat on the floor you will need to maintain some tension in your legs to keep them together. The disadvantage of extending your legs and crossing your feet is that you may have a tendency to sit back in the chair, rather than maintain a straight back. The chair should be a straight-backed chair that is neither too hard nor too soft.

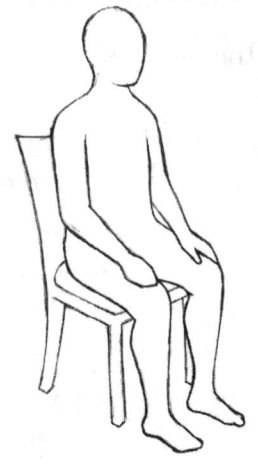

Whether you are meditating on a cushion or on a chair, it is most important that you keep your back straight. Keeping your back straight keeps your body centered and your mind calm and clear. There is a strong relationship between body and mind.

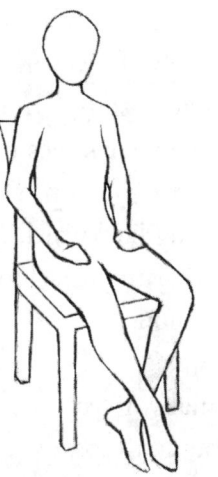

Consider how easy it is to fall asleep if you try to read a book lying down or in a chair that is too soft and comfortable. Try smiling and notice how your mind lightens up. Lean forward and notice how you feel a sense of anticipation. Mind and body are connected. Keeping your back straight all the way up through your neck has a calming effect on your mind. In order to keep your back straight, you should tilt your head forward slightly so the spine in your neck is in line with the rest of your back. It is also helpful to keep your shoulders straight—you should not have one shoulder higher than the other and your shoulders should not be shrugged forward.

With respect to your hands, simply rest them lightly on your thighs. In the alternative you can place your hands in a meditative posture (one on top of the other one, palms up, in your lap). If you do this, however, do not let your hands drag your shoulders forward so that you are shrugging and your back is not straight. You will be most comfortable if you keep your mouth slightly open with your tongue resting on your palate.

Finally, with respect to your eyes, there are several options. Many people try to meditate with their eyes closed. I strongly recommend keeping your eyes open because closing them is likely to cause dullness, sleepiness, or dreaminess in your meditation. A recommended approach is to lower your gaze and focus your eyes softly on a spot in the air about a foot in front of your chest. This helps reduce the distraction that you may experience if you look around the room without creating the tendency to sleep associated with closing your eyes completely.

Another approach is to look straight out in front of you. It is generally best to begin with a softly focused downward gaze to reduce distractions. If, however, you are able to look straight in front of you without being distracted, that is fine. I will discuss what I mean by not being distracted as I present this meditation instruction.

The Practice – Following the Breath

You may find it useful to begin your session of meditation with an aspiration expressing your motivation for practicing. Why are you practicing meditation? What do you hope to accomplish? Your aspiration could be to become more calm, peaceful, and content. Or it could be to become more present and non-distracted. Or you may have a meditation aspiration to be less judgmental or to work more skillfully with others. Or you may aspire to deal more effectively with the stress in your life or to deal more skillfully with clients and others in your life.

Whatever your motivation, it can be helpful to state your aspiration (out loud or in your mind) at the beginning of your meditation session. Stating your motivation helps you reach your goal because it provides the motivation to meditate. Simply by expressing your aspiration every time you meditate you may find yourself changing and moving in the direction of accomplishing your aspiration. Aspirations can have a powerful impact on your habitual patterns and on your outlook on life.

It will be helpful at this point if you sit in the meditation posture described above and treat the instruction that follows this paragraph as a guided meditation. (The instruction continues through the next five paragraphs). Try to find someone else to read these instructions to you *very slowly* while you begin to meditate (settle into the posture of the body as previously explained before the instruction is read).

Meditation is about becoming familiar with our own mind. Meditation practice is about knowing oneself. It is about discovering the qualities of your mind. The meditation technique is simple: rest your mind on your breath as it flows in and out of your nostrils. Feel the breath flowing down into your lungs and back out again through your nostrils. Feel your chest rise up and fall back down as you breathe. There is no need to change the way you breathe.

Simply follow your breath as it flows in and out. Appreciate your breath. Breathing is a precious experience of being alive in the moment. Appreciate that moment, rest in that moment. Breath is momentary. Breath is always changing. Each moment brings a new breath. Appreciate the present moment of your breath.

When thoughts arise, simply acknowledge them and return to your breath; do not label your thoughts or engage them or follow them. At the same time, don't try to repress them. Simply notice them, acknowledge them, and return to following the breath. If you become distracted and engaged with your thoughts, simply return to following the breath once you recognize that you have become distracted.

This practice is both deceptively simple and deeply profound. This practice allows your mind to be present. Ordinarily our minds are anticipating the future or reviewing the past. We are so busy making plans for the future that we are never present. We are busy regretting the past, trying to relive the past, or obsessing about some hurt we experienced in the past. Or we are busy worrying about something we need to do in the future. We are so busy with the past and the future that we never experience the present moment—NOW. Simply follow your breath and appreciate *nowness*.

You may find yourself distracted by many thoughts--perhaps you are under a deadline at work and are unable to get a project out of your mind. Remember your aspiration and remind your-self that now is the time you have set aside for meditation. There are twenty-three other hours during the day that you can spend thinking about your work projects. Another way to deal with obsessive thinking driven by anxiety is to stop meditating for a moment and write your thoughts down. Placing them on a piece of paper may help you let them go during your meditation session. However, thoughts should not be viewed as an enemy when you are meditating. Thoughts are your friend. They remind you to return to the breath. They are a reminder to return to the present. Meditation is simply about being present. The meditation instruction is simply to establish the intention to use your thoughts as a reminder to return to following your breath; a reminder to return to the present. Without this intention, we almost always ignore this reminder and ignore the present. But if we use thoughts as a friendly reminder to return to the present, they can help us follow our breath and appreciate *nowness*. More than that, noticing and being fully aware of your thoughts is your first experience of meditation. Ordinarily, we think without even realizing that we are thinking. Ordinarily we are "lost in thought."

When you complete your meditation session, it is good to end with a dedication based on the motivation for practice that you expressed in the beginning. Simply dedicate your practice to accomplishing your aspiration. You may find it particularly motivating and profound to dedicate your practice to developing skills to benefit others. What I mean by this is that through meditation practice you can become more skillful in the way you relate with others, including your clients, other individuals you encounter in your work world, and also your family and friends.

How Long & How Often Should You Meditate?

Even five minutes of meditation on a daily basis can be very beneficial. Meditating for a longer time is even better as long as you don't try to meditate beyond the point when you are appreciating the meditation. It is best to leave the meditation with a positive rather than negative feeling. It is wonderful if you can meditate for a short time both in the morning and in the evening. It can also deepen your practice substantially if you meditate for a longer time each day (up to one hour) or attend a weekend or even a week-long retreat and meditate for many hours each day for several days in a row.

It can be helpful to locate others who are interested in doing the meditation practices in this book together with you in a group. There are several advantages to meditating with a group. First, setting up a regular group meeting time makes it much easier to maintain a regular schedule of meditation practice. Second, some of the exercises suggested in this book require more than one person. Finally, for some of the practices and exercises in this book you will find it helpful if you can discuss the practices with a group of meditators. You can particularly enhance the benefit of these practices if you find a group of lawyers to meditate with you. The fact that you all share the same work experiences and face the same workplace challenges will make your discussions with each other extremely useful.

Each practice described in this book should be practiced for many days. For example, I recommend that you complete at least fourteen daily sessions of Following the Breath before beginning the next practice (Counting the Breath). It is a good idea to create a practice schedule to help you keep track of your meditation so you know when to move on to the next practice. A schedule for this practice can be found in the Practice Schedule Appendix. You can check off one box each time you complete a practice session. Your sessions can be as short as five minutes, but it would be good to develop an aspiration to meditate for at least fifteen minutes each time you sit. Longer is even better.

In the Appendix you will find practice schedules for all of the practices taught in this book. The practice schedules suggest a minimum number of sessions for each practice and in some cases suggest circumstances that would make more practice sessions appropriate and helpful.

There is a post-meditation practice that accompanies this formal meditation practice. The post meditation practice is described later in this Chapter and should be practiced for the two weeks during which you are practicing Following the Breath in your formal meditation sessions.

What Can You Expect to Accomplish by Meditating?

How meditation practice will work for you depends on a number of factors. The first relevant factor is how you generally related to life before you started meditating. Some people are naturally calm and mindful. Others experience a great deal of anger, judgment, and stress. Some people are very conceptual and analytical. This is true of many lawyers. Others approach the world from a more experiential perspective. Where you are when you begin to meditate will affect your perception of how meditation works for you.

A second relevant factor is motivation. Your motivation determines the results of practice to a significant degree. For example, if you are primarily motivated to reduce stress and achieve some sense of calmness, you are less likely to develop compassion as a result of your meditation than if your initial motivation for meditating is to benefit others.

A third factor is diligence. If you rarely practice you are unlikely to see results. In this sense, how diligent you are about practice is not simply a matter of how much time you spend sitting on a cushion or chair and "meditating." Diligent practice means actually following the meditation instructions while you are sitting rather than using the time to develop a *to do* list for your day. Again, you may find it much easier to be diligent about practice if you practice with a group.

Another aspect of diligence is whether you make a good faith effort to bring these practices into your daily life by making an effort to do the post-meditation practices associated with each formal practice of meditation. Therefore, two additional factors that relate to how meditation will impact your mind and life are the environment in which you work and live and how you apply meditation to your world.

I will talk more about these factors after presenting some of the post-meditation practices associated with tranquility meditation. In short, however, the only way to know if and how meditation will work for you is simply to try it.

When I teach this practice, I am amazed at how many of the people I teach experience significant insights as a result of meditating for just a few short weeks. The following comments are taken from journals written by individuals shortly after they started meditating:

> "Meditation helped me relax for the rest of the day from the first time I tried it, but recently I have been finding other effects of meditation, such as clarity, calm assertiveness, confidence and a general sense of wellness during most of my day. It is not that I am becoming a Zen master or anything, but I find myself processing things differently because I am opening up

to the possibility that things can be better and more productive through calmness."

(Participant, Contemplative Lawyering 2005)

"When I pause and focus on a few breaths during the day, some stress is relieved. Therefore, I am more relaxed at the end of the day than I otherwise would be. By staying more relaxed, I also remain more energetic."

(Participant, Contemplative Lawyering 2005)

"Your mind is really *all* that you can control and your ability to control your mind can have a positive impact on your relations with others and your outlook. . . . The tape that plays in my mind is that I'll be happy when I finish . . . , when I get . . . , when I accomplish . . . . I think that this tape is playing in many peoples' minds. . . I'm hoping that through meditation I will develop an ability to greater appreciate the here and now."

(Participant, Contemplative Lawyering 2006).

"The night before, my feelings were hurt and since I am not usually able to let go quickly, I came to meditation with a heavy heart. However, I left feeling a little better. Resting on the breath really does help. In fact, I found that I was not repeating the scenario in my head over and over again like I often do only to burden my spirit."

(Participant, Contemplative Lawyering 2006)

"During meditation today, I discovered that I am definitely too emotionally attached to external rewards. I need to change my mindset. Those words, "Great job" may not come even if I have in fact done a great job. I want to try to break myself out of the "needing approval" cycle and learn to be satisfied with knowing that the job I have done was the best I could do in the circumstances."

(Participant, Contemplative Lawyering 2006)

"When we meditated, I realized that the source of a lot of my stress is that I try to be in control of every situation that I am in. Being out of control or even thinking of being out of control causes me anxiety and stress. I formulated the idea in my mind that my aspiration (for meditation) will be to recognize the things I cannot control . . . and accept those things without getting stressed out about it."

(Participant, Contemplative Lawyering 2006)

Others experienced some difficulty with meditation at the outset:

"I found it very difficult to concentrate on just my breathing. The more thoughts popped into my head, the more I fidgeted, and the more I became agitated with the whole process of trying to focus on just my breath."

(Participant, Contemplative Lawyering 2006)

"I found it particularly difficult to acknowledge my thoughts and let them go. I found myself having arguments in my head about concentrating only on my breath or reprimanding myself for not being able to do it. I think one of the hardest things about meditation is getting rid of my judgments about myself because I have spent most of my life judging my performance and basing my self worth on those judgments."

(Participant, Contemplative Lawyering, 2006)

"Today was my first experience with meditation and it was frustrating because I had a hard time relaxing. As I focused on my breath and the present I found myself holding my breath and not being able to find a natural rhythm to my meditation. Every time I inhaled I felt like I was gasping for air and as I exhaled I felt my chest become heavy."

(Participant, Contemplative Lawyering 2006)

"I find it is simply harder to meditate when you have a lot going on or are more stressed out than when you are already relatively calm. It seems like a pretty obvious point, but recognizing this helped me when I started to get down on myself for not being able to concentrate."

(Participant, Contemplative Lawyering 2006)

Most people experience mixed results in their first attempts at meditation:

"I found it interesting how my mind raced. First, I rested on the breath. I listened to myself breath in and out. I imagined all of the particles going through my nose and throat, my lungs expanding, every part of me knowing what to do on its own. I thought that was nice. These visuals—the picture of the breath—appeared again today. Then I found myself thinking, "Stop thinking and just focus on the breath! Stop talking to yourself. Focus on your breath. Stop visualizing. Just focus on your breath."

You mentioned that there was no reason to be upset with yourself if you realized that your mind wandered or you lost focus—just acknowledge it and go back to your breath and maybe be amazed at how easily your mind can wander or how much information is flowing through your mind. There is no reason to feel like you've failed or done anything wrong. I like that.

So far, in two days of minimal meditation, this is my pattern. First I think about my goal. Of course I have a million goals—be happy, relieve stress and anxiety, understand myself better." Then I question myself, "Is this the right goal? Am I doing it right? Am I asking too much? Should I just be in therapy? What is the right goal?" Fortunately I also acknowledge this and laugh at my craziness. Phew. Then I focus on my breath. I visualize the breath. I am amazed by my breath. Then my mind races."

(Participant, Contemplative Lawyering 2006)

Study Resources

I have provided you with meditation instruction here, but you may find it helpful to supplement what I have taught with some reading about meditation. The first source I would suggest that you look at is pages 1-24 of *The Miracle of Mindfulness* by Thich Nhat Han.[22]

I encourage you to read and re-read *The Miracle of Mindfulness* many times. This is not a book to skim through. Break it down into small chunks--no more than three to five pages at a time. Read and contemplate sections of this book each day, reading each section more than once and slowly. Thich Nhat Han's writings are meditation instructions. This book should be read like a guided meditation. This particular text was written in the context of the extreme conflict of war. It is, therefore, directly applicable to working with conflict, which lawyers do all the time.

Another excellent source of meditation instructions can be found in *Bodhi*, Volume 7, numbers 1 and 2. These magazines include a series of articles instructing on tranquility meditation.[23]

---

22   (Beacon, 1975). This book can be purchased at any major bookstore.

23   Bodhi is no longer published and no longer available for purchase. It can be found

Both Thich Nat Han and the articles in *Bodhi* talk about other tranquility practices. Try them out as you read those materials, but in your formal practice sessions, stay with the practice of following your breath until you have completed the recommended number of sessions. Some of these practices will be discussed and recommended later in this book. For example, Thich Nat Han talks about counting the breath and being present with listening.[24] Those practices will be discussed and recommended later in this book.

POST-MEDITATION PRACTICE EXERCISE

During the two weeks that you are spending some time each day meditating (Following the Breath), it will be very beneficial if you also engage in a post-meditation practice of Following the Breath periodically throughout the day. One way to help you remember to engage in this post-meditation practice is to establish a "mindfulness reminder".

Of course, identifying a "mindfulness reminder" will not help if you don't use the reminder. Therefore, along with identifying your reminder, you should establish an aspiration to use the reminder. With respect to establishing this aspiration, remember that formal meditation provides a protected environment where we can *practice* calming our minds. We practice calming our minds in order to provide the space and non-distraction required to look at and work with our minds. We work with our minds in order to bring calmness and equanimity to our post-meditation world, improve

---

in some University Libraries including Naropa University, Columbia University, The University of California at Berkeley, The University of Connecticut School of Law, and Cornell University.

24   *Miracle of Mindfullness*, at 80-83.

our ability to work with stress in our post-meditation world, or to improve our relationships with others in our post-meditation world. The mindfulness reminder can help you bring the results of your meditation practice into our post-meditation world.

There are many options for mindfulness reminders. One option is to purchase a digital watch or cell phone and set it to beep once every hour. Whenever you hear the beep, rest your mind on your breath for a few breaths to bring yourself into the present. When you follow your breath in post-meditation, it is good to keep your eyes open and continue to engage whatever visual object you were looking at before your mindfulness reminder brought you back to the present. Think that you are placing 25% of your attention on your breath.

Other possible mindfulness reminders can be drawn from your environment. Thich Nhat Hahn suggests that we use the ringing of the telephone as a mindfulness reminder.[25] Try allowing the phone to ring several times before you answer it. This way you can calm your mind prior to engaging the person on the other end of the line in conversation. This can have a beneficial effect on the quality of the conversation.

This approach is very helpful for lawyers whose practice includes lots of phone conversations. Many lawyers have shared with me the stress associated with these constant interruptions. Using the phone ringing as a mindfulness reminder allows us to appreciate and be present with these phone conversations rather than resent them as an interruption of whatever we are doing. Another possibility for your mindfulness reminder is to use stop signs or stop lights that you encounter while driving. This approach can convert encountering a

---

25   Thich Nhat Hanh, *Peace is Every Step: The Path of Mindfulness*, at 29-31. (Arnold Kotler ed., Bantam Books, 1991).

stop sign into a lesson. The stop light or stop sign is telling you something. It is telling you to stop and be present. Again, it is best to keep your eyes open during post meditation mindfulness stops.

Anything you encounter regularly in your life can be your mindfulness reminder. If you have frequent visitors to your office, you can use the knock on the door as your reminder. Checking email can be your reminder. The face of your child or spouse can be your reminder. The point here is to establish a reminder and use it. When you use your mindfulness reminder, you may find yourself amazed at how often your mind is not in the present—how often you are thinking of something else while someone is speaking to you. If you use these various encounters with others as your mindfulness reminder you may find that being present allows these encounters to become more meaningful.

The benefits of bringing mindfulness into your post-meditation world can be amazing. Every moment that you are present is a moment that you are content. Our habit of ignoring the present is based on dissatisfaction with the present. We rush through the current task in order to move on to the next task. When we get to the next task, we rush again anticipating what we will do after we finish. Because we are always trying to get to the next item on our list, we never appreciate the present moment. We never appreciate what we are doing now. Living in the future or the past means we never actually live at all. The past is gone and the future is not here yet. When we rest in the present, there is no "getting this done" in order to go on to something else. When we are content to rest in the present, there is no dichotomy between work and play. We simply appreciate whatever is happening now; appreciate the present moment.

Several years ago I taught a small seminar. After several weeks, I knew each of the students reasonably well. Whenever I spoke with them after class, I found I was able to engage in the conversation, being present and open to whatever questions or comments they had. As I prepared for class one day, however, I realized that I was viewing the class as a "task to be completed" so I could go on to whatever else I was doing that day. I realized that I was viewing the students in the class as a group that I needed to work with for the next hour and a half, not as individuals. I realized that I approached all of my classes that way and that it would be wonderful if I could be present and fully engaged with each student in the class while I was teaching rather than plowing through the material to simply "get it done." This was a profound realization for me.

This is how it can be for lawyers meeting with clients or conducting meetings or litigating cases or mediating disputes. Each encounter can be a precious opportunity to engage another individual or group of individuals—a precious opportunity full of possibilities.

Setting and using a mindfulness reminder makes it possible to fully experience each present moment. As Thich Nat Hahn has said, "when you are washing dishes, you are washing dishes."[26] Whatever you are doing, simply be there, whether you are eating an orange, hugging your child, taking a shower, advising a client, conducting a trial, or meeting with a colleague or group of colleagues. Fully experience the moment. Each moment can be a profoundly beautiful experience.

> "When I do dishes, I frequently find myself thinking of other things and longing for the task to be over. I think it might be this longing that is what makes it beneficial to simply wash the

---

26 *Miracle of Mindfulness* 3-4 (Beacon, 1975).

> dishes in the moment—because while I am longing to be doing
> something else, I am becoming increasingly unhappy that I am
> not doing something else."
>
> *(Participant, Contemplative Lawyering 2006)*

You may find that you are first able to experience the benefits of this post-meditation practice in the context of reasonably simple activities such as eating, driving, washing dishes, or running. Using your mindfulness reminder in these contexts will ultimately make it possible for you to bring mindfulness into the more complex world of interacting with others in your work as a lawyer.

Will your meditation accomplish these results? The results you experience will depend in part on your diligence. Diligence includes working with the formal practice in your post-meditation environment. In addition, how your post-meditation practice develops depends in part on the work and home environment you experience. For example, if you work in a very frenetic work or home environment, you may have difficulty remembering to use a mindfulness reminder at all. On the other hand, if you can remember to be mindful in an environment such as this, the benefits of the practice will be even more dramatic than if your world is generally peaceful.

The impact of your work and home environment will become more apparent later when we work with practices designed to cultivate empathy and to work with strong emotions like anger. For those practices, a work or home environment that includes argumentative, critical, and judgmental individuals may be so overwhelming for you that you find it difficult to work with your anger and generate feelings of empathy. On the other hand, difficult environments provide significant opportunities to work with strong emotions and a substantial need to develop genuine empathy. If you can manage to bring post-meditation practice into this kind of environment, the results can be extremely beneficial for you, as well as for the other people in your world.

"My daily reminder has been my wedding ring, and it has worked very well—almost too well in fact. I naturally play with my ring while it's on my finger, so I have found myself twirling it often, forcing me to pause and focus for a few deep breaths to help clear my mind. It has actually made me realize exactly what it was supposed to make me realize. I spent almost none (perhaps none at all?) of my time in the present. Rather, I spend all my time obsessing and ruminating about something in the past (distant, recent, embarrassing, conquests) or planning for the future (to-do lists, playing out future situations in my head). What a waste!"
(Participant, Contemplative Lawyering 2006)

"The benefits of meditating each morning this week have been readily perceivable. Specifically, my patience has increased dramatically. For example, while working at the Tax clinic, I was put on hold by an IRS agent. When I was put on hold for extended periods of time last semester, I would typically become angry and would frequently stare at the clock as the minutes ticked away. After meditating this week, however, I used the time on hold to reflect and to concentrate on my breathing. As a result, I was calm and better able to communicate with the IRS agent who ultimately assisted me. Furthermore, focusing on the present has increased my ability to concentrate. For example, while reading in the library, I often am tempted to check my email or to browse the internet. Through being aware of my breathing, however, I was better able to focus on the text that I was reading."
(Participant, Contemplative Lawyering 2006)

"Last weekend, during a long drive, I remembered to concentrate on my breathing and to drive for the sake of driving (like Thich Nhat Han's practice of "washing dishes in order to wash dishes"). The trip that I have done countless times became an entirely new trip. I looked around and saw the mud, the houses of all types—farm houses (dilapidated, both beautiful and quaint and yet at times sad), other large modern homes, small trailers, etc. The mountain tops were hidden by the clouds, the snow was left in patches, the colors all muted. I noticed a car that was clean. It stood out because it didn't have the grime and salt blanket that every car in this region is coated with. I enjoyed my surroundings. I enjoyed the moment. I breathed deeply and realized that I had stopping thinking about and worrying about anything."

(Participant, Contemplative Lawyering 2006)

Continuing with instructions on the practice of following the breath, meditation is getting to know your mind which is ordinarily somewhere else—in the past or the future. Meditation is bringing our minds to rest in the present. Meditation is seeing, acknowledging, and letting go of distracting thoughts and emotions.

What does it mean to be present? Whenever I take a shower, I notice how long it takes for me to realize that I am in the shower. I may be planning how to spend my day. I may be planning a class or simply spacing out. It usually takes a minute or two before I actually see the water coming from the shower head or notice it splattering against the tiles. Once I am present, I feel the warmth of the water against my face and body. I see the water drops glistening on the surface of the glass shower door. I feel the shampoo on my hands and in my hair. I see the water drops shining in the light as they fall from the shower head. When I leave the shower, I feel the air on my wet body, feel the soft bathroom rug under my feet, feel the towel rubbing against my body, and see the drops of water against my skin.

Similarly, when I sit down to eat breakfast, it takes a few minutes to let go of my wandering thoughts and notice that I am eating cereal and fruit or notice that my husband is sitting next to me.

This is the way we approach our lives most of the time. We are lost in thought. It is as though we have eyes in our minds that are looking elsewhere—anywhere other than where we are at the moment. The list of tasks to do later today is running through our minds. We are lost in fear and anxiety about an upcoming meeting or presentation. Meanwhile, breakfast happened without our knowing it. When my mind is lost in thought, I miss the taste of cooked cereal and fruit. I have been known to actually forget whether I ate or not. I miss seeing and relating with the amazing person who is eating breakfast next to me.

The thoughts that remove us from the present frequently revolve around hopes and fears. We experience anxiety about how we are doing and fear about what others will think. We experience annoyance and pass judgment on ourselves and on others. Meditation allows us to let go of hope and fear and just reside in the present. When hope and fear come up, simply acknowledge them and return to the breath. There is no need to repress these thoughts or push them away. Simply notice and return to following the breath.

> "I cannot recall ever deliberately taking the time to stop and clear my mind. It is amazing to stop and recognize the stream of consciousness inside my head. While the instructions seemed

simple, it was very challenging to calm myself down, to count my breath, and to simply acknowledge any thoughts that arose.

During those *few* moments that I was able to focus on my breath and practice mindfulness, I felt like I was more aware of everything. I was not lured away by thoughts of my grocery list, of the fight I had with my sister last week, or of how much I was regretting taking Commercial Paper this semester. Instead, I heard the sound of the heater, the reverberation of a classmate's cough, and the rise and fall of my own chest. I felt like I was hyper-aware of my surroundings—but not in a way that was annoying or distracting. This is proving difficult to explain but I felt like I was equally aware of my surroundings and myself."

(Participant, Contemplative Lawyering 2006)

One of the participants in my Contemplative Lawyering course applied meditation to the experience of watching the birth of his first child:

"I haven't been able to stop thinking about how incredible the birth of my son was and how "present" I was during the labor process. I'd like to think it was due in part to this class, but I also think it was a function of the gravity of the situation. In other words, it was such a momentous event that I focused my energy and mind on what was happening and all else faded away— my egocentric worrying about something I said or did, and my prospective anxiousness about my to-do list in the future. I was able to focus completely on my wife and our lives and this process of bringing life into the world and it was an incredible experience, unfit for words. But it provided me a glimpse of how freeing life could be if I lived in the present, focusing on the here and now and letting go of the past and future and those

> things I cannot control or change. Granted, there has to be some forward-looking planning to get through life, but I (and probably most people) engage in far too much of it."
>
> *(Participant, Contemplative Lawyering 2006)*

This person had a profound insight. He is correct that many of us, even without meditation training, are able to be present in extreme situations such as the birth of a child. Most of us fail to realize, however, that we can appreciate the present moment *all the time*, not just during extraordinary events like birth and death. Meditation practice makes it possible to connect with the profound experience of *now* even in the context of our ordinarily lives.

> "If one is mindful of each discrete act in the present, when is there room for other thought such as reflection or planning?"
>
> *(Participant, Contemplative Lawyering 2006)*

Sometimes people ask whether resting in the present means that we should never make plans for the future. Making plans for the future is not inconsistent with being present. Resting in the present without distraction means that you are fully aware of what you are doing, seeing, or thinking. Most of the time, we aren't particularly aware of the thoughts running through our minds. We are lost in thought, following one thought and then another until we finally wake up and can't figure out how we got around to the thought we are on when we finally become aware of it. When we are driving along a familiar route we are lost in thought, unaware of our environment or of what we are thinking.

Being present means knowing where you are, what you are doing, and what you are thinking. It is quite possible to be present with the process of planning for the future. A good example is the process we go through to make sure we get to work on time in the morning. This process starts the night before. You need to gather together the items you will need to bring with you. You need to set your alarm so you will get up in time to take a shower, get dressed, and drive to work. You need to get yourself to bed early enough to get up in the morning. All of this activity requires mindfulness. All of this activity relates to something you will do in the future, but the planning process is accomplished in the present. It is very helpful to be present with your preparations for the following day.

The same is true for more distant future events. When you are online purchasing your airline tickets for your summer vacation, you need to be present with the process of purchasing those tickets. If you are not fully mindful and present with that process, you may make a mistake and buy tickets for the wrong dates or the wrong location.

LETTING GO OF EGO ATTACHMENT

One of the benefits of tranquility or mindfulness practice is that it helps us begin to let go of ego attachment. How does mediation practice accomplish this? The thoughts that distract us from the present involve relating to the world from a perspective of ego involvement. For example, while engaging in a conversation, we often simultaneously engage in a running commentary in our mind about how to respond to what we are hearing. If the conversation is part of a meeting with colleagues, we may be considering what we can say that will impress the group or we may be anxious and fearful that we will have nothing to add to the discussion.

While listening to a client, we are busy thinking about the legal relevance of what we are hearing. We may be worrying that we won't have a good question or answer for the client at the end of his or her story. While writing a brief, we may be concerned that our colleagues won't be impressed. Nearly every encounter with another person includes some kind of judgment.

Mindfulness meditation is a practice of seeing, acknowledging, and letting go of thoughts. If we are able to see and let go of distracting thoughts while in conversations with others, we will automatically be more attentive to what they are saying because we will be less involved in our own story line. If we can learn to let go of thoughts during meditation, we can apply what we have learned in post meditation. For example, we can let go of anxiety about how we appear to others while writing a brief or presenting an argument. Mindfulness meditation is a practice of acknowledging thoughts without judgment. If we can let go of judgments during formal meditation, we can let go of judgments during post meditation when we encounter other people. In this way tranquility or mindfulness meditation begins to undermine our tendency to interact with the world from a self-centered perspective.

Letting go of the distractions associated with attachment to our own agenda has a profound impact on our ability to work effectively as lawyers. The result is improved focus on whatever task we are performing, and undistracted listening to clients, colleagues, opponents, judges, and others.

CHAPTER 2:

CAUSES, QUALITIES & BENEFITS OF TRANQUILITY MEDITATION[27]

The material presented in this chapter is good to read when you start meditating. You may find it helpful to return to this material and review it periodically.

CAUSES OF TRANQUILITY MEDITATION

There are three basic causes of tranquility or mindfulness meditation: aspiration, guidance, and environment. An additional condition that promotes non-distraction in meditation is letting go of attachments.

Aspiration

Aspiration comes from understanding the purpose of meditation. Understanding the purpose of meditation means understanding

---

27 The material presented in this Chapter is based on written and oral teachings I have received from Dzogchen Ponlop Rinpoche. Some of this material can be found in Dzogchen Ponlop Rinpoche, *Secret of Mind*, 7(1) Bodhi, 32-33, 51-53.

that happiness and suffering depends on our state of mind rather than situations we face in our world. Looking to the outside world to achieve happiness or avoid suffering won't work.

Consider people you know personally or know about from media or other sources. Think of individuals who appear to have everything from a material perspective—money, talent, power and influence, respect, and all the material comforts money can buy. It is easy to see that some individuals who are blessed in this way appear to be genuinely happy. Others, however, are miserable in spite of their material wealth and success. They continue to acquire more and more possessions and seek more and more power and prestige in an effort to reach some sense of contentment and satisfaction. Perhaps you have seen this tendency in some of your legal colleagues—never satisfied, always seeking more. They are depressed and angry. Sometimes they turn to alcohol and illicit drugs, or get into legal difficulties. Sometimes they even commit suicide to escape their misery.

Consider also individuals who appear to have it all in terms of relationships. They have supportive families and have met and married a wonderful person. Some people who are blessed with these circumstances are genuinely happy. Others are miserable in spite of their apparent good fortune. They soon tire of their marital relationship. They fight with their spouse or engage in extra-marital affairs or get a divorce and seek another relationship in hopes of finding the perfect situation.

Consider also individuals who enjoy perfect health. Some individuals are satisfied with their bodies. They eat and exercise to maintain health, but are not obsessed with their physical appearance or condition. Others are never satisfied. From a positive perspective, their addiction to running or weight lifting or healthy eating results in significant health gains. Nevertheless, they may suffer from the perception that they are still not beautiful enough, not strong enough, not quick enough, etc. At the extremes this form of attachment and obsession can be physically unhealthy. For example, for some individuals the obsession with appearance results in an eating disorder such as anorexia or bulimia.

The lesson to be learned here is that even the best of circumstances in life do not guarantee happiness. No matter how much one has—material wealth, prestige, influence, good relationships, good health—this does not guarantee happiness.

On the other hand, I am sure you have known or become aware of people who have experienced difficult circumstances, including the death of a young spouse or child or perhaps a life threatening illness or a significantly disabling accident or condition. Or perhaps they have experienced a financial disaster that has taken them from wealth to extreme need. Some of the individuals who have experienced extreme hardships are angry and unhappy. However, you probably know or know of individuals who have transformed their unfortunate circumstances into a basis for significant personal growth. Their experience of personal disaster has helped them develop compassion for other individuals who suffer. Their brush with death has brought them a profound connection with the blessing of every precious and fragile moment of existence. Their financial disaster has helped them move in a different and more positive direction with their lives. They experience a great deal of contentment and happiness.

Considering all of this, it becomes clear that happiness and suffering do not depend on external circumstances or even bodily health. The difference between individuals who experience lasting happiness and contentment and those who suffer from anger, depression, and anxiety lies not in their external circumstances, but rather in how they perceive and relate to their circumstances. The difference is in their minds.

You can see less extreme examples of this truth by observing how individuals experience nearly everything in life. For some people a trip to the beach is a vacation with fun in the sun including swimming, running, Frisbee, collecting shells and rocks, building sand castles with kids, and enjoying a picnic in a beautiful location. For others a trip to the beach is an uncomfortable misadventure with sunburn, excessive heat, headaches, burned feet, and sand in your picnic lunch. The experience is not in the external environment. The experience is in how we relate to that experience with our minds.

The same is true in our everyday experience of life and work. Whether we are taking care of our personal world (shopping, cooking, cleaning, paying bills, mowing the lawn, maintaining the house, etc.) or our work world (meeting with clients, attending meetings with colleagues, conducting research, answer the phone, filing motions, attending hearings, conducting trials, etc.) we can be present, mindful, and content or we can be stressed, angry, and unhappy.

Understanding this reality means understanding that it is only through working with our minds that we can transform our view of the world. This understanding, together with an awareness that the purpose of tranquility or mindfulness meditation is to become familiar with and work with our minds, makes it possible to generate the aspiration to practice tranquility meditation.

Guidance

It is best to learn contemplative practice, including tranquility/ mindfulness meditation from a qualified instructor. Learning meditation practice from books can be very beneficial if the books contain genuine teachings and instruction on meditation practice. Most books simply teach *about* meditation rather than actually teaching the practices. This book provides detailed instruction on a variety of practices. If you practice what is taught in this book (both the formal meditation practices and the post meditation exercises) and read and apply the supplementary materials recommended in this book, you can make significant progress with meditation.

Nonetheless, it would also be beneficial to have instruction from a living person. Such instruction has an "alive" quality that is missing from instructions in a book. Such instruction also provides you with a context in which you can ask questions about your practice. For this reason, I encourage you to seek further guidance from a qualified instructor to supplement what you are learning by reading this book and engaging in the practices that are suggested here. In the Resources Appendix you will find a list of resources for meditation instruction.

Environment

Meditation practice requires an appropriate place to meditate. This pre-requisite to meditation practice concerns the outer environment where we practice meditation. It is important at the outset to have a peaceful, calm, positive environment for meditation. An experienced meditator can practice anywhere. At the outset, however, we are easily distracted and therefore need a quiet, safe place. Meditating at home can be difficult because of distractions presented by phones ringing, coffee in the kitchen, the computer and TV beckoning, books to read, dirty laundry to wash, pets and children to feed, etc.

If you are planning to meditate at your home, the distractions mentioned in the previous paragraph can be minimized by creating a space within the home that is dedicated to meditation practice and away from the major activity centers in the home. This space doesn't need to be elaborate. It simply needs to be uplifting (not too dark), comfortable (not too hot and not too cold), and provide you with a stable seat for meditation (a cushion or a chair). Having few distractions in this room (e.g. books, computers, television, or telephone) will make this space more conducive to meditation.

Another option that has worked for some meditation practitioners is to meditate in your office during your lunch break or when you first arrive in the morning. This can work if you have an office that is reasonably quiet with a door that can be closed (perhaps with a sign discouraging interruptions).

It can be helpful to locate a meditation center where group practice sessions are held. This approach has the advantage of providing a physical location relatively free from distractions. In addition, simply being with a group of meditators can facilitate meditation. On the other hand, finding a group with a meditation schedule that works for you may pose difficulties. One way to find a group to meditate with you is simply to create one. If there are other lawyers in your office or neighborhood who are interested in meditating, you could create a space at your workplace or find a place to rent that is conducive to meditation and create a schedule of group meetings (perhaps during the lunch break) that works for the group.

Meditating at home has the advantage of being on your own schedule. It can be particularly powerful, for example, to meditate first thing in the morning. In a busy household, this may be the best time of the day to meditate because it provides an environment free from distraction. Ordinarily, the telephone doesn't ring early in the morning. The computer is not yet turned on. In addition, the rest of the household is still in bed. This means less distraction from the household and also less temptation to engage in activities like washing dishes, watching TV, or doing laundry that will disturb your sleeping family or roommates.

Early morning meditation also sets the tone for the entire day. If you are not a "morning person" you may find early morning meditation a good way to start the morning. Often our resistance to getting up is based on a negative attitude towards what we expect to experience during the day. By making meditation the first activity of the day you can begin the day on a positive note which may make it easier to get up.

Thich Nhat Han suggests a way to work with early morning lethargy and resistance. He encourages us to start the day with a smile. You can simply set your intention to smile when you wake up in the morning.[28] A more powerful approach is to post a small sign on your alarm clock or on the wall next to your bed that simply says "smile." Just a half smile is enough to lighten your mind and awaken your anticipation and enthusiasm for the new day. Try it. You may be surprised at the result.

Finally, you should meditate in a place where you feel safe. It is extremely difficult to meditate if you are distracted by biting bugs, dangerous people, or threatening animals. Meditating outside in a

---

28   *Miracle of Mindfulness*, at 79-80.

park or in the woods on a mountain top can be a wonderful experience, but you should choose a location where you feel safe and comfortable with no fear of being attacked by animals, thieves, or muggers.

Abandoning Attachment

The less attached we are, the easier it will be for meditation to arise because we aren't plagued by anxieties, plans, and worries related to our attachments. Attachment to activities also prevents meditation from happening because attachments tend to leave us with no time to meditate. For example, if you are attached to working 70 hours a week, you will have very little time left to meditate. Attachments also prevent meditation because if we have strong attachments we see no reason to practice meditation.

It is important to understand that our attachments are really about wanting to be happy. We engage in all of the activities we are attached to because we believe that they will either bring us happiness or help us avoid suffering. If you consider your life from birth until the present, you will see that everything you have done was motivated by a desire to be happy and free from suffering.

This condition for meditation is about understanding that the happiness achieved through engaging in these activities is transitory and that, in fact, this transitory happiness is simultaneously a source of suffering.

For example, we believe that acquiring certain material possessions will bring us happiness. Unfortunately, this is not the case. Consider our desire for the home of our dreams. First, we experience the difficulty of acquiring the money necessary to purchase a home. We may need to work many years to accumulate enough money for a down payment and acquire a job with sufficient income to support the monthly payments on a mortgage. Then we must find the home, which can involve countless hours of searching for the right house that is within our financial limitations and located in the right neighborhood. Once we locate the "perfect" house, we suffer through the process of making offers. We may lose the house to another bidder and find ourselves starting all over again on the search for a home that meets our needs (desires?).

After we finally find a home and secure a contract, then we must arrange for inspections and financing. This process may result in another failed attempt. However, even if we finally succeed in purchasing the home that we believe will be perfect for us, our difficulties have only just begun.

As soon as we move in we discover all the problems we failed to notice prior to purchase. Perhaps the basement leaks or the sewer line is broken or the insulation is inadequate. These problems result in more worry and expense. Once we get the home in order in terms of its' aesthetic appeal and underlying mechanical sound- ness, we have satisfied our desire to acquire something we wanted very much.

Unfortunately, this is not the end of the story. Now we begin worrying about losing what we have acquired. We insure the home and maintain it, but its' gradual demise is inevitable. It requires constant effort to retain its value and appeal. But, no matter how diligent we are about maintaining this home, there is always the fear that we will lose it. We could lose our job and therefore our ability to pay the mortgage. The home could be destroyed in a fire or flood or it could simply lose significant value in an economic downturn. We tend to worry about all of these possibilities.

This is what is meant about transitory happiness. If happiness or contentment is dependant on acquiring and keeping what we want and escaping or avoiding what we don't want, that happiness will always be temporary. Change is inevitable. It is not possible to control all aspects of our lives.

Understanding this reality is the basis for abandoning attachment. We turn towards meditation when we understand that tranquility and mindfulness practice promotes contentment and understand that lasting happiness depends on contentment. This is what is meant by *abandoning attachment* as a condition for developing meditation.

QUALITIES OF TRANQUILITY MEDITATION

The Waterfall

In the beginning, it is almost impossible to calm our minds, almost impossible to rest without thoughts. Our mind is flooded with thoughts, lists, concerns, and anxiety. In the beginning, you may find yourself thinking, "What am I trying to do? Is it possible for me to really experience the calmness, the tranquility, and the mindfulness of meditation?"

Recognizing the overpowering flood of thoughts is the first experience of meditation. This experience is described by the analogy of a waterfall. The powerful experience of thoughts and distractions feels like a strong, beautiful, powerful waterfall. We are standing underneath this rush of water. The water is flowing strongly, aggressively and continuously, bubbling and roaring with white foam sparkling in the sunlight and rushing over us. Our mind is like this huge powerful waterfall—full of thoughts. There are millions of thoughts. We can't even count them, can't even look at them. There are so many, simultaneously arising.

This is our first experience of meditation and it is very positive, very encouraging. Experiencing this flood of thoughts is not a reason to be discouraged. This is not a negative experience. We are *experiencing* our thoughts. This is the beginning of experiencing the peacefulness and calmness of tranquility meditation. Calmness is not different from the experience of the waterfall of thoughts. This is a very positive experience of meditation. We are seeing how busy our minds are and how much we are *unaware* of these thoughts in our ordinary daily experience. Mindfulness allows us to *see* how busy our minds are. Mindfulness allows us to *experience* our thoughts. We are bombarded by thoughts, emotions, one after another. It is a very powerful experience. We wonder how it is possible that we never noticed before.

The Peaceful River

In the middle, our experience in meditation becomes like a fast flowing river. It is peaceful on the surface, but there is a strong current. There are waves and ripples, like a river with rocks underneath, but not so close to the surface that the water actually breaks.

The Calm Ocean

In the end, the experience of meditation is like the ocean on a very calm day. Out in the bay on a calm day, the surface of the water is smooth with an occasional wave. Tranquility meditation becomes like this. Thoughts arise, but like the waves in a calm sea, they don't disturb the calmness and clarity of the mind.

THE BENEFITS OF TRANQUILITY MEDITATION

Meditation is not about trying to eliminate thoughts. Meditation is simply about making thoughts and emotions more workable. Meditation is letting go of hope and fear. Meditation practices are like weight lifting. The point of weight lifting is to develop muscles. The exercises themselves have no meaning. They are simply techniques. Similarly, meditation practices are methods to make our minds more spacious and workable. Once our minds have become more workable, we are able to see more clearly how our minds work. Seeing clearly makes it possible to generate insight about how we view and react to the world.

When we bring the mindfulness of meditation into our post-meditation world, we are able to understand more clearly our interactions with other people. For example, if you are working with a group of lawyers on a litigation project and one of the lawyers fails to provide his or her part of the materials needed for trial in a timely manner, mindfulness allows you to stop and consider the situation from a non-judgmental perspective.

Being present and non-distracted means being less judgmental and ego involved. From that perspective, you may see that the instructions you provided to the non-performing lawyer were not clear. Or, you may see that this colleague is buried in work for another litigation team or has recently experienced a significant loss or a debilitating illness. These insights may help you avoid assuming that this individual is simply untrustworthy and irresponsible. Mindfulness meditation makes it possible to see in this way because we are less distracted by our own mental chatter and story line.

Not only does settling the mind allow us to see more clearly, it puts us in touch with our basic nature which is wise and compassionate. Research confirms that there is a connection between being present and being open to seeing situations from the perspective of others.[29]

---

29   This example came from Steven Keeva, *Transforming Practices: Finding Joy and Satisfaction in the Legal Life* 68-69 (Contemporary Books, 1999).

CHAPTER 3:

MEDITATION OBSTACLES & REMEDIES[30]

There are a variety of obstacles to meditation practice. This chapter discusses several obstacles and provides remedies for overcoming them. It is helpful to read this chapter when you first learn about meditation, but you may find that as you experience meditation practice, these instructions become more meaningful because you encounter obstacles in your own meditation. On the other hand, it is helpful to read about obstacles before you encounter them in order to help you recognize them when they occur.

DULLNESS AND TORPOR

Dullness in meditation may simply mean falling asleep. Even if you are awake, your mind may lack clarity and focus. There is no power in your focus on the object of meditation and you may experience the sensation of sleepiness. This is the obstacle of *dullness*. Torpor describes a meditative state that is lacking in crispness. There is a dull, heavy feeling to the mind.

---

30 The material in this Chapter is based on written and oral teachings I have received from Dzogchen Ponlop Rinpoche. See, e.g., Dzogchen Ponlop Rinpoche, *Investigating the Mind of Meditation*, 7(2) BODHI, 30-37.

The primary remedy for dullness and torpor is watchfulness. This means setting up an intentional watchfulness to recognize the presence of dullness. Simply watch for these obstacles and recognize their presence when they appear. This is like having a guard dog trained to watch for robbers—robbers who steal our mindfulness.

Three additional remedies use the body to combat dullness and torpor in the mind. First, movements such as walking meditation or yoga promote clarity in the mind. A second approach is to straighten up one's posture. This means putting some physical exertion into maintaining the meditation posture. It may help to raise your gaze up high. Gaze into the sky if you are outside. Opening your eyes wide may prove helpful as well.

Physical exhaustion contributes to dullness. Finally, sitting in a room that is hot and stuffy contributes to sleepiness. The remedies, of course, are to get more rest and to meditate in a cooler room.

WILDNESS

Wildness is simply distraction. When your mind is wild, you are drawn to some object other than the object of meditation. For example, you may think, "I need to get something to eat." Then you think about going somewhere and selecting items to eat while your body remains sitting in the meditation hall, supposedly containing a mind that is meditating.

Coarse wildness refers to a distraction that is so strong that even if you recognize that you are distracted and recognize that distraction as an obstacle to your meditation, you are unable to come back to the object of meditation. Subtle wildness means your mind is generally clear and able to maintain awareness of the object of meditation, but your clarity and awareness is not unbroken. It is continually interrupted by distracting thoughts.

A more precise description of wildness defines five levels of distraction. Defining these levels of distraction is instructive because the definitions can help us see more clearly our own state of mind during meditation.

Agitation

The coarsest form of wildness is called agitation. Agitation refers to the mind being distracted by an external event. For example, if you are meditating in your home, the phone may ring or a truck may drive by outside or you may smell something burning on the stove. Agitation is when you hear the sound or smell the smell and your mind goes out to that object.

Excitement

Excitement is absence of stability, meaning that the mind is unable to remain at rest. The mind does not actually go out to the distracting object, but it is disturbed by the distracting object.

Feeling Scattered

Feeling scattered means the mind is distracted by thoughts relating to the present, past, and future.

Undercurrent of Thought

The undercurrent of thought doesn't become apparent until after the mind has come to rest to some degree so that the coarse distraction of manifest thoughts and agitation has settled down. Once the mind is settled to this degree, meditators become aware of the subtle undercurrent of thought or potential for thought that is occurring all the time.

Getting Lost in Itself

Getting lost in itself is a very subtle form of wildness that occurs when, having come to rest, one generates a thought or concept of rest. That thought or concept distracts you from the state of rest.

As with dullness, the first antidote for wildness is watchfulness, which means maintaining an intentional awareness or watchfulness to notice when one of these forms of wildness is present. Simply recognizing the presence of wildness is an antidote for wildness.

Another way to work with wildness is to refrain from analyzing too much. This means not putting too much intentional effort into the practice. The instruction is to *relax* the mind, not *stress* the mind. Too much effort will generate thoughts. You can work with wildness by relaxing. Let the mind settle and relax naturally. Physically, relax within the meditation posture. Mentally, do not try too hard to keep the mind settled. Just let it settle. Lowering your gaze or closing your eyes gently may also be helpful.

> "Last week, I thought I picked up the meditation exercise with a certain amount of ease. This week it felt completely different. At first, I was not really certain of why this was. Then I realized

that maybe it was because on Monday before class I had a cup of coffee (well a travel mug—so more like 3 cups). I thought being "wired" from the coffee was keeping me from being able to focus. My mind was just running wild ... On Wednesday, I started with hope. I did not have coffee in my system and that helped tremendously (some people should just be banned from coffee!)."

(Participant, Contemplative Lawyering 2006)

As suggested by the person who drank too much coffee, wildness, like dullness, sometimes results from something you have had to eat or drink, including medications. Stress also may contribute to wildness.

Meditation can help you recognize the impact that food, drink, exercise, and workload have on your mind. Becoming aware of the impact of food, drink, and other environmental factors can be helpful to you in your post-meditation world as well. The "wired" coffee-drinking individual who could not relax in meditation probably also had trouble focusing on reading legal research materials.

CHAPTER 4:

TRANQUILITY MEDITATION – COUNTING THE BREATH & MEDITATION ON AN OBJECT

There are many different forms of tranquility meditation practice. Each practice has a slightly different focus or emphasis. In addition, different approaches to tranquility practice are taught because meditators do not all respond the same way to every practice. A practice that is extremely effective for one person may not be helpful for another person.

In this book I provide you with three different tranquility meditation instructions. You will find additional approaches to meditation instruction in some of the books I recommend in the Resources Appendix. You will find excellent instruction on various methods of tranquility meditation in the books and magazine articles I already suggested.[31] I encourage you to try these methods after you have some experience with the methods I introduce in this book. Additional sources of meditation instruction and practices include

---

31   Thich Nhat Han, *Miracle of Mindfulness* (Beacon Press,1987); *Feature: The Mind of Meditation*, 7(1) BODHI, AT 22-63 (2004); *Feature: Shamatha, The Mind of Meditation*, 7(2) BODHI INSERT, AT 12-37 (2005).

The Practice of Tranquility and Insight, by Khenchen Thrangu Rinpoche[32] and *Stages of Meditation* by the Dalai Lama.[33]

TRANQUILITY MEDITATION INSTRUCTION: COUNTING THE BREATH

For the practice of Counting the Breath, begin by reviewing the instruction on meditation posture that appears in Chapter 1. Counting the Breath is, like Following the Breath, a very simple practice which is at the same time quite profound.

First consider your motivation for practicing. It can be very helpful to have an aspiration that you contemplate or verbalize each time you sit down to practice. This aspiration should not be a fixed or solidified goal in the sense that you feel like a failure if you don't progress quickly. Settling your mind in meditation takes time and does not proceed in a completely linear progression. Developing an aspiration for your practice is wonderful and beneficial, but if you become too attached to your aspiration, it becomes an obstacle. Try to relax and be gentle with yourself.

It is helpful to reconsider your motivation periodically. Over time you may be able to more accurately pinpoint what you wish to work on. For example, perhaps your initial aspiration was to experience less stress in your life. Then, as a result of meditation you begin to recognize the source of your stress. For example, you may see that your stress results from dwelling on past mistakes. This insight might cause you to adopt and aspiration to be less judgmental of your own mistakes.

---

32 (Snow Lion Publications, 1993).

33 (Snow Lion Publications, 2001).

In order to engage in the practice of Counting the Breath, each in and out breath is mentally counted as one breath. Each in and out breath is counted sequentially, starting with one, until you reach ten. If you lose track of the next number, return to one and start again. It is important to be really honest with yourself. If you think you know what the next number is, but are unsure, you should return to *one* and start again. As with Following the Breath, if you are distracted by a thought, return to the object of meditation, which in this case is counting the breath. Whenever you are distracted, you should resume counting at one.[34]

Making it to ten is not the goal of this practice. In some ways, meditation is like weight lifting. Weight lifting is an exercise designed to help you develop your muscles. Becoming a skillful weight lifter is not the goal of weight lifting. Similarly, meditation is an exercise or practice that helps you develop the skill of being present in all of your daily activities. The meditation practice itself is simply an exercise or tool. Doing the practice well is not the goal.

The practice of Counting the Breath is beneficial for several reasons. First, Counting the Breath provides the practitioner with a more substantial anchor or focal point for meditation than Following the Breath alone. The breath alone is sometimes perceived as extremely insubstantial, which can make it difficult to maintain focus. Counting the Breath focuses the mind by engaging the mind in the counting process. This allows the mind to settle more easily. Your mind is not capable of truly multi-tasking. If you are paying attention to more than one thing at a time, your attention to each item tends to be impaired to some degree. Ordinarily, you handle more than one focus of attention by jumping back and

---

34   Thich Nhat Han, *Miracle of Mindfulness* 21 (Beacon Press 1987) (provides instruction on Counting the Breath).

forth between the two different focal objects. Therefore, if your mind is fully engaged with following the breath or counting the breath, this will vastly reduce distracting thoughts. It is for this reason that counting the breath can be a very effective method for settling the unsettled mind.

Second, Counting the Breath is helpful because it includes a built in feedback mechanism. When you are distracted while following the breath, you may not notice that you are distracted. When you are distracted while counting the breath you will lose track of the next number. Losing track of the next number lets you know that you have been distracted.

If you maintain your focus and count all the way to ten, simply return to *one* and start again. The reason for limiting the practice to *ten* is to combat our habitual tendency to turn a practice like this into a game or contest—"How high can I count before losing focus?" Approaching the practice in this way (with attachment to the result) promotes an attitude of pride (when we succeed) and negative self-judgment (when we fail). Approaching the practice in this way mirrors our habitual patterns in life. But, Counting the Breath is not a game or contest. It provides an opportunity to experience working on a task without attachment, without hope and fear. It is simply a method for stabilizing your mind. If you succeed in reaching ten, all that means is that you are following the instructions.

If you find that you are able to count to ten easily, stop counting and continue your meditation session using the method of Following the Breath. If you find you are having difficulty reaching ten, don't be hard on yourself. Relax. Again, counting is not a contest. It is simply a method to help you rest your mind. If you find that counting your breath is extremely effective in terms of settling your mind, you may want to use this practice as an antidote for wildness when you are engaging in other forms of meditation. If you encounter dullness and wildness while counting your breath, apply the remedies discussed in Chapter 3.

Finally, whenever you end a meditation session, it is helpful to dedicate your meditation to accomplishing your aspiration for that meditation session. This reminder of your aspiration may help you take what you have learned from meditation into the rest of your day.

What to do with Thoughts in Meditation

Thoughts continue to be a challenge for meditators even after many years of practice. Remember that eliminating thoughts is not the goal of meditation. Meditation practice is designed to tame the mind by making thoughts more workable. Ordinarily we are controlled by our thoughts. Meditation practice makes it possible to observe our thoughts. Mindfulness allows us to work with our thoughts. For example, when someone says something hurtful to you, your habitual response may be anger. Mindfulness meditation allows you to look at your anger and consider the situation and your response to the situation rather than simply feeling hurt or acting out in anger.

Therefore, don't try to repress your thoughts. The more effort you expend trying to stop them, the more thoughts you will generate. Relax and observe your thoughts. Acknowledge them and return to counting. Your thoughts are like the pictures in a museum. They are beautiful. Look at them and then move on. Don't reach out and touch them or possess them. Meditation is appreciating the present, resting in the present—experiencing *Nowness*. Meditation is letting go of hope and fear.

Counting the Breath – Practice Schedule

It will be very beneficial if you do this practice of counting the breath interspersed with following the breath for at least 14 practice sessions. Even five minutes of meditation each day will be beneficial. It will be even more beneficial if you can do this practice twice a day and/or extend your sessions to 15 minutes or even longer. Again, I have provided you with a Practice Schedule Appendix to help you keep track of your meditation sessions.

Post-Meditation Practice Exercise

During the two weeks that you are practicing counting the breath, you can extend the benefit of this practice into post-meditation by continuing to use a mindfulness reminder as discussed in Chapter 1. Continue with the reminder you have been using or select a new one. A traditional approach is to keep a small pebble or rock in your pocket. Feeling the rock in your pocket is your mindfulness reminder. Of course there are many other possibilities, including stop signs, ringing telephones, digital watch alarms, the face of your child or spouse, email, etc. Anything that occurs regularly in your life can serve as your mindfulness reminder.

For this post-meditation practice exercise, whenever you encounter your mindfulness reminder, look at your mind and notice whether it is in the past, the present, or the future. Then, simply return to the present by bringing your awareness back to your breath. Rest about 25% of your attention on your breath and notice the present world around you.

You may find it helpful to keep a journal about your experiences with the post-meditation practice. A daily journal helps you establish a habit of considering each day at the beginning and at the end. If you begin your day with meditation practice, you can make an aspiration at the end of your practice session to use your mindfulness reminder throughout the day. At the end of the day, you can make an entry in your journal about the post meditation exercise. What did you discover when you looked at your mind?

I think it is important to note here that it is very ambitious to aspire to bring your meditation into your post meditation world when you have only just begun meditating. I have learned, however, from teaching these practices and post-meditation practices that selecting and using a mindfulness reminder is a very powerful and profound practice right from the beginning. Combining daily meditation with the post-meditation practices using a mindfulness reminder helps you see the benefits of tranquility meditation and mindfulness much more quickly than if you do either of these practices alone.

Therefore, if you were unable to settle on or remember to use a mindfulness reminder during the first two weeks of practice, I encourage you to make the effort again. If you take the time to purchase a journal in which you record your meditation experience and any insights you gain from the post-meditation practice this can help you remember to use your mindfulness reminder.

> "This exercise has shown me that I am hardly ever in the present. I find that I am mostly in the future thinking about what I have to do next, when I will do it, how I will do it, etc. If I am not in the future, then I am in the past worrying about things I cannot change—thinking I should have done this or worrying about

the consequences of what I did not do. I find that thinking and worrying about the past and the future is quite draining because it affects my concentration and my ability to relax. I have noticed over the course of the week that my mindfulness reminder is a good check on this. By having a reminder, I am aware of what thoughts are going through my mind and can make a more conscious effort to focus on the present."

(Participant, Contemplative Lawyering 2006)

"For the practice exercise, my mindfulness trigger was a ringing telephone. Throughout the week, I noticed that my mind was in the future each time the telephone rang. For example, I was working on editing a document. When the telephone rang, I realized that I was thinking about things I needed to do at home. I was editing the document simply to check it off my "to-do" list instead of editing in order to edit (like Thich Nhat Han's dishwashing example). In fact, I was barely aware of the process of editing while I was doing it. Because I was consumed with concerns about the future, the time I spent working on the document was lost.

As the week progressed, I used the ringing telephone as a signal to take a breath and bring my focus to the present. I chose the ringing telephone because I receive so many calls—and they annoy me no end. Before I picked up the phone, I would take a deep breath and practice mindfulness. I frequently get exasperated when I receive calls during the dinner hour. Sometimes I am rude and then I feel guilty about it later. As the week went on, I found that taking the breath and acknowledging my annoyance helped me to be less rude. I became more aware of the person on the phone as a person and not just as a nuisance. For the first time, I consciously thought about productive ways to approach the situation."

(Participant, Contemplative Lawyering 2006).

A DAY OF MINDFULNESS & OTHER INSTRUCTIONS FROM THICH NHAT HAN

In *The Miracle of Mindfulness*, Thich Nhat Han describes a practice of dedicating an entire day to mindfulness.[35] I am fully aware of how difficult it is for lawyers to carve out a day during which the telephone is turned off, the computer is shut down, and no paid work is done. Nonetheless, I suggest that you read Chapter 3 of Thich Nhat Han's book and consider finding a way to use this practice in your life. While it is hard to convince yourself that you have the time to do this practice, it is a gift of relaxation and contentment. It can sooth your soul. Even if you can only spend part of a day mindfully, that would be wonderful.

Even if you cannot manage a day (or part of a day) of mindfulness, short sessions of daily meditation can provide you with much-needed rest and contentment. When you are preparing to meditate, it can be helpful to read and re-read chapters from *The Miracle of Mindfulness*. Chapter 2 (The Miracle is the Walk on the Earth) and Chapter 4 (The Pebble) are particularly helpful. These chapters should be read as guided meditations. Do not just skim through these chapters. Read a few pages at a time, slowly. As you read the material, follow Thich Nhat Han's meditation instructions. Alternatively, ask someone to read to you from these chapters while you meditate.

---

35   *The Miracle of Mindfulness*, at 27-31.

TRANQUILITY MEDITATION INSTRUCTION: MEDITATION ON AN OBJECT

Like the first two tranquility practices, this practice is deceptively simple. The focus or object of meditation in this practice is a small rock or other simple object. You can also use a small dot drawn on a piece of paper or a short stick.

Place the object in front of you at a distance that will make it possible to view the object comfortably. You will probably find that you need to place the object some distance away from you so that you aren't looking down too much, which can be uncomfortable after a while. It would be good to treat the following instruction as a guided meditation. You may find it helpful to have someone else read the instruction to you very slowly.

Take a moment at the outset to generate an aspiration for your practice. Why are you meditating? Your aspiration may be to improve your focus or to achieve some sense of calmness and contentment in your life. Or perhaps your aspiration is to interact more skillfully with others, let go of attachments and judgments, or to work with strong emotions. It is very beneficial to consider your aspiration whenever you practice.

While sitting in a proper meditation posture rest your mind on your breath for a few minutes until you mind is settled.

After your mind has settled, look at the rock or other object. Your gaze should not be too intense. Rest your mind on the object. Simply see the object clearly. You don't need to analyze the object or consider its color or shape or where it came from. Simply see the object clearly. Seeing the object clearly means resting your mind on the object without and labels or judgments. Simply see it. When thoughts arise, acknowledge them and return your attention to the object. You may find it grounding to allow a small amount of your attention to follow your breath.

Seeing an object clearly, without thoughts or labels, brings your mind into the present. The object is an anchor for resting your mind in the present. Appreciate this experience of the present. Relax and rest your mind in this experience of *nowness*. Let go of hope and fear. Do not dwell on thoughts of the past—the past is gone. Do not anticipate the future—the future is not here yet. Simply be here now—relaxed and spacious. See the object clearly.

If you find that you are having difficulty settling your mind, return to the practice of resting on your breath. Once your mind is settled, try meditating on the rock or other object again.

This practice can be done with other visual objects, including virtually anything in the room. The difficulty you may encounter with other visual objects is that they may cause you to generate more thoughts. However, if you find you can work with other objects, this would be very beneficial. In addition, this practice can use sounds, smells, tastes, or bodily sensations as the object of meditation.

The Benefits of Meditation on an Object

Like the meditation practices of Following the Breath and Counting the Breath, this practice is very simple and yet very profound. Again, this practice brings your mind into the present. Working with an object rather than the breath has several advantages. First, for some people, the insubstantial nature of the breath causes them to lose focus and become dreamy. An object like a rock provides a clear anchor for your mind. A visual object has a solidity that can be very grounding.

For some people, however, this practice is difficult because they find that having their eyes fully open is distracting. The object and the environment give rise to distracting thoughts. If this practice is difficult for you, try alternating Following the Breath with Meditating on an Object during your meditation session.

Even if you find meditating on an object to be difficult, I encourage you to try this practice for at least fourteen sessions. The benefit of continuing to work with this practice is that it is a powerful bridge to post meditation. This practice gives you the opportunity to learn to be present with objects in a formal meditation setting where there are minimal distractions. A simple object like a rock or a dot on a paper is used because you are unlikely to have many thoughts about these simple objects. This practice provides you the opportunity to learn what it means to rest in the present experience of an object without concepts, analysis, labels, attachments, or aversions. Having experienced resting with an object in formal meditation, you can then take that experience into your post-meditation world.

Our world is full of objects and beings. We tend to respond to those objects and beings with attachment, aversion, or neutrality. These responses interfere with our ability to see and experience our world clearly. For example, if we encounter another person we tend to immediately judge that person. We make assumptions about others based on their appearance or based on something they have said or even based on someone else they remind us of.

These assumptions interfere with our ability to see others clearly and cause us to relate to others unskillfully. For example, if we encounter someone who reminds us of a family member we don't get along with, we may approach that individual with suspicion. By working with objects in meditation, we can begin to experience responding to our world without attachment and aversion and without labels. We can then take that experience into our post-meditation world. We can respond more skillfully because our minds are not distracted by our constant mental discourse.

Furthermore, this practice can provide the basis for truly seeing and experiencing the world we live in. When we walk or drive through the world, we are often lost in thought, not noticing the flowers and trees we are passing. We miss the clouds in the sky or the smile on a child's face. We don't notice the taste of our food or the sound of the birds singing. We are too busy with our thoughts to notice and experience our world.

Post-Meditation Practice Exercise – Meditation on an Object

In order to bring the practice of Meditation on an Object into your post-meditation world, continue to use a mindfulness reminder. When you encounter your mindfulness reminder, stop and rest your awareness on an object in your field of vision. Rest your gaze and awareness on the object for the time it takes to breathe in and out 5 or 10 times. Try to select a mindfulness reminder that you will encounter frequently throughout the day. Of course it is important to actually use your reminder. You may find it helpful to keep a journal about your experience with meditation and with the post-meditation practices. If you sit down to write about it, you will be reminded to do it. Another approach might be to make a note on your practice schedule or post a note on your computer screen or refrigerator or inside your front door or in your calendar reminding you of your intention to use a mindfulness reminder. You can also set reminders in your cell phone.

I suggest that you engage in the formal practice of Meditation on an Object for at least fourteen sessions. The post-meditation practice of using a mindfulness reminder to be present with objects should be practiced on the days when your formal practice is Meditation on an Object. If you skip a day (or more) of formal practice you should continue to engage in the post-meditation practice. I have provided a practice schedule in the Practice Schedule Appendix.

2nd Post-Meditation Practice Exercise — Meditation on an Object

While you are practicing meditation on an object during your formal meditation session I recommend that you engage in a second post-meditation practice.

In post meditation, use whatever materials you are reading (or writing) as an object of meditation. Whenever distracting thoughts arise, simply return to your reading material or writing project. You may find yourself surprised by how often your mind wanders when you are reading or writing. By applying your meditation skills, you may find that you are not very present with these tasks or that you are frequently distracted by a desire to check your email or get up and get a snack. Our inability or unwillingness to remain present is an indication of dissatisfaction with what we are doing. It can be helpful to remind yourself why you are engaging in this work and how fortunate you are to have the opportunity to do the work you are doing. This can help motivate you to remain present with your work. Your meditation practice can help you identify distractions and return to your work in the same way you return to the object of meditation during formal practice. Many meditation practition-ers have been amazed at how much more efficient they can be in completing reading assignments and writing projects when they apply mindfulness.

> "The practice assignment for this week was to be fully present while reading legal materials. I am blown away by what a significant change I've realized when I read. I am actually able to read significant portions in far less time and having absorbed far, far more than I have prior to meditating and making the effort to be mindful. I used to find it almost impossible to focus while reading legal materials because I'd allow my mind to wander, usually to worries and stresses related to work. In the past, in order to deal with this I've literally had to write out what I was reading in order to keep focused. This would sometimes take hours. I am so pleased that I am able to focus now, take notes and not have to write what I'm reading verbatim in order to absorb the material. I'm amazed."
>
> *(Participant, Contemplative Lawyering 2005)*

> "In general, I have been more aware of how often my mind is wandering off. I have noticed that I have a habit of wandering while reading, especially while reading difficult legal materials. However, I have been able to recognize that my mind is wandering off, stop, focus on my breath, and then return to my reading in a more present state. It has been very helpful."
>
> *(Participant, Contemplative Lawyering 2006)*

> "I now read for understanding rather than just to get the reading completed. Before applying this post-meditation practice, if I read something that was unclear, I would just go on reading,

hoping someone else would explain it to me. But now, I will reread the unclear text until it makes sense to me. I have also noticed that I can concentrate better in meetings by following my breath for a few moments during the meeting. This helps me tune out distractions that may surface while I am trying to pay attention to what others are saying."

(Participant, Contemplative Lawyering 2006)

"I decided to try mindfulness while reading about Commercial Paper, which is notoriously dense and frequently uninteresting. This kind of reading always takes me forever to get through and then I have a hard time recalling what I read. On Friday I tried to be present as I read each word about cashier's and teller's checks. I found that in short order my mind wandered to a conversation I had earlier which had not gone well. I thought about what I should have said, how I could have argued well, and how I wasn't really listening to the other person. Instead of getting angry at myself for not staying focused on my reading, I tried to find value in the fact that I was learning how my mind works and how I got distracted from the present.

After reading a few paragraphs and still finding my mind wandering, I realized that I was just going through the motions of mindfulness. Instead of setting my aspiration to stay mindful while reading all 40 pages, I set my aspiration to be present with one paragraph at a time. I said each word aloud in my head as I worked through a sentence. At the end of the paragraph, I summarized what I had just read. This worked a lot better. I was present and really learning the material. Even though this method seems slow and arduous, I moved through this material more quickly than I ever had before.

When I read the materials about mindfulness engendering efficiency, I don't believe I grasped the full magnitude of this. I see now that mindfulness is really a way to live a more productive life. By slowing down my reading and focusing on each word, I ended up saving myself time. I didn't spend half my time daydreaming about the past. I also ended up understanding the information on the first pass and I feel confident that I won't need to speed read it again in order to use this information."

(Participant, Contemplative Lawyering 2006)

Other Post-Meditation Practice Exercises — Meditation on an Object

In *The Miracle of Mindfulness* at pages 3-6 and 85-86 you will find several additional post-meditation mindfulness practices that relate to meditation on an object, including washing dishes, eating a tangerine, cleaning house, and making tea. Try any of these exercises or make up your own. You may find it helpful to keep a daily or weekly journal of your experiences with meditation and post-meditation practices and exercises.

WHY DID PHIL JACKSON INTRODUCE MEDITATION TO THE CHICAGO BULLS?

Phil Jackson, the extremely successful coach for the Chicago Bulls and the Los Angeles Lakers, uses meditation to improve his teams' performance.[36] From what you know about meditation at this point, why do you think that meditation would help a professional basketball team perform better? How do you think it helps

---

36   Phil Jackson & Hugh Delehanty, *Sacred Hoops: Spiritual Lessons of a Hardwood Warrior* (Hyperion, 1995).

individual players perform better? Do you think meditation will help players work better as a team? Why? Why not?

This question works well as the basis for a group discussion. If you do not have access to a group, you can work with this question by contemplating your own experience engaging in sports activities, including competitive team sports. Consider how your state of mind has impacted on your ability to compete.

In this book, I would like to make your experience of exercises and discussion questions as beneficial as possible. My view is that you will benefit the most if you actually consider the questions I pose prior to reading my comments on those questions. For this reason, I strongly encourage you to engage in practice exercises and think through your own answers to those questions both before and after you read my comments.

If you are meditating with a group, this question can provide a wonderful basis for a group discussion about the benefits of meditation on an object. Whether you consider this question on your own or with a group I suggest that you also consider how this question relates to the practice of law.

COMMENTS ON WHY MEDITATION IS HELPFUL FOR SPORTS (AND OTHER) COMPETITORS

There are aspects of engaging in sports that are very meditative. When you engage in extreme sports such as rock climbing, it is important to pay close attention to the cliff you are climbing and also to where your body is in relationship to that cliff. Successful rock climbing requires the climber to be present and undistracted.

The same is true (but with less danger involved) for most sports, especially those that are competitive. A slalom skier must be completely present with her body, the snow and ice, the course, her skis, and the gates. She can't be lost in anxiety about the time. She can't be thinking what she will do when the race is over. If you have ever played a sport, you know what I am talking about.

The players on a professional basketball team probably made it to that level of play in part because they already have learned to be present and non-distracted when they are playing basketball. On the other hand, they may not be consciously aware of the mental dimension of their playing ability. By engaging in meditation, they will be more aware of distractions and consciously develop the ability to acknowledge their thoughts and let them go.

When one plays professional basketball, there are many sources of distraction. The stands are full of shouting fans, some hurling insults and others trying to get the attention of an adored famous player. Players may be distracted by anger at what they perceive as an unfair call by the referee. Players also may be distracted by anger at other players—opponents who commit fouls or team-mates who play poorly. Players may be distracted by personal difficulties, such as an argument with a spouse shortly before the game. Players may be distracted by the pain of an injury or by concern about the score. All of these distractions can turn a player's mind away from being present with the game and contributing to the team. Meditation can provide them with the skill of acknowledging distracting thoughts and emotions and then returning to the present.

Staying present with playing basketball is a form of meditation on an object (the ball, the basket, your body, the other players, and the game). Obviously, playing basketball is a much more complex situation than the formal practice of meditating using a rock as the focal point for your meditation. Nonetheless, the same skill is involved. The formal practice environment allows you to work with being present and non-distracted when there is very little going on to distract you. Practicing in this protected context allows you to learn the skill of acknowledging thoughts without being distracted by them. Practicing meditation helps you learn to recognize what it means to be resting in the present, which can then be applied in the post-meditation world, including the world of sports. In sports, being fully engaged in playing a sport like this is sometimes referred to as playing "in the zone."

In the same way, meditation is helpful for lawyers. If you can let go of distracting thoughts (including anger, hope and fear, attachments, and aversions), you can perform much more effectively, whether you are reading, listening to a client, delivering an oral argument, writing a brief, or examining a witness. You can work "in the zone."

Kris Shaw is a criminal defense attorney in Seattle, Washington. A long-time meditator, he puts it this way:

> "During trial, there are things I repeatedly see that help me. I can feel the energy of the prosecutor, their myopic focus on one issue. Specifics are hard to describe, but innumerable. It is more like a football player talking about the "field slowing down" which you can experience but it is hard to describe. But rather than be speedy, I can be with my client, take a minute out to look them in the eye. In trial I can look the jury in the eye and be present and kind of see the field more clearly and slowly than I would without meditation."

Another aspect of meditation that relates to playing basketball is the impact that meditation has on one's ability to be a team player. Mindfulness meditation is a practice of seeing, acknowledging, and letting go of thoughts. If we can learn to let go of thoughts during meditation, we can apply what we have learned in post meditation by letting go of anxiety about how we appear to others while playing a sport as part of a team. Letting go of distracting thoughts allows us to be more aware of the actions of our teammates—less involved in our own story line. We are able to work well with the team because we are not distracted by our thoughts.

Mindfulness meditation also is a practice of acknowledging thoughts without judgment. If we can let go of judgments during formal meditation, we can let go of judgments during post meditation when we encounter other people, including teammates and opponents. In this way tranquility or mindfulness meditation undermines our tendency to interact with the world from a judgmental perspective. In this way, meditation can make us better team players.

What I have said about sports teams applies to legal teams as well. Letting go of distracting thoughts makes it possible to be more attentive to what our colleagues in law practice are saying. Letting go of judgments allows us to see our colleagues more clearly. For example, rather than jumping to the conclusion that a colleague has not performed assigned work out of laziness or incompetence, we might see that we failed to explain the assignment clearly. Letting go of our ego-centric need to be acknowledged as the best team member makes it possible to work collaboratively. A group that respects each others' contributions rather than always trying to outperform each other tends to be much more successful.

"Meditation is slowly making me less judgmental of others, as well as less judgmental of myself. My experience with law has been difficult. . . I wonder everyday why I am here. Instead of scolding myself for being unsure, I am able to acknowledge and think rationally about such thoughts. Meditation is not only helping me live in the present, my mindfulness reminder (my cell phone) is helping as well. Whenever it rings, I listen to it and acknowledge my thoughts. I am always in the past (worrying if I said something wrong or did something to offend someone) or in the future (lists and more lists of things to do). I am beginning to realize that I can let things go. It's a wonderful feeling."

(Participant, Contemplative Lawyering 2006)

As this person suggests, mindfulness meditation helps us let go of ego attachment. Most of our distracting thoughts relate to hopes, fears, attachments, and aversions. With mindfulness we can let go of our attachment to winning or fear of losing.

We tend think of attachment to winning as productive because it helps us move towards goals. In fact, strong attachment to winning interferes more than it helps. When we are attached to succeeding (whether in sports, in personal relationships, in the courtroom, or in our career), we become anxious and worried about our performance. Our worry makes it difficult to work without distraction. And when we don't perform as well as we hoped we would, we are deeply disappointed. When we let go of clinging to success, it is possible to perform much better. This is what being "in the zone" is about. When a player lets go of distracting thoughts about performance she or he is able to be fully present with her body, the ball, her teammates, and her opponents. Being fully present allows a player to perform at peak capability.

This point also is relevant to the practice of law. If you can let go of attachment to personal success, you will be a much more effective worker. If you can let go of fear of losing, you can work without distraction. Many of us who have been extremely successful, whether in sports, in academics or in a profession, think that our drive for personal success has been a critical component of our accomplishments. Actually, our need for personal accomplishment distracts us from performing well by creating anxiety, hope, and fear. It is quite possible to have aspirations to perform well without having a personal stake in the result and without being attached to the result. For example, when you represent a client, you can work hard simply because it is the right thing to do given the amount of money the client is paying you not because winning will make you look good. Or, you can work hard simply because you wish to benefit the client.

Even when your motivation is to help your client, you can get caught in the trap of attachment—attachment to winning for the client. The trick is to have aspirations rather than goals. When I refer to aspirations, I mean that you work towards an objective— you believe that it will be beneficial for something to happen and you put effort into moving in that direction. When I refer to a goal, I mean something much more solid. A goal is something that you believe you *need* in order to make you happy. If you do not meet your goal, you will be distressed. Having an aspiration is recognizing the benefit of moving in a certain direction without clinging to the result.

This is the attitude that meditation helps us adopt. Meditation helps us see the insubstantiality of our solidified goals and attachments. Meditation helps us recognize that it is the solidity or clinging nature of our goals that causes us to suffer.

"In discussion you posed the question why Phil Jackson would employ meditation with his team. After contemplating, I have concluded that it really comes down to selflessness. In basketball, selflessness is sine qua non. An avid sports fan will frequently hear commentators praise a player for "making the extra pass" that led to a basket. This is selflessness. And ultimately, isn't meditation too? Isn't it about looking outside of yourself, outside of your egocentric world, outside of your own needs and desires for a moment? These same principles, applied in basketball or any other team sport or endeavor, are invaluable."

(Participant, Contemplative Lawyering 2006)

"When I played competitive tennis, I was distracted by critical thoughts and doubts about my game. I never understood why sometimes I played 'in the zone' and other days I mentally checked out of a match. Through this class, I appreciate that mindfulness is a way to achieve what my coaches called mental toughness. By practicing meditation, one can connect with and understand the mind and thereby train it to stay focused on the present moment. Because I am prone to negative thoughts and self-doubt, my aspiration for meditation is not to let those thoughts control me. During the past week, I had a lot of difficulty meditating on the rock. When a negative thought would creep in ("Why is this so difficult for me? I'm terrible at this."), I tried to acknowledge those thoughts but not let them consume me or distract me. When negative thoughts seep in during a future tennis match, I can take the skills acquired in meditation and apply them on the court. While some people may be more athletic or better equipped at getting in the zone I appreciate that with practice anyone can improve both her backhand and her ability to focus on the present."

(Participant, Contemplative Lawyering 2006)

CHAPTER 5:

LISTENING

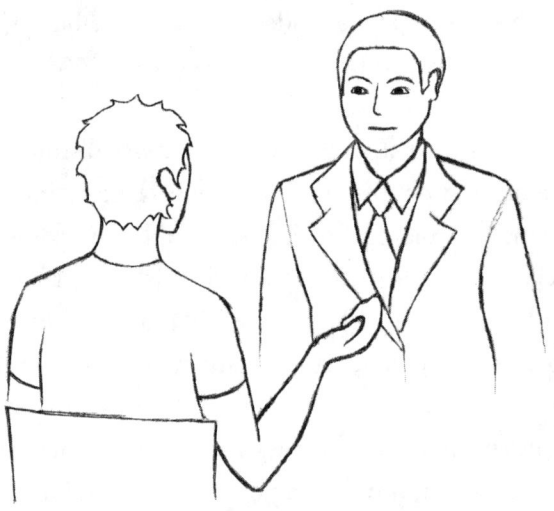

When we think of lawyers, we think of people who are skilled at asking questions, making arguments, presenting positions, and providing advice. However, if we define ourselves in terms of our ability to speak and present issues skillfully, we neglect an essential component of legal practice, listening. Listening is a necessary foundation for negotiating, mediating, arbitrating, litigating, discussing cases with our colleagues, meeting with clients to learn facts and goals, and many other legal functions. In addition, if we neglect listening, we miss opportunities to benefit our clients and others simply by providing them with an opportunity to tell their story and be heard. This may be more important to some clients than anything we can do for them based on our legal training.

Unfortunately, even those of us who count ourselves as good listeners spend much of our listening time considering how we will respond rather than genuinely listening. Listening with an open, engaged, and undistracted mind is an extremely difficult, but deeply rewarding skill to master. The exercises in this chapter will help you evaluate your own listening skills, discover the thoughts that get in the way of genuine listening, generate an aspiration to engage in deep listening, and develop the skill of deep listening.

Formal Meditation Practice as a Basis for Mindful Listening

The listening practices taught in this chapter are post-meditation exercises. In order to provide a foundation for these practices, it is important to continue to practice daily one of the three tranquility meditation practices you already have learned—Following the Breath, Counting the Breath, or Meditation on an Object. Choose the practice that works best for you or alternate between them. For example, if Meditation on an Object is challenging for you, use one of the other practices to bring your mind to rest and then try changing your focus to an object once you have settled down. If your mind becomes distracted again, return to whatever practice is easier for you.

You can further support your post-meditation listening skills by starting your formal meditation sessions with an aspiration to improve your listening skills. It is helpful as well to end your meditation session by dedicating your practice session to improving your listening skills for the benefit of your clients and other individuals in your life. This aspiration and dedication helps you carry your experience of meditation into the rest of your day and serves as a reminder of your intention to practice mindful listening during post-meditation.

During your formal meditation session, if you find that you are able to maintain present awareness of your breath or an object with minimal or no distraction, simply let go of the meditation practice and allow your mind to rest. What I mean by this is that you can let go of the intensity of your focus on the object of meditation (breath or physical object). If you are meditating on an object, allow your eyes to take in more of the room. Expand your awareness to encompass more than your chosen object of meditation. For example, you might allow yourself to become aware of the visual objects in the room beyond your object of meditation. Alternatively, if there are sounds where you are meditating, your awareness can be extended to include them. Similarly, if you are resting your awareness on your breath, expand your awareness to encompass the visual space in front of you. Again, you can also encompass sounds and other sensations into your awareness. Simply rest your mind in your present space. If you become distracted, return to resting on your object of meditation. By distracted I mean engaged in thought or lost in thought.

You may find it helpful to take a few minutes right now to meditate and experiment with the suggestions in the previous paragraph while it is fresh in your mind. If you are meditating with a group, you may find it helpful to have one member of the group read the previous paragraph slowly to the rest of the group as a guided meditation.

Listening Practices Group

Most of the listening exercises that follow require two or three other individuals in addition to you. Some of the exercises are fun. Others are challenging. Others require trust between the participants. If you have already created a meditation group to work through this book together, you are all set.

If you are working through these materials alone, this would be a good time to gather a group of friends, family members, or colleagues together to work with you. Doing these exercises together will help everyone in the group begin to understand the skill and benefit of mindful listening. In addition, working on these exercises together will provide everyone in the group an opportunity to get to know each other better. Finally, these exercises provide group members with opportunities to listen, but also provide them with an opportunity to be heard.

If you are putting a group together for this purpose, a good approach may be to simply ask for their help. You could tell them that you recognize that mindful listening is an important skill that you want to improve both for your work and for your personal life and that these exercises will help you learn listening skills.

Schedule of Listening Practices

The following schedule indicates the post-meditation listening exercises I am suggesting that you engage in over a three week period. The listening exercises are explained in the reading material following this practice schedule. As I have already mentioned, you will find these exercises more effective if you engage in a daily practice of tranquility meditation (Resting on the Breath, Counting the Breath, or Meditation on an Object) throughout this three week period. This schedule also appears in the Practice Schedule Appendix.

Post Meditation: Listening Exercises

1ST Competing Voices	2ND Just Listen	2ND Just Listen	2ND Just Listen	3RD Suffering	3RD Suffering	4TH Prepare
4TH Prepare	4TH Prepare	5TH Speak	5TH Speak	5TH Speak	Listen & Speak	Listen & Speak
Listen & Speak	Listen & Speak	Listen & Speak	Listen & Speak	Listen & Speak	Listen & Speak	Listen & Speak

COMPETING VOICES EXERCISE – INSTRUCTION

Ask two of your friends, family members, or meditation group members to tell you what they did last weekend. Both of them should tell you their story at the same time. Try to listen to both of your friends at that same time. Let them talk for at least two or three minutes. You probably will have difficulty tolerating this exercise for much longer than that.

After you have finished this exercise, consider whether you were you able to hear what either person was saying. Were you able to hear what both of them were saying? Did you listen to one person and tune out the other person? After doing this exercise, can you draw any conclusions about effective listening? You may find it helpful to discuss these questions with your meditation group or with the individuals who helped you with this exercise.

JUST LISTENING – INSTRUCTION

This exercise can provide an interesting opportunity for you and your listening group to get to know each other a little bit better. In this exercise the speaker tells the listener(s) something to help them understand the speaker better. While the speaker is talking, simply listen *without any follow up questions or comments*. While listening, notice any thoughts, judgments, or emotions that come up in your mind. Consider how this exercise relates to the previous exercise.

BENEFITING FROM THE LISTENING EXERCISES

The Competing Voices exercise takes only a few minutes and should generate an interesting discussion. Just Listening extends over many classes when I use these materials to teach a course on Contemplative Lawyering. The Just Listen exercise results in extensive discussions about the components of mindful listening and also about fears and anxieties related to speaking in front of a group. These exercises provide participants with an opportunity to learn about mindful listening from an experiential perspective. By watching our own minds while listening, we can learned how our state of mind impacts on our ability to listen. During these group discussions, I provided input and guidance about mindful listening. This approach made it possible for the group members to learn by experience, while at the same time benefiting from my comments.

In my view, you will receive the most benefit from the listening exercises if you make sure to engage in each of the exercises I teach in this Chapter at least once prior to reading my comments about what you can learn from these exercises. For this reason, my comments appear in a separate section from the instructions for doing the exercise.

I encourage you to do these exercises with a group and think about or discuss the questions I have asked both before and after you read what I have to say about the exercises. Once you have completed the first exercise and at least one session of the second listening exercise and contemplated what you observed about listening, then read my comments.

I will be providing you with a variety of listening exercises as you proceed through these materials. Each exercise has its own questions and comments. The comments on the earlier exercises also apply to the later exercises and vice versa. The commentary is cumulative.

COMMENTS ON THE FIRST TWO LISTENING EXERCISES

When we listen, we often simultaneously engage in a variety of mental activities including evaluating what is being said, thinking about similar experiences we have had, thinking about what to say in response, or thinking about our next appointment.

When we think like this while someone speaks, it is like listening to two speakers at the same time. We can't hear the speaker because we are busy listening to our own mental chatter.

Later in this book I will talk about listening in the context of legal practice. At the outset, however, it is helpful to practice listening in simpler contexts such as someone telling you about their day. Listen without distraction. Let go of your interest in responding or questioning. Just listen deeply. Don't worry about having something to say when the speaker stops talking. If you listen deeply you will know what to say without planning it out while the other person is speaking. Feel free to pause and consider your response once the other person has stopped speaking. Give the conversation some space.

You can also practice mindful listening while watching the nightly news. Try listening without being distracted by your thoughts. Treat listening like meditation on an object. When thoughts arise, dismiss them and return to listening. Let go of judgments.

Listening in this way is a practice of applying meditation on an object to a post-meditation situation. When you listen, the object of your meditation is the sight of the other person, the sound of the other person's voice, and the content of their speech.

> "Though I pride myself on my listening skills, I am not always a good listener. I will occasionally stop listening when I think I've gotten the gist of what someone is saying and start list making. If I'm not truly concentrating on what someone is telling me, I'll also start formulating a response to them before they've finished talking. I am really impressed by what happens when I concentrate on someone's story the same way I rest my mind on an object during meditation. I have much more interesting and helpful things to ask them and I don't waste so much time worrying that I won't have a good response."
>
> *(Participant, Contemplative Lawyering 2006)*

"I had a positive reaction to the listening exercises. One observation I have is that our class, and in turn the world, consists of individuals with widely different backgrounds and experiences. Seeing these differences, I came to realize that each individual will necessarily have a differing perspective and opinion on issues than I do. I must admit that I have often been quick to assume that another's beliefs were the same as mine based on the fact that the individual had an upbringing similar to mine. This assumption, however, did not take into account those experiences of another of which I may be unaware. Ultimately this experience emphasizes the non-judgmental aspect of mindfulness. That is, I should not assume the intentions of someone else simply by projecting my experiences on to that person."

(Participant, Contemplative Lawyering 2006)

"I switched my mindfulness reminder so that I returned to the breath whenever I began listening to someone. This worked very well. I tried this with the people who I usually tune out as soon as they start talking. I also tried this at the Capitol during my work, listening to many people during public hearings. I noticed that my perception of these individuals changed, in part because I wasn't constantly judging. By focusing my listening I was able to gain a more objective view of these people." (Participant, Contemplative Lawyering 2006)

LISTENING TO SPEAKERS IN DISTRESS – INSTRUCTION

Recruit one or more people to do this exercise with you. Again, this exercise provides you with an opportunity to become closer and more open with the person or people you select to help you.

In this exercise, the speaker tells the listener(s) about a very difficult situation or occurrence he or she has experienced. The "listeners" simply listen. Whatever is revealed during this exercise should be kept confidential. This exercise will be most comfortable if everyone in the group shares a difficult experience with the others.

Most people are grateful that someone actually is interested in listening to them, especially if they are sharing painful and difficult experiences. People have a strong need to talk about difficult experiences. When we listen to an individual talk about grief or illness or some other difficult situation, we often want to say something comforting. However, simply listening with an open heart is a wonderful gift that will be deeply appreciated.

As you listen to each speaker tell his or her story, watch your mind. There is no need to generate thoughts. There is no need to plan a response or give a response. Notice when thoughts or emotions come up, simply notice and return to listening. Complete at least one session of this exercise prior to reading the comments below. If you are doing this exercise with a group of meditators, you may find it helpful to discuss your experience of listening. After you have read my comments, complete this exercise again several more times. You may want to reread my comments between practice sessions.

Listening to Speakers in Distress — General Comments

As lawyers we spend a great deal of time listening to clients. Clients come to us in a context of conflict. Often, the situation they are dealing with is very painful for them. Marital and custody disputes are inherently difficult. Tort lawsuits often involve working with clients who have suffered significant losses. Even a simple contract dispute can be emotionally painful because it involves a breakdown in a formerly harmonious business relationship. Income tax cases often involve clients who fear that the outcome will include compliance with onerous financial obligations. Working with clients frequently involves hearing about situations that are emotionally difficult for them. This exercise relates to this aspect of law practice and also to interactions that you have in your personal life with individuals who are experiencing physical pain, emotional pain, or financial loss.

"I deal with situations of intense suffering and emotional intensity all the time. The ability to stay present helps me be more present for my clients and do a better job rather than getting hooked in all the static or emotional dramas that are inviting me to think of them as more important."

(Kris Shaw, Criminal Defense Attorney, Seattle, Washington)

"Clients seem so relieved just to be able to tell their story to someone who is willing to listen. I think this is particularly true in the tax clinic because many of the clients have dealt with the IRS, which in my experience tends not to be particularly receptive to what people have to say. I think Steven Keeva is quite right in suggesting that as attorneys we should consider listening to be one of the services that we provide.[37] In addition to helping lawyers get accurate and complete information, it helps clients feel like someone really cares what they have to say. This can be just as helpful to them as actually solving their problem."

(Participant, Contemplative Lawyering 2006)

There are three important points to learn from this exercise. First, this exercise allows you to begin to understand what it means to be genuinely empathetic. Second, this exercise can help you understand the importance of being comfortable with suffering if you wish to help others who are experiencing suffering. Third, this exercise provides an opportunity to see how we confuse fear with compassion.

Genuine Empathy means Hearing Their Story, Not Yours

"The stories I listened to made me both angry and sad. I find it very difficult to just listen. I think my emotional reactions to the stories, though empathetic, are a manifestation of a personal attachment. My ability to empathize is one of my best qualities and one of the reasons I want to pursue pubic interest and legal services work. But is it possible that if I allow emotion to govern empathy, I may fail to be mindful?"

(Participant, Contemplative Lawyering 2006)

---

37   *Transforming Practices*, at 111-124.

What is genuine empathy? Often when someone relates a difficult situation, we associate that experience with similar experiences of our own and imagine that this person is reacting in the same way that we reacted. Although this approach to listening provides a basis for compassion, it can interfere with our ability to understand the other person's experience. We may even get so engrossed in thinking about our own experience that we don't hear what the other person is saying at all. When this happens it is definitely not possible to work skillfully with the other person.

People experience trauma in different ways. For some people a death, serious illness or injury in their family awakens an appreciation for every precious moment. They see clearly what is important in life and let go of concerns about small inconveniences and difficulties. The death or pending death of a relative also can provide the basis for generating compassion for other individuals who are experiencing the same loss. The same is true when an individual experiences their own significant health problems or pending death.

Others respond to death or serious illness with anger. They may be angry at doctors for alleged mistakes or at someone who contributed to causing the death, serious illness, or injury. They may simply experience anger at the situation. Other individuals respond to situations like this with fear—fear of their own death, serious illness, or injury.

Your personal experience of difficult situations can color what you hear when someone tells you about some difficulty in their life. For example, suppose someone tells you her mother died of cancer. If you have lost a close relative to a serious illness, you may assume that you understand this person's feelings. You could be completely off base. How a mother's death is experienced depends on many factors including the illness that took her life, the mind set of the mother and of the child, the age of the mother and of the child, and the relationship between them. Your experience of death may provide you with insight, but first it is important to listen without imposing your experiences on the other person.

Listening with genuine empathy means listening without judgment, without fear, and without labeling. To use Thich Nhat Han's language, it is "listening in order to listen."[38] Only when we listen in this way can we really hear. When we listen in this way, our empathy is free from egocentricity. Our experience of a similar situation may provide us with helpful insight, but that similar experience will be helpful only if we first listen and fully understand the other person's situation.

> "Today we shared life changing experiences. One person shared the loss of her husband and another shared her mother's fight against cancer. I could easily relate to each of the shared stories and feelings because I have lost a loved one, watched my grandmother fight cancer and struggled with crippling feelings of empathy. While listening to the stories I thought I was listening in the present. By eliciting empathy through my past experiences I was partially in the past and not listening in the present. I was reliving my own sadness. I always thought that my ability to relate through my past experiences brought me closer to understanding what was shared with me. Now I am considering what "carrying around my own sadness" does to my present appreciation for what someone else is saying."
>
> *(Participant, Contemplative Lawyering 2006)*

---

38   *Miracle of Mindfulness,* at 3-4, 23-24.

The Gift of Listening

One obstacle to skillful listening is the discomfort we may experience when we feel there is nothing we can do to help someone who is relating to us an experience of grief, pain, depression, illness, or other suffering. Our discomfort results from fear or a feeling of helplessness.

When we encounter a suffering person, we want to relieve their suffering. We become uncomfortable if we feel we don't have the skill to relieve their suffering. It is even more uncomfortable to realize that the individual's distress, pain, or illness can't be relieved because their emotional pain is too deep or the illness is incurable. This discomfort may approach unbearable when the suffering person is a close family member. Our discomfort results from feeling helpless. This reaction is typical when we encounter someone whose spouse, parent, or child has died recently. We are afraid to say anything because we think we can't possibly say the right thing. We feel that we can't say anything that will help this person.

Often the most helpful thing we can do for someone who is suffering is to simply be there, willing to listen.[39] The suffering person doesn't expect you to relieve his or her suffering. A grieving widow may cry for months or even years after the death of her husband. She may repeatedly retell the story of his death and how it affected her. She may want to bring back memories of her husband that cause her to cry yet again. She may need to revisit unresolved conflict in her marital relationship. You can help simply by listening, simply by being unafraid of her deep anguish.

---

39   See Claxton, J.W., *Paving the way to acceptance. Psychological adaptation to death and dying in cancer.* Prof Nurse (Jan. 1993) ("By offering support and being prepared to listen, nurses can help patients and their families express their feelings and possibly proceed onto acceptance.")

In these circumstances you need to understand that you are not helpless. You can help by listening. Your meditation practice can help you develop the skill of deep listening. Listening is a form of meditation on an object. Simply let go of distracting thoughts and return to listening to the speaker. Let go of your need to "fix" the situation. Let go of your fear of not being able to help by reminding yourself that you are providing a great service by listening. Simply listen with an open heart.

From a practice perspective, there are several ways to develop comfort with your own suffering and with the suffering of others. Later in this book, I will offer additional practices for working with your own sadness and the sadness of others. However, the listening practice we are working with in this section relates to meditation on an object. This is the practice you should work with at this point.

> "As I listen to people tell me their stories, problems or anything else, I find myself looking for the solution: what to say, what to do, how the person should react? Apparently, this reaction is not limited to me. In response to my panacea-type responses to my wife's work problems, she has often said that she doesn't tell me about her work so I can help solve the problems, but only because she needs someone to tell. She wants to get it out. This is very much in line with your comments that it is powerful just to be heard and to be a listener—no evaluation, no response, no solution—just listen. I will have to pay more attention to this."
>
> *(Participant, Contemplative Lawyering 2006)*

Fear is Not Compassion

When you listen to people talk about their suffering, you may be working not only with distracting thoughts, but also with distracting emotions. For example, if someone very close to you tells you they have a life threatening illness, you may experience fear of loss. Or you may fear that you will experience the same kind of illness. Mindful listening means letting go of ego-centric concerns. It is impossible to listen if we are distracted by our fears. It is easy to confuse fear and associated feelings of distress with love and compassion. As you listen, watch your mind. Is the distress you are experiencing based on concern about the other person's suffering or is it based on your own fear of loss? Or are you distressed because you are afraid of experiencing the misfortune this person is speaking about? Acknowledge and let go of your thoughts, hopes, and fears relating to what you are hearing and return to simply listening with an open heart.

PREPARING FOR MINDFUL LISTENING — INSTRUCTION

An important aspect of listening is preparing for a conversation with another person. Often, we are not fully present because we remain lost in whatever activity we were engaged in prior to a meeting or phone call with another person. Alternatively, we may be on a tight schedule

and thinking about what we need to do next rather than being fully present to the conversation.

When you know you are scheduled to speak with someone in person or on the phone, you can engage in a centering practice to prepare yourself to listen mindfully. Stop what you are doing a few minutes before the other person arrives or calls. While you are waiting, rest your mind on your breath. Once you have settled on your breath, contemplate the pending interaction. You are about to encounter another human being. The interaction is full of potential. You have a precious opportunity to listen deeply and in doing so, to provide immeasurable benefit. You have a precious opportunity to learn about another person's world. Generate an aspiration to welcome this person into your presence and give this person your undivided attention.

When the phone rings, whether you are expecting the call or not, don't answer it right away. Allow the phone to ring at least three times. While it is ringing, drop whatever you are doing, bring your mind to rest on your breath, and generate an aspiration to be fully present with the person on the phone, giving this person your full attention and listening deeply. The person you encounter on the other end of the phone may be trying to sell you something you don't want or trying to solicit a contribution for some organization you don't support. It is easy to be angry at this interruption. Remember, however, that the caller is simply attempting to make a living. Having

prepared for the conversation, you can politely decline, rather than say something hurtful. On the other hand, the caller may be a family member in need or a client or colleague with important information. If you have paused and reflected prior to picking up the phone, you can be fully present and appreciate the wonderful opportunity to interact with this person.

For this listening exercise, do the centering practice in preparation for a scheduled meeting or phone call. Also, whenever the phone rings, try to allow it to ring two or three times before answering. While the phone is ringing, generate an aspiration to be fully present with the caller. Finally, try to engage in mindful listening in all of your conversations.

> "For our listening assignment this week, I knew I was meeting with someone at work to talk about revamping or retaining certain procedures. I anticipated that we might have different opinions on the subject so I arrived at the meeting early and made a concerted effort to calm myself. With my eyes closed, I thought about the importance of listening to the other person's viewpoints and staying open and receptive to her ideas. I decided that this meeting was a unique opportunity to focus on the opinions and ideas of someone completely different from myself. I reminded myself that interrupting or leaping in with my opinions or judgments could prevent me from seeing the whole picture. Just before the meeting started, I focused on counting my breath and bringing myself to the present.
>
> This preparation was enormously helpful. I was focused on the other person and her opinions about the process and her ideas for improving it. I made an effort not to judge whether I thought these ideas were good or bad. Instead I asked questions to make

sure I understood what she was saying. As she explained her reasoning, I realized that she had a unique perspective and that she had thought of things I never would have considered. If I had not engaged in centering meditation I probably would have leapt in with my ideas earlier in order to prove myself. I was able to let go of my ego by consciously focusing on the other person. As a result, we achieved an outcome from the meeting that we probably would not have managed or, at least, it would have taken a lot more time to get there."

(Participant, Contemplative Lawyering 2006)

"Last week I went to New York for interviews at a job fair. I focused on my breath for a few minutes before each interview in order to center myself and bring myself into mindfulness before the interviews. I found that I was better able to really listen to the interviewers than I have been in the past. Also, I made an effort to not be distracted by what I would say next. I was able to listen and respond more effectively. Rather than just saying what I thought the interviewer wanted to hear, I feel I was able to actually respond to the interviewer's questions and comments and the interviews, therefore, flowed rather smoothly."

(Participant, Contemplative Lawyering 2005)

DEALING WITH FREQUENT INTERRUPTIONS

Many lawyers tell me that one of the most difficult aspects of their job is the constant interruption from phone calls and visits. They complain that they never have enough uninterrupted time to complete their research and writing projects.

If you are faced with this difficulty, one way to deal with it is to set a time during the day when you make and receive calls and visits. Make sure that all of your colleagues and clients are aware of this schedule. When you receive calls during other times, simply allow the caller to leave a message. It is better to delay speaking with the caller than to pick up the phone and be angry or impatient. If you take this approach, make sure you return any calls you receive, just wait to do this during the portion of your day you have set aside for phone calls.

Another way to work with this difficulty is to practice being fully present with your written work as well as with the calls that interrupt you. What often happens is that a two minute call results in a fifteen minute distraction from work because you continue thinking about the call after it is finished or allow the call to distract you from your original project so much that you launch into a new project or take a break. With mindfulness meditation you can learn to be fully present with your work. This will make you much more efficient. When the call comes, you can make a quick note to yourself about where you are in your written project and then be fully present with the call. When the call is over, you can make a quick note to remind you about anything that needs to be done as a result of the call. Then return to your project.

As you develop the skill of being fully present with your work, you may see that you often are distracted whether people call or not. As a result, you may find that the calls and interruptions that come from outside are not the reason why you have difficulty completing your work. Rather it is your own distracted mind, including your tendency to allow the interrupting calls to distract you more than is necessary.

Mindfulness meditation can help you see and identify distractions and then dismiss them just as you do in formal meditation practice. Mindfulness meditation can help you remain present with your work and therefore more efficient and less stressed.

MINDFUL SPEECH INSTRUCTION[40]

So far we have been working primarily on exercises that involve listening without any comments or questions. Obviously when you are practicing law, you will need to combine listening with speaking. Speaking is an important part of interactions with clients, legal colleagues, and court personnel. Introducing speaking into mindful listening increases the difficulty of remaining present and non-distracted.

Our habit of considering what we are going to say in response to another person during a client interview or even during a casual conversation is a distraction that impairs our ability to listen mindfully. Included in this distraction is our ego-centered concern that we won't have anything intelligent to say. This concern is especially pronounced in the context of law practice because we have set ourselves up as the expert with the answers.

For many of us, every context in which we will be required to speak is full of anxiety and fear about how we will appear to others. When we are introduced to the practice of listening without distraction, we worry that if we clear our minds to listen we won't have anything to say when it comes our turn to speak. This is an unwarranted concern. You will find that if you listen mindfully you will actually be in a better position to speak in a way that is helpful to the

---

40   The materials in this section are based on a talk given by Dzogchen Ponlop Rinpoche to students of the New York Nalandabodhi Study Group (August, 2005). This talk is not available in print.

other person than when you are distracted. When you *really hear* what the other person is saying, your response will be more appropriate and on point. When you truly listen, you will not forget what you have heard. There is no need to jump in quickly with your comments and responses when the speaker stops talking. Also, it is fine to leave some space in the conversation to provide you with time to consider your response once the other person has finished speaking.

Mindful speech begins with calmness. As was discussed in the previous section, it is helpful to engage in a short meditation practice prior to a meeting with a client or any other person. Remember that this meeting provides a precious opportunity to interact with another person. Generate an aspiration to listen, speak mindfully, and be helpful.

Speaking mindfully means watching your thoughts before you speak. Pause and think before speaking and make an effort to say what you have to say in a positive way. This is difficult at the outset, but gets easier with practice. When you watch your thoughts, what you should be watching is your intention. Consider whether what you are about to say is coming from your own ego-centric interests, or whether the purpose of your speech is to benefit others. If your motivation is ego-centered, there is no need to speak. Try to develop a pattern of speaking mindfully and with a pure motivation. By pure motivation I mean a motivation to provide benefit to the person you are speaking to.

It is good to always start any conversation with a positive statement. Even if the situation is quite negative, try to find some way to begin with a positive statement. This statement needs to be genuine in order to be effective. It will not help the situation to begin with a positive statement that is fabricated. If you are not genuine, the other person will know and your attempt to be positive will make things worse. However, if you start with a negative, accusatory statement, the conversation definitely will not go well. Make an effort to genuinely see the positive qualities of the other person. It should be possible to find something positive to say no matter how difficult the person or the situation. Nobody is completely bad. Then speak with an intention to benefit, not from ego. Try not to speak from a place of pride, jealousy, anger, or need.

Mindful speech is very important. Often we open our mouths to speak too quickly, without mindfulness. When we do that, we end up thinking, "Why did I say that?" Thoughtless speech often creates confusion and unhappiness. Mindful speech is important in law practice, but it is also important everywhere. Mindful speech is very beneficial when you are dealing with family, children, friends, colleagues—everyone you encounter in life. Mindful speech is a wonderful opportunity to help others. Mindful speech is based on mindfulness developed in meditation.

The following comment by Chogyam Trungpa Rinpoche talks about how wonderful a conversation can be if we listen and speak mindfully[41]:

> "The process of communication can be beautiful, if we see it in terms of simplicity and precision. Every pause made in the process of speaking becomes a kind of punctuation. Speak, allow space, speak, allow space. It does not have to be a formal and solemn occasion necessarily, but it is beautiful that you are not rushing, that you are not talking at tremendous speed, raucously. We do not have to churn out information and then stop suddenly with

---

41   *Chögyam Trungpa, Cutting Through Spiritual Materialism* 157(Shambhala, 1973).

a feeling of let-down in order to get a response from the other person. We could do things in a dignified and proper way. Just allow space. Space is as important in communicating to another person as talking. You do not have to overload the other person with words and ideas and smiles all at once. You can allow space, smile, say something, and then allow a gap, and then talk, and then space, punctuation. Imagine if we wrote letters without any punctuation. The communication would be very chaotic. You do not have to be self-conscious and rigid about allowing space; just feel the natural flow of it."

For this post-meditation practice exercise, prepare for a planned meeting as in the previous exercise. During your preparation, generate an intention to speak mindfully. During the meeting, watch your mind whenever you plan to speak. What is your motivation? During this week, try to engage in mindful listening and mindful speaking in all of your conversations.

"I applied this listening and speaking exercise to a meeting with one of my co-workers. Last semester he and I had several disagreements about procedures. At this meeting, the other person wanted to review the problems from last semester and make sure they didn't happen this semester. As he spoke, I made an effort to observe my emotions so I could choose to respond instead of react. It was very difficult for me not to become defensive and assign blame to others during this conversation. But, I think I was able to approach the discussion with a clear head and accept responsibility for my part. Instead of being defensive and reactionary, I tried to work with this person on reviewing our processes to see what changes we could make to improve them. I also listened fully. I made an effort not to interrupt when I disagreed or to try to spin the facts. I was also conscious of my facial expressions. Part of listening fully is controlling your non-verbal communication as well. As a result, I think that he felt heard and had a sense of having benefited from the discussion. At the same time, I had several issues I wanted to address with him. I had to be careful in how I presented these issues so that it did not seem like an attack and raise his defenses. I think that because I made an effort to be aware of him and listen to him as well as be present in the situation, I appeared engaged and I was able to convey that the conversation was a joint effort instead of an effort by me to assign blame. As a result, I think some progress was made in what otherwise would have been a very difficult conversation."

(Participant, Contemplative Lawyering 2006)

ACTIVE LISTENING

It is likely that you have heard of active listening. This approach to listening involves reflecting or repeating back what you have heard in order to communicate to the other person that you have heard what has been said. A further benefit of active listening is that by repeating back what you believe you have heard, you can check to see if you have heard the other person accurately.

Active listening is a very powerful tool. It is a methodology that forces you to listen closely enough to be able to accurately reflect what you have heard. Active listening is also helpful because using this approach communicates to the other person that he or she is being heard.

On the other hand, one could characterize active listening as "fake it until you make it." It is a methodology that is designed to make you appear to be truly listening to the other person. When I taught mindful listening to one lawyering process professor, she commented that active listening teaches students to appear to be listening while mindful listening teaches them to actually listen. This is true.

One point of active listening is to communicate to the other party that you are hearing what he or she is saying. However, it is not necessary to engage in "active listening" in order to communicate that you are listening. If you engage in mindful listening so that you are fully present with what the other person is saying, he or she will know that you are truly listening even if you never say or do anything. Think about how often you have had conversations with another person who is distracted. You have to repeat what you are saying several times. You know they aren't listening because of the vacant look in their eyes. It is easy to tell when someone is really listening.

If you engage in mindful listening, you will not need to worry about demonstrating that you are listening by reflecting what you have heard. You will naturally empathize with the other person. Mindfulness meditation provides the foundation for mindful listening. Rather than reflecting, you can ask an open question. This accomplishes the same thing. By asking an open question that is related to what the person has just said, you communicate that you are listening and you solicit more information at the same time.

On the other hand, the aspect of active listening that involves checking the accuracy of your perceptions by repeating what you have heard is an excellent way to ensure that you have understood what has been said.

Another aspect of active listening concerns body language and the set up of the room. The advice often given is to maintain eye contact (unless this makes the other person uncomfortable). This is good advice. Your body language can communicate that you are fully present with a conversation. In addition to maintaining eye contact, it is helpful to sit with nothing between you and the other person (e.g. no desk or table). You can also communicate that you are listening by sitting facing the other person and leaning slightly forward. This posture communicates your interest in the other person. It is good to refrain from fidgeting or glancing at your watch or computer screen. If you are really present with the other person, this will come naturally.

MINDFUL LISTENING & SPEAKING – SUMMARY

The main point to remember is that being present with someone and listening without distraction is much more important than any stylized listening skills. There is no greater gift that you can give to another person than listening deeply without distraction. Listening deeply means going beyond the facts and really hearing what the other person is experiencing. Listening mindfully means not having a second sound track running in your mind. Listening mindfully means not judging, evaluating, or analyzing. Listening mindfully means resisting the urge to comment and clarify. When you engage in mindful listening you let go of ego-centric hopes and fears. When you engage in mindful listening, you are fully present and listening for the benefit of the other person. Mindful speaking shares these same characteristics.

I have dedicated many pages to the skills of listening and speaking, but it all boils down to a few points that are easy to state, but difficult to practice. If you can simply be present and non-distracted and act for the benefit of others, you will listen and speak skillfully and beneficially. These skills can be practiced with great benefit in any context. The foundation for mindful listening and speaking is mindfulness meditation.

Mindful listening and speaking is much easier to do if you have a genuine feeling of empathy for the person you are working with. Genuine empathy has been identified as an important prerequisite for skillful relationships with clients.[42] Chapters 7 through 12 present practices designed to help us generate genuine empathy for others.

---

42   Robert M. Bastress & Joseph D. Harbaugh, *Interviewing, Counseling and Negotiating: Skills for Effective Representation* 116-130 (Aspen, 1990).

CHAPTER 6:

USING MINDFULNESS PRACTICE TO WORK WITH EMOTIONS

In this chapter we will learn to use a post-meditation practice to work with strong negative emotions. Negative emotions are emotions that cause us distress and that cause us to engage in unskillful speech and conduct that harms others. The emotions we will be working with are anger (including impatience), jealousy, pride, and obsessive desire.

If you consider the mental states that cause distress, you are likely to also mention sadness and fear. These feelings often underlie the negative emotions I have mentioned, especially anger. However, sadness and fear by themselves do not tend to cause us to engage in unskillful speech and conduct. On the other hand, sadness and fear often contribute to other emotions (including anger, pride, and jealousy). In addition, many individuals, including many lawyers, suffer from feelings of sadness and fear. Therefore, in order to help you work skillfully with these feelings, I will talk about contemplative practices that work with sadness and fear later in this Chapter and again later in the book.

This Chapter presents a mindfulness-based practice that is designed to help us avoid the negative consequences of anger, jealousy, pride and obsessive desire. In preparation for learning about this practice, you will find it very helpful if you take the time to watch the video recording of a talk presented by Dzogchen Ponlop Rinpoche.[43] This talk (*Mindfulness and Working with Emotions*) provides a wonderful summary of mindfulness or tranquility meditation (also called shamatha or calm abiding). In addition, this talk provides an introduction to using mindfulness meditation as a foundation for working with negative emotions. Rinpoche's talk can be found online at YouTube at the following link: http://www.youtube.com/watch?v=1em8i1Ysqwc&feature=youtu.be.[44]

After you have watched this talk, it would be helpful for you to spend some time contemplating the negative emotions I have mentioned (anger, jealousy, pride, and obsessive desire). Consider why it is that they are characterized as negative. If you are meditating with a group, I encourage you to have a discussion about why you think I have identified these emotions as negative.

This is what one person said about Rinpoche's talk:

"I found this video extremely helpful. Who would have ever thought that you could use your emotions as a mindfulness

---

43   Dzogchen Ponlop Rinpoche is a leading Buddhist teacher in North America and an advocate of American and Western Buddhism. Rinpoche is acknowledged as one of the foremost scholars and meditation masters of Tibetan Buddhism in his generation. Fluent in English and well-versed in Western culture and technology, he is known for his sharp intellect, humor and the lucidity of his teachings. Dzogchen Ponlop Rinpoche, www.dpr.info.

44   This YouTube video is a twenty-minute excerpt from Talk 2 of a weekend teaching by Dzogchen Ponlop Rinpoche, *Compassion Without Limit: The Courageous Heart and Lojong Practice*. The Title of the Rinpoche's Talk on YouTube is *Mindfulness and Working with Emotions*. The complete recording of the weekend teaching is available in DVD and MP3CD format at www.varjaechoes.com.

reminder? All this time, I have been trying to come up with a mindfulness reminder that I would use consistently. It is so true that when thoughts arise, we carry them with us throughout the day. I have a tendency to dwell on everything, and the video really hit home. I've been carrying these thoughts with me, and I have turned them into a burden. I wake up every morning with them, and then I keep them with me when I go to sleep at night. It is no wonder I am always so tired. I am going to try something new this week. Every time I sense an emotion of anger, impatience, worry, pain or sadness, I am going to stop, take a few breaths and go back to whatever I was doing."

(Participant, Contemplative Lawyering 2006)

SLOW REVERSAL – INTRODUCTION

Slow Reversal is a mindfulness-based post-meditation practice designed to help us work with negative emotions. I learned this practice when I attended *Transforming Mental Afflictions*,[45] a weekend teaching presented by Lama Kathy Wesley.[46] Based on that teaching, I incorporated this practice into my life. The presentation here is based on what I was taught, what I have experienced applying this practice to my own life, and what I have learned by teaching this practice to law students and lawyers.

Later in this book, we will spend time working with negative emotions using other meditation and post-meditation methods.

---

45 *Transforming Mental Afflictions* is available on DVD and CD from Vajra Echoes at www.vajraechoes.com.

46 Lama Kathy Wesley is a long-time student of Khenpo Karthar Rinpoche of Karma Triyana Dharmachakra Monastery in Woodstock, New York. She participated in a three-year retreat at Karme Ling Retreat Center, completing the retreat in 1996. She serves at the Columbus, Ohio, Karma Thegsum Choling as its resident teacher.

Slow Reversal is a good starting place for this process. I will begin presenting this practice in the context of working with anger. Later, I will talk about adapting Slow Reversal practice to work with pride, jealousy, and obsessive desire.

Recognizing the Negative Attributes of Anger

The first step in Slow Reversal is to recognize the negative attributes of anger. We need to clearly see the kind of trouble anger gets us into. The difficulty with anger is that we have strong habitual patterns of dealing with conflict. We believe we have no choice other than to prolong negative experiences. We believe it is necessary and important to clearly identify that we have been wronged. Whenever things don't go well, we engage in mental elaborations, running the difficult scenario through our minds over and over again.

For example, suppose you represent a client who accuses you of overcharging for work you performed. Assume that the work you did was complex, of very high quality, and competitively priced. Assume as well that you worked many long hours for this client and perhaps have not charged the client for all of the hours you put in.

In a situation like this, you may feel you are being insulted by your client's accusation. You may run the situation over and over in your head, justifying your position and generating anger at the client for not understanding and appreciating the quality of your services. This is how anger works. Elaboration is our problem. We think, "This awful thing happened to me." We tell ourselves about it over and over. We run it around in our minds. This is a very uncomfortable feeling. Sometimes we are so obsessed by the problem that we cannot sleep at night.

In addition to creating discomfort, anger often causes us to engage in unskillful speech and actions. While numerous examples illustrating this point could be cited from news and other sources, if we think about it, we can remember times when we ourselves have responded to another person in anger or maybe just annoyance. We can recall how our unkind words or sharp tones hurt someone or maybe even contributed to ending a relationship. We may have yelled at the client and insulted him or her. Sometimes we become so angry we throw and break things or actually threaten to hurt someone.

In extreme cases anger can result in one person hurting or killing another person. The news is full of examples of individuals injuring others in anger. The widely reported incident, in which Chris Brown savagely beat his girlfriend, Rihanna, allegedly because she confronted him with a text message from another woman, clearly shows the damage an angry individual can cause.[47]

Anger also interferes with our ability to see clearly what is really going on. Fear and distress cause us to misperceive what is happening. Perhaps the client in the scenario mentioned above did not intend to insult you. Perhaps the client simply has run out of money and is embarrassed to admit that he cannot pay the bill. If you are angry, you probably won't realize that embarrassment, not

---

47   See State of California, County of Los Angeles, Search Warrant and Affidavit (Mar. 2, 2009), available at http://i2.cdn.turner.com/cnn/2009/images/08/25/brown. warrant.pdf. An online search using search terms "angry killed family" yields multiple articles about angry individuals killing others. See, e.g., Kim Janssen, *Cops: Woman Kills Man in Argument over Son*, Chi, Breaking News Ctr, May 19, 2009, available at http:// www.chicagobreakingnews.com/2009/05/harvey-homicide-douglas-collins-shooting-domestic.html. Criminal cases provide examples of defendants who kill or assault others in anger. See, e.g., State v. Guthrie, 461 S.E.2d 163 (W. Va. 1995)(Guthrie stabbed a co-worker after becoming enraged by his persistent taunting); Keeler v. Superior Court, 470 P.2d 617 (Cal. 1970) (Keeler assaulted his ex-wife enraged by her relationship with another man; the assault caused the death of her unborn fetus).

offense, has motivated the client's accusations. You will be too busy demonizing the client and justifying your own conduct.

If you look at situations in which you have become angry, you will see that anger tends to include these three negative attributes. First, it is uncomfortable. Second, it causes us to speak and act unskillfully. Third, it interferes with our ability to see things clearly. This is true both in our personal lives and in our dispute resolution at work.

Making a Conscious Choice to Transform Our Anger

Once we recognize anger as a negative emotion, the next step in the Slow Reversal Practice is to make a conscious choice to transform our anger and distance ourselves from this emotion. The method is Slow Reversal or mindfulness in daily life. How do we take conscious control and choose constructive over destructive responses? Meditation allows us to see emotions coming. We can see anger coming. We can see hurt coming up in us. Because we can see these strong emotions coming, we can reject our destructive default reactions and choose a "different direction," a different response to deal with the distressing situation.

We can apply this practice in all areas of our life, both personal and professional. The facility we gain with taming our emotions in personal situations will be there for us when we need it in a stressful lawyering situation.

"I helped a friend move to New York City from Darien, Connecticut all day on Saturday. We woke up incredibly early, packed up the truck, drove to NYC, unpacked and then drove back to Darien to drop off the truck. At this point it was nighttime and had been a very long day, yet we still had to drive back to NYC. Of course something had to happen to prevent this. As I backed out of the driveway, I drove over a large rock that scraped the bottom of my car and became stuck underneath, causing damage to my car. At first I lashed out at myself in frustration, was angry with my friend for no reason at all and almost lost it completely. However, just a few minutes into this escapade I became aware of the situation and stepped back from my emotional response as if I were watching it from afar.

This immediately helped change an extremely frustrating situation to an amusing event. We ended up having quite an adventure digging a big hole, trying to use a jack (which we quickly learned we had no clue how to use), rocking the car to the side and pulling a gigantic rock out from under the car. All this happened with laughter. It was amazing. Honestly, at this point in the day most people would have had a serious breakdown, but I was somehow able to laugh it off. And my attitude made her attitude much better as well. It was a nice way to experience something so annoying."

(Participant, Contemplative Lawyering 2006)

The Slow Reversal practice begins with an aspiration. Start by promising yourself that you are going to try to tame this particular mindset. This is not about repressing or eliminating anger. Rather it is about slowing the emotional process and walking it back to the point of ignition. Anger, like all emotion, starts with a thought. That thought leads to another thought and another and gradually anger flares. With this practice we walk the anger back to the point of ignition and insert an aspiration to tame this emotion once it arises. I am talking first about anger because lots of people experience anger. It is a common problem.

"I think my emotional reactions could be properly identified as a manifestation of wildness. As a result of these emotional occurrences, I feel scattered and agitated. Reviewing the remedies for wildness, I realize I should probably set up a watch dog. (I thought I had a pseudo watchdog in place, but I guess he has not been quick enough). This upcoming week, I will specifically enlist a new watchdog to be on guard for this emotional wildness. I think in order to make him most effective and real, I must give him a name and a breed—he will be a St. Bernard named Max."

(Participant, Contemplative Lawyering 2006)

SLOW REVERSAL – PRACTICE INSTRUCTION

When you wake up in the morning generate an aspiration for the day: "Today I will tame my anger." You will find it easy to generate this aspiration if you have looked at your experience and, on that basis, recognized that anger is a destructive force in your life. For example, I experienced profound insight into the destructive nature of anger after my first husband died in a motorcycle accident. Contemplating my grief and my loss, I realized that I lost the wonderful relationship I had with my husband *long before* he died. Our relationship had been destroyed by hurtful and angry interchanges. This insight provided me with the basis for generating an aspiration to transform my anger.

If you recognize that you are plagued by jealousy, pride, or obsessive desire rather than anger, generate your morning aspiration to tame whatever emotion is most difficult for you. Maintain your aspiration throughout the day.

If you maintain a daily formal practice of tranquility or mindfulness meditation you will develop your mindfulness skills so that during the day you can see your anger or other emotion coming up. The practice of meditation is the foundation that will help you maintain mindfulness throughout the day.

When the anger (or another emotion) comes up, use that anger as a mindfulness reminder. Slow the process down with mindfulness. Rest your mind on your breath. Counting your breath is a good way to slow things down. Hold yourself back from responding with negativity. Do not engage the anger or act on it. Then in the space created, use an antidote to work with the situation. There are many antidotes that you can use.

First, ask yourself, "How important is this really? Is this the end of the world, as we know it?" We tend to exaggerate the importance of things all the time. For example, following sports teams involves manufactured intense feelings. How important is it really? Getting stuck in a traffic jam on a highway is a situation that often causes extreme rage, but really isn't all that important. How important is it that we get to our destination so quickly? We can use the space created by slowing down our reaction to consider how important this issue really is.

Second, if you are angry because you have been criticized, think about what has happened. Is the criticism correct? If so, there is nothing to be angry about. We can be grateful when someone lets us know that we are doing something incorrectly. Our response can simply be to try to do better next time. If you think about the criticism and determine that it is incorrect, why does it bother you? The person who spoke was mistaken. Our response can simply be to calmly correct the misimpression or let it go. We can use the space created by slowing down our reaction to consider whether the criticism we have received is justified.

Third, compassion is a powerful antidote for anger.[48] Think back to our hypothetical lawyer whose client accused him of overcharging. If the lawyer realizes that the real problem is the client's inability to pay, the lawyer can generate compassion for the client's difficult situation rather than express anger at the perceived insult. Similarly, when you are stuck in a traffic jam on the highway, one way to diffuse anger is to generate compassion for the other individuals who also are stuck in the traffic jam or for the individuals who

---

48   Many sources talk about the power of compassion as an antidote for anger and teach contemplative practices that can awaken that power. See, eg. Thich Nhat Hahn, *The Miracle of Mindfulness: An Introduction to the Practice of Meditation*, 93-96 (1987); Sharon Salzberg, *Loving-Kindness: The Revolutionary Art of Happiness* (2002).

have caused the traffic jam, perhaps by having an accident. Because it is impossible to be angry and compassionate at the same time, compassion is a powerful antidote for anger.[49] We can generate compassion in the space created by slowing down our reaction.

Fourth, look to see if your anger is based on a misperception. This is what could be happening with the hypothetical lawyer who is being accused of overcharging. The lawyer perceives an insult when in fact something different is happening—the client simply cannot pay and is embarrassed to admit that inability. We often read insult into someone else's speech and conduct when in fact no insult is intended. For example, a clerk at a retail establishment may be short with us, not because she is angry, but rather because she is tired or hurt by her dealings with a previous customer. If we take the clerk's bad mood personally, failing to recognize that it is not aimed at us, we may feel angry or hurt.[50] We can use the space created by slowing down our reaction time to identify misperceptions that may cause us to be angry and thereby recognize that the anger is unnecessary.

At the end of the day consider how the day went. If it went well, you can rejoice and renew your aspiration for the following day. If it did not go well, recognize that it did not go well, regret that it did not go well, and develop an aspiration to do better tomorrow.

---

49   I have experienced this reality on countless occasions. I have watched my heart soften and open when compassion arises towards a source of annoyance and anger. Annoyance at the shrieking baby on the airplane transforms into a loving desire to relieve the child's suffering. A spark of anger at a phone call interrupting my work transforms into a heartfelt desire to relieve the tears, suffering, or anger of the person I encounter when I pick up the phone. Annoyance at a spouse whose work schedule is interfering with vacation plans transforms into understanding that the spouse is suffering and an aspiration to help in any way I can to relieve that suffering.

50   See generally, Elaine Hatfield, John T. Cacioppo & Richard L. Rapson, *Emotional Contagion* (Cambridge Univ. Press, 1994) (offering evidence of emotional contagion, a phenomenon in which people communicate their mood to others.)

Rejoicing strengthens your practice. Regretting weakens your habitual patterns.

This is called Slow Reversal because every time we choose the skillful approach we gradually strengthen our ability to tame the negative emotion. However, there is no "quick fix" to instantly transform strong emotions. It takes time.

> "I was so blown away by a hate-filled verbal insult I heard that I actually closed my eyes and started to focus on my breath and it did calm me down. But whenever I stopped following my breath, I'd start to get worked up again. I also tried to remember that remarks like these come from a place of confusion and that the hate communicated through them is predicated on this confusion."
>
> *(Participant, Contemplative Lawyering 2005)*

> "I am having difficulty with the Slow Reversal practice. This past week I found myself in a few situations where I was angry or annoyed. Each time, however, I did not think about Slow Reversal immediately. Instead, I reacted in an emotional way. Only after a sufficient amount of time, up to an hour afterwards, did I think of the Slow Reversal process. I think it will take some time to change ingrained patterns and ways of reacting. I expect that I will continue to improve in my reactions as I continue to focus on the Slow Reversal process."
>
> *(Participant, Contemplative Lawyering 2006)*

> "Working with internal conflict is one of my biggest challenges. Anger in particular, is a common emotion for me. It erupts very quickly and causes me to react very, very unskillfully. As a result it creates negative outcomes that leave me with intense feelings

of guilt and negative emotions. I carry these with me for an extended period of time—like a long slow burn, or like a weight of sadness or discontent. The story of the two Zen monks in Rinpoche's talk provided insight into this tendency of mind. I spend too much time acting as the first monk did and then allowing unskillful actions to burden my mind for hours, weeks and sometimes MONTHS.

This week, I have tried to use the Slow Reversal practice. I am trying to get myself to take a (figurative) step back when my anger arises and *watch* it unfold, trying to unravel the feelings caught up inside of it. To describe what I *see*—it is like a flash of red. This red ball of energy is a response to something, usually someone else's conduct or words or simply their presence. Wrapped up in the flash is the assumption (misperception!) that this other person, who is the source of my anger, is aware that he or she has caused my anger and knows exactly why I am upset. This is what causes me to lash out or react unskillfully. With Slow Reversal this week, I have thankfully been able to give some of that anger some *space* as you described it in class and not react immediately.

However, I am not able to catch myself in time in all situations. It seems to depend on the severity of the conflict and the history behind the feeling of anger. The deeper or more severe it is, the more difficult it is to slow my anger down when it arises."

(Participant, Contemplative Lawyering 2006)

Comments on "Justified Anger"

After considering what you have read so far, you may be thinking, "But what about *real injustice*?" When we see *real* injustice, we get angry. How should we deal with this? Lawyers often encounter real injustice. For example, we may represent a client who was injured by someone else's negligent or even intentional act. Or we may represent a client in a situation that involves an ongoing threat of physical or psychological harm.

A good approach is to consider, "What is the most useful response to *real* injustice?" Is it a good idea to hit someone? While hitting someone could be a skillful response in a context of physical attack, we ordinarily are not going to be effective in dealing with injustice if we become angry and react with physical violence. And if a strongly worded verbal response is needed, nobody is going to listen to what we have to say if it comes from a place of ego-involved anger. Whenever ego is involved and we feel personally hurt or insulted, our ability to speak and act effectively diminishes. We tend to attack. When people are under attack, they do not listen. They simply become defensive. Remember the earlier discussion about speaking mindfully. The most effective way to communicate with someone, even in a difficult situation is by starting with something positive. This is very difficult to do if you are angry and argumentative.

Patience can be helpful even when we encounter a situation that is truly worthy of our concern. For example, we may see that someone is treating another person badly at work and that it is not deserved. Or perhaps we see someone being mistreated on the basis of their race or sex. These are serious and important concerns, but if we can somehow prevent ignition into flame, we will see the injustice clearly and deal with it skillfully and calmly or at least not make things worse.

Even if we are faced with a situation of danger, anger may not be the most skillful response. For example, suppose you encounter someone who is drunk and aggressive. If you become angry in return, this will simply escalate the situation. Speaking calmly is much more likely to keep you safe from harm because it may calm the aggressive individual.[51] In addition, if you become angry, you will not be able to think clearly about the best way to approach the situation.

Nevertheless, there are times when strong words can be helpful. For example, when a small child tries to run across a road, strong words may be necessary to stop the child from getting hurt. However, even in this circumstance, you will be more effective if any strong and loud words are spoken out of genuine concern for the child's safety rather than anger.

Impatience & Annoyance

People sometimes tell me that they do not get angry. Usually, however, further conversation reveals that they frequently experience impatience or annoyance. Impatience and annoyance are subtle forms of anger. It is possible to cause an amazing amount

---

51   The Crisis Intervention Team's approach to policing provides a profound example of the benefits of approaching dangerous and aggressive individuals with calmness. The Memphis Tennessee Police Department adopted this approach following an unfortunate incident during which a mentally ill individual was shot and killed by police. The centerpiece of the Memphis program is training officers to communicate with mentally ill individuals in ways that de-escalate rather than escalate conflict and aggression. The officers learn that calm speaking de-escalates while confrontation tends to escalate aggressive behavior. The program in Memphis has resulted in reduced injuries and arrests and increased diversion of mentally ill individuals into treatment programs. The Memphis Program has been nationally recognized and has encouraged other jurisdictions to adopt a variety of training programs designed to work more skillfully with aggressive mentally ill individuals. See Crisis Intervention Team, http://www.memphispolice.org/Crisis%20Intervention.htm (last visited Mar. 14, 2010); Joanne Silberner, *Morning Edition: Training Police to Handle Mental Illness Cases*, NPR (May 21, 2009), http://www.npr.org/templates/story/story.php?storyId=104350808.

of pain and anguish by acting on your annoyance or impatience. The usual result of impatience or annoyance is a quick, judgmental, cutting remark to another person. If that other person is a spouse or child who craves your love and approval, this cutting remark may be just as hurtful as full blown yelling or even hitting. Annoyance and impatience, like anger, also cause the person who experiences them a great deal of discomfort. From a practice perspective, it is best to treat annoyance and impatience as anger. You can work with these reactions in exactly the same way you would work with full blown anger.

The Dangers of Venting & Repressing Anger

It is important to understand that the Slow Reversal practice is not about repressing anger. Rather it is about slowing it down and looking at it. Slow Reversal is about learning from our anger. Repression is an approach to anger that never admits or acknowledges anger. Repression does not allow anger to manifest or even be recognized. When we repress anger, we may not even be aware that we are angry. This is the opposite of using mindfulness to look at anger and at the situations that make us angry.

Repressed anger can cause us to be depressed without knowing why. It is possible to repress anger for many years without being aware that we are experiencing it. Therefore, it is important not to take this approach to anger. It is important to be aware of anger when it arises.

At the other extreme, venting is not an effective way to work with anger. Venting involves expressing anger and perhaps even acting it out by punching an inanimate object. Venting means we are not repressing the anger. At the same time, however, venting does nothing to help us understand the roots of anger or work with it in a productive way. Instead, venting promotes a habit of expressing anger. Venting increases our tendency to get angry. Venting teaches us to view expressing anger as a positive activity. When we vent our anger we experience all of the negative feelings and discomfort associated with anger.[52]

Any emotion has two extremes—suppression and expression. Blind expression is as harmful as blind suppression. Blind expression is harmful to us and to others. Blind suppression is unhealthy. The goal is to look for a healthy way to react to emotions. Neither blind expression nor blind suppression is healthy. What we need to do is find a middle way, find a healthy way.

It is foolish to think that we can free ourselves from anger by blindly lashing out and saying whatever we want to say. The healthy way to work with emotion is to acknowledge the anger without acting out and hitting someone. We need to be willing to stay with the pain of anger without expressing it and without denying it. We need to sit with it and then choose a response that is healthier. If we can sit with anger, we have the freedom to choose a healthy response. Mindfulness and Slow Reversal provide the space in which to choose how to respond. It gives us the space in which to apply an appropriate antidote.

---

52   For an excellent discussion of the dangers of venting, see Thich Nhat Han, *Anger* 115-117, (Riverhead Books, 2001).

SLOW REVERSAL PRACTICE –
OTHER EMOTIONS

So far, I have presented Slow Reversal primarily as a practice for working with anger in post meditation. This practice also is appropriate for working with pride, jealousy, and obsessive desire. As with anger, the first step is recognizing the negative attributes of these emotions.

Pride and arrogance arise when we fail to see the positive qualities of others. Pride harms others by making them unappreciated and uncomfortable. Pride may be a way of covering up our feelings of inadequacy. Considered from this perspective, pride is a form of personal suffering because it is based on lack of confidence or feelings of self-hatred.

It is typical for lawyers to approach their clients with pride and arrogance, an approach that harms clients by making them uncomfortable. A lawyer's effectiveness is impaired by viewing clients with arrogance. Because the lawyer perceives clients as inferior, he or she will not seek (or benefit from) the client's input.

Jealousy is harmful in much the way anger is harmful. It sometimes results in extreme negative conduct such as war. Jealousy often underlies negative interactions on a personal level as well, especially in the context of love relationships, but also in the context of work relationships. For the person who experiences jealousy, it is a very uncomfortable feeling based on a poverty mentality. A poverty mentality is an experience of deep dissatisfaction. In the context of jealousy, poverty mentality means feeling inadequate, especially in comparison with others.

Obsessive desire is the suffering of not having what we want. Desire for money is the basis for theft and inflating billable hours. Obsessive desire undermines generosity. Desire is based again on a poverty mentality. We never seem to have enough of what we want. Obsessive desire is also harmful because it is the basis of sexual misconduct, including rape.

All of these negative emotions are ego-centered distractions from focusing on benefiting others (including clients).

Antidotes for Pride

When you apply the Slow Reversal practice to working with pride, there are some antidotes you can employ that are specific to pride.

First, it is helpful to begin by remembering that whatever you have accomplished in your life is based on an enormous element of good luck. We tend to think we deserve what we have achieved or acquired because we worked for it. Try to remember that the reason you have been able to work hard is because you had the good fortune of being born with intelligence and good health. Try to remember that you could not be what you are now if it were not for the support you received from your parents or from other individuals who helped you prepare for and pay for your education. These are just some of the lucky aspects of being better educated, healthier, or wealthier than others.

Look at your own situation and consider how much of what you have attained is the result of your own work and how much is the result of other factors. Consider that even your ability to put hard work into developing your life and career results from lucky circumstances of birth and the assistance you have received from others. In light of this, how does it make any sense to feel superior to others who are less fortunate than you?

A second antidote for pride is to see what is good about other people. In order to maintain our prideful attitude, we must discount the value of others. Seeing what is good about others reduces pride and arrogance. See how many positive adjectives you can come up with that describe the other person, using words such as determined, kind, courageous, loving, patient, loyal, compassionate, adventurous, capable, enthusiastic, generous, honest, imaginative, modest, original, spontaneous, tactful, thorough, charming, clever, friendly, happy, fair-minded, spunky, resourceful, talented, tolerant, joyful, dynamic, quiet, reflective, careful, curious, eager, energetic, precise, responsible, sociable, calm, witty, tenacious, light-hearted, organized, reliable, or zany. It may take some effort to perceive these qualities at first, but once you begin to look you will find many admirable qualities in others that you never noticed before.

Third, you can work with pride by realizing that while you may be highly competent with respect to some skills, there are many skills that others possess in much greater measure. For example, perhaps you are a very skillful corporate lawyer. This is no reason to feel superior to others when you consider the many skills that you do not have, skills that others possess. For example, it is likely that there are others who possess much more skill than you in the areas of auto mechanics, art, music, carpentry, sports, business, science, medicine, etc. The list is endless. No matter how talented you are in one or more ways, there are many other people who are more skillful than you in other ways.

Finally, we can work with pride by remembering that for most of us pride is a cover for deep uncertainty about our own self worth.

Pride generally indicates that we are suffering from a deep need for affirmation. Therefore, the most powerful antidote for pride is to recognize your own self worth and see that recognizing your own self worth does not require putting others down.

Antidotes for Jealousy

When you work with jealousy using the Slow Reversal practice, you will need to apply some antidotes that are specific to jealousy.

One way of working with jealousy is to contemplate all the suffering that arises as a result of jealousy. Jealousy can cause wars, marital break-ups and even murder. Once we have recognized the harm that jealousy causes, we will be able to generate a strong aspiration to tame this emotion.

Another powerful antidote for jealousy is to rejoice in the merit of others. In other words, when you encounter someone else who has better circumstances than you (more money, better grades, a better job, etc), instead of experiencing jealousy, feel happiness for that person and rejoice in their good fortune.

Finally, the most fundamentally powerful antidote for jealousy is simply to recognize and appreciate your own self worth.

Antidotes for Obsessive Desire (Passion)

Again, a good place to start is to contemplate the suffering that comes from desire, including theft, embezzlement, abuse, over eating, rape, and other forms of sexual misconduct. Seeing clearly the harm that comes from this emotion can help us generate a strong aspiration to let go of obsessive desire.

Another antidote for desire is to contemplate impermanence. If you can remember that everything you want will soon be rendered useless or valueless, you may be able to lessen your desire.

A powerful antidote for desire is to cultivate generosity. The more you focus on benefiting others, the less you will desire for yourself. Finally, tranquility meditation is an antidote for desire because it cultivates contentment.

SLOW REVERSAL PRACTICE SCHEDULE

Most people find this practice to be extremely helpful. I suggest that you work with this practice for at least two weeks with the aspiration to make it part of your life for a very long time. While this practice stands on its own, it will be even more effective if you combine it with a daily practice of tranquility meditation. A practice schedule for Slow Reversal can be found in the Practice Schedule Appendix.

DEALING WITH GUILT USING THE FOUR POWERS

The process of working with strong emotions is extremely slow. We have deeply ingrained habits that are difficult to reverse. It may take years of practice to finally come to a place of contentment and selflessness that allows you to work skillfully with disturbing emotions like anger. There is no quick fix. Slow Reversal is a first and significant step towards working with anger and other strong emotions. However, it is important to understand that you will not be able to tame your anger in a week or even in a year. The effectiveness of this practice depends on the strength of your aspiration to work with emotions and your confidence in the practice of working with emotions balanced against the strength of your habitual pattern of emotional reactivity.[53]

It is wonderful progress if this practice simply helps you recognize your strong emotions as negative and notice when they arise. Even if you do not catch your anger until you have said or done something really unskillful, you *noticed*. This is amazing and very beneficial because noticing is the necessary first step to working skillfully with emotions. It is important to be gentle with ourselves as we work with strong emotions. It is important not to expect to progress too quickly. It is important to maintain an aspiration to work with strong emotions without turning that aspiration into an expectation that brings more suffering because we find ourselves unable to meet that expectation.

As a result of this practice, you may find that you notice your unskillful actions more than you have noticed them before. Having noticed your failure to be mindful and kind, you may find yourself experiencing guilt and regret. Try to be gentle with yourself. We gain nothing when we suffer from guilt which is a form of self-condemnation. When we entertain guilt we label ourselves as evil, unworthy persons who must suffer as a result of our bad deeds.[54] A more positive approach is to acknowledge how wonderful it is that you noticed your unskillful actions.

---

53   See, Dzogchen Ponlop Rinpoche, *The Secret Mind*, 7 Bodhi 27. Bodhi Magazine is no longer published and no longer available for purchase. It can be found in some University Libraries including Columbia University, Naropa Universtiy, University of California Berkeley, University of Connecticut School of Law, and Cornell University.

54   B. Alan Wallace & Steven Wilhelm, *Tibetan Buddhism from the Ground Up: A Practical Approach for Modern Life 101* (Wisdom Publications`1993).

There is a four-part practice that is designed to transform this lapse in mindfulness into a beneficial experience:

- **First,** recognize and acknowledge that you have made a mistake.

- **Second,** generate genuine regret for your lapse of mindfulness and the resulting unskillful speech or conduct.

- **Third,** generate an aspiration not to repeat this mistake.

- **Fourth,** you can enhance the power of your aspiration by making your aspiration known to someone you respect deeply.[55]

Engaging in this practice makes your mistake useful and beneficial because you use your mistake to lay the foundation for a more mindful and skillful approach in the future. You take your mistake and use it to inspire and motivate better conduct in the future. This is wonderful. Every time you do this you increase the possibility that you will catch your rising anger earlier next time.

Guilt over unskillful actions accomplishes nothing. Using unskillful actions as the basis for a generating a genuine aspiration to be mindful and skillful has the potential to accomplish something wonderful.

---

55   Id. at 100-102. See also Tulku Damcho Rinpoche, *Talk 3*, on *The Complete Path of Practice: A Teaching on the Kagyu Lineage Prayer* (2009). This recording is available on CD, DVD, and MP3CD format at http://www.vajraechoes.com.

PART II

GENERATING GENUINE
EMPATHY:

Mind Training Practice

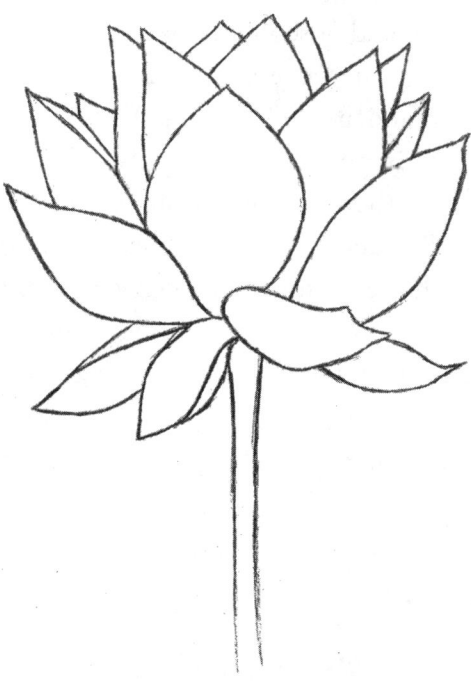

CHAPTER 7:

CULTIVATING GENUINE EMPATHY

WHAT IS GENUINE EMPATHY & HOW DOES IT RELATE TO GOOD LAWYERING?

In Robert Bastress and Joseph Harbaugh's book, *Interviewing, Counseling and Negotiating: Skills for Effective Representation*,[56] they set out the fundamentals of a helping relationship. They begin by citing the importance of empathy which they define as understanding how the client views the world from his or her vantage point.[57] The authors also emphasize the importance of genuineness, which they define as being aware of and comfortable with yourself.[58] A third characteristic they emphasize is having respect for your client, which means "genuinely valuing the client as a person, viewing him or her as a person who exists beyond the legal context with which you deal."[59] Further, the authors make it

---

56   Aspen, 1990

57   *Id.* at 116-18.

58   *Id.* at 126-128.

59   *Id.* at 130.

clear that open and effective communication between a lawyer and client depends on establishing and maintaining a relationship that meets these fundamental requirements. Other important factors that facilitate communication are non-judgmental acceptance and sincere recognition or approval.[60]

The practices in this chapter are designed to help cultivate empathy that is characterized by genuineness, respect, non-judgmental acceptance, and sincere recognition as described by Bastress and Harbaugh. The genuine empathy discussed in this chapter includes these characteristics and more.

Earlier we considered the importance of genuine empathy in the context of mindful listening and speaking. Whenever we listen to someone, we will hear more clearly and deeply if we are fully present and not distracted by our own thoughts, hopes and fears. Whenever we speak, we will be more skillful and beneficial if we speak with an aspiration to benefit others. Every time we get caught up in egocentric thought, it becomes more difficult to hear, evaluate, analyze, or advise clearly.

There are a variety of personal agendas that can interfere with skillful representation. If we act out of pride, we may choose a course of action that will impress others, rather than an approach that meets the needs of the client. If we are motivated by a desire to earn higher fees, we may spend more time on lucrative cases than on other worthy endeavors. If we are motivated by fear of making mistakes, we may be unnecessarily cautious in our advice. If we develop a desire to have a close personal relationship with a client, we will have difficulty providing neutral advice. If we dislike a client and allow that to color our representation, the client's

---

60   *Id.* at 188.

interests will not be well served. If we become too entangled in the client's financial affairs, our advice will be impacted by our own personal interests, hopes, and fears. The list goes on and on.

What a client needs is someone who is genuinely concerned about the client's well being without being obsessively attached to the success or failure of the client's case. This is genuine empathy. Genuine empathy encompasses both genuine loving kindness (the wish for others to be happy) and genuine compassion (the wish for others to be free from suffering). Loving kindness and compassion are "genuine" when they are not colored by egocentric needs and agendas. This attitude will make it possible for us to provide the best possible service to our clients. In addition, if we can develop this attitude towards our colleagues, employees, court personnel, legal adversaries, friends, and family we will work more skillfully with all of these individuals as well.

You may be thinking that it is not possible to change our view of other people, not possible to cultivate genuine empathy. However, there are powerful practices designed to awaken our innate loving kindness and compassion for other beings. In fact, some scientific studies have found evidence that long-term meditators who engage in compassion practices show more brain wave activity in the areas of their brains that are devoted to compassion than individuals who do not meditate.[61]

Many people find that simply by engaging in tranquility meditation their compassion for others increases. This happens because tranquility meditation calms our minds and quiets the ego-driven

---

61   Lutz, Antoine, Greischar, Lawrence L., Rawlings, Nancy B., Ricard, Matthieu, Davidson, Richard, *Long-term meditators self-induce high-amplitude gamma synchrony during mental practice*, 101(46) Proceedings of the National Academy of Sciences of the United States of America, 16369-16373 (Nov. 16, 2004).

judgments, thoughts, and distractions that prevent us from fully attending to the needs of others. By quieting our minds, tranquility meditation puts us in touch with our inherent loving kindness and compassion.

The following sections provide you with contemplations and meditation practices that build on the foundation of tranquility meditation and that are specifically designed to cultivate loving kindness and compassion.

CULTIVATING GENUINE EMPATHY — A GUIDED CONTEMPLATION[62]

Genuine empathy does not need to be brought in from outside our mind. We can generate genuine empathy by reflecting on our own experience. Consider your entire life from birth right up to the present moment. If you consider carefully how you have approached your life, you will see that all you really want out of life is to be happy. Everything you have done has been for the purpose of making you happy. You have never, not even for a moment, wanted to suffer and be miserable. You have never wished for problems, worries, and harm. This is obvious if you simply think about it.

Once you have considered this point thoroughly, ask yourself the following question, "Are you the only person who is like that or is everyone the same in this regard?" Consider first those people you know best, for example your family and friends. When you think

---

62   This guided meditation is based on a talk by Khenpo Karthar Rinpoche at Trinity College in Hartford, Connecticut on September 9, 1998. This talk was published in the 4th issue (Oct. 1998) of *The Precious Jewel* Hartford Karma Thegsum Choling. A recording of this talk is available from Vajra Echoes LLC (www.vajraechoes.com).

about them, what do you see? Isn't it clear that they are just like you? Isn't it clear that they only want to be happy and do not want to suffer? In fact, you will never find anyone who really wants to suffer. You will never find anyone who really does not want to be happy.

Look around you at the wider world. Consider human beings in any country or culture. What you will find is that all of them are very busy from birth until death and that all of this activity is caused by wanting to be happy. Everyone tries to acquire objects and situations that they think will make them happy. Everyone tries to remove or avoid situations that they believe will cause suffering. These are the only two reasons we do anything at all.

You are not alone in your wish to be happy and your wish to be free of suffering. All people are fundamentally the same in this respect. Understanding this helps us understand the fundamental equality of all individuals.

Consider beyond human beings. Think about animals, including birds, fish, and animals of all types. All of them are very busy from waking until sleeping, from birth until death. Why? They all are trying to stay alive and protect themselves. They are trying to obtain food and shelter. Why? They want to acquire situations that will make them comfortable and happy, situations that will keep them safe from hunger, cold, and danger. Like us, they want to be happy and free from suffering. Animals may not be consciously aware of what they are doing and why they do it, but all of their activities are aimed at the same result. Their strategies for attaining happiness and removing or avoiding suffering are less elaborate, but the purpose is the same.

All beings without exception are fundamentally the same in wishing to be happy and wishing not to suffer. Unfortunately, the methods used to *obtain* happiness and *avoid* suffering often *bring* tremendous suffering. Humans and animals consistently do the wrong things in their effort to achieve happiness and remove suffering. The result is that they destroy their own happiness.

How does this happen? This happens because of egocentricity and disturbing emotions. We approach the world with attachment and aversion. We want what we believe will make us happy and do not want what we believe will make us suffer. We live in fear of not getting what we want, losing what we have, getting what we do not want, and not keeping what we have. These attachments, aversions, and associated fears and suffering are the product of our egocentric view.

If you understand that all beings without exception wish to be happy in the same way that you do and take that to heart, this will awaken a profound sympathy and love for other beings—they are just like you. This love will naturally reduce your selfishness and attachment. Similarly if you remember that all beings have the same innate desire to be free from suffering and misery that you have, this will give rise to compassion and a wish for beings to be free from suffering. That compassion will cause your hatred, aversion, and anger to diminish automatically.

Selfishness and hatred come from rigid obsession with our own happiness and the fear that this obsession produces. Expanding our minds to consider the needs of others and wanting others to be happy and free of suffering will automatically make us less aggressive.

You may ask, "How can I do this? How can I care for others in this way? I need to take care of my own needs."

The answer is that you have the potential for limitless love and compassion. This potential is always there. For example, parents love their children wholeheartedly. If they have other children, they love them wholeheartedly as well. No matter how many children they have, they love them all. The capacity to love is not like a pie that must be divided up. Loving one person does not diminish your ability to love other people. Rather, the more you love, the more you are capable of loving.

You may ask, "What is the point of having an aspiration to bring about the happiness of all beings and free all beings from suffering when it is not possible for me to do that?"

The answer is that generating this aspiration is not useless. If you help any sentient being as a result of your aspiration, this is useful. Having this wish or aspiration weakens your aggression and selfishness. Having this wish or aspiration will make you more empathetic, loving, and compassionate towards others.

Finally, the world is a mirror. If you are less aggressive and more loving, others will imitate you and respond to you in positive ways. This improves the quality of your life and of those who are around you. How can this be anything but beneficial?

SENDING AND TAKING PRACTICE – AN INTRODUCTION

Sending and taking is a practice that is specifically designed to help people cultivate genuine loving kindness and compassion.[63] By genuine, I mean not motivated by egocentric needs and interests. There are many different varieties of sending and taking practice. The series of practices I am presenting here build on each other. These practices begin by building a foundation of impartiality and then progress through a series of practices designed to help us see and appreciate the kindness of others and finally generate pure loving kindness and compassion for others.

---

63 This practice has a variety of names. In Tibetan, it is called Tonglen. You may also see it referred to as sending and taking meditation. The series of sending and taking practices taught in this and the following chapters are based on a teaching on *Compassion Without Limit*, delivered by Dzogchen Ponlop Rinpoche at Naropa University in Boulder, Colorado in April, 2003. A DVD of this teaching is available from Vajra Echoes Dharma Recordings (www.vajraechoes.com).

CHAPTER 8:

TRAINING IN IMPARTIALITY

It is important to cultivate impartiality before or along with culti-vating genuine empathy, which includes loving kindness and compassion. Without impartiality, when we develop compas-sion and loving kindness, it becomes biased and limited. That is our usual approach. Ordinarily we love some people and not others. Love and compassion that prefers some over others is not a genuine and limitless heart of loving kindness and compassion. This limited form of love and compassion will not help us approach all of our clients, co-workers, adversaries, court personnel, family, and friends with the genuine empathy that promotes skillful and mindful interactions.

Therefore, training first in impartiality is important. Impartiality does not mean bland neutrality. Impartiality means extending the *positive*, *non-clinging* aspects of the love and compassion we have for family and friends to all beings.

In this practice, impartiality also means letting go of our aversions. It means giving up the hatred and aggression that we experience towards some beings. At the same time cultivating impartiality means letting go of the clinging, need, and obsessive attachment that characterizes our relationship to other beings. When we label someone as bad we have the first problem—hatred, aggression, and aversion. When we label someone as good, we sometimes have the second problem—attachment, clinging, grasping, and obsession.

It may be easy to see how hatred and aggression leads to unskillful speech and conduct, but how is it a problem to approach someone from a "positive" place of attachment? This is what we ordinarily refer to as love. Unfortunately, when our positive feelings come from a place of attachment or need, this is not genuine love. Actually, it is not *love* at all—it is need. When our relationship with someone is based on need, it is very difficult to be skillful. Because we are needy and clinging, we act in ways that are designed to help ourselves rather than help the other person. Genuine love and compassion (genuine empathy) is not ego driven. Rather, genuine empathy means acting with an intention to benefit the other person. This is not possible if we are needy, clingy, and attached.

An excellent example of this can be seen in the context of close family relationships. We all know people who have relationships that are primarily based on need. Those relationships tend to be rocky, argumentative, and judgmental. A needy "lover" operates from a place of fear and anxiety, worrying about losing the love of her partner. She is defensive and jealous. She perceives neglect as intentional hurt. When her partner is unhappy or sick, she is annoyed because he is no longer fun to be with. When he is busy with work, she becomes angry that he is not spending time with her. The list goes on and on.

On the other hand, we all have known couples and families who approach each other primarily from a place of genuine love and compassion rather than egocentric need. These relationships tend to be gentle, loving, and forgiving.

This is what we are trying to develop with the impartiality practice. We are training to develop an attitude towards all beings that is equally loving and compassionate. We are training to cultivate impartial love and compassion rather than our usual hatred and aggression for some and attachment and obsessive clinging for others.

This meditation practice is the first in a series of practices designed to cultivate genuine loving kindness and compassion. This first practice is designed to cultivate impartiality, equanimity, or equality. Without impartiality, pure compassion and loving kindness does not arise. Impartiality is the necessary first step. It is the necessary foundation practice. The other practices in this series build on this first practice.

Everyone Has the Same Potential & the Same Confusions

You may be thinking, "How is it possible to generate genuine empathy for everyone?" You may be especially skeptical about your ability to generate genuine empathy when you encounter individuals in your life who are hard to deal with.

The key to generating loving kindness and compassion for everyone you encounter is understanding that we all suffer from the same confusions that keep us from recognizing our own inherent nature of limitless wisdom and compassion. We all suffer from the same confusions that keep us from achieving the happiness we all are seeking.

The fundamental problem we all share is attachment and aversion. The attachments and aversions that we think will bring us happiness cause us to suffer. Our attachments to people, things, money, health, achievements, and "favorable" circumstances cause us to become angry and engage in unskillful speech and actions when we can't get what we want or lose what we have. Our aversion to people, things, poverty, illness and injury, loss, and 'unfavorable' circumstances cause us to become angry and engage in unskillful speech and actions when bad things come our way.

Once we recognize the source of our own unskillful speech and actions it becomes easier to understand that when others engage in unpleasant speech and behavior it is not because they are evil. Rather, like us, they are victims of their own egocentric thinking (attachments and aversions). They are simply trying to achieve happiness in unskillful ways.

In this practice we are training to transcend and transform our rigid concepts that see some people, things, and circumstances as favorable and friend and other things as unfavorable and enemy. We are training to transcend seeing some people and things as good and others as bad. From these labels we get many emotions and thoughts and suffering and unskillful conduct. We are training to generate loving kindness and compassion for others who, like us, also suffer from labels, emotions, and unskillful conduct.

IMPARTIALITY PRACTICE INSTRUCTION

Visualizing a "Neutral" Person

This practice is complex. It has five stages. The focus of this meditation is a visualized image. You will do this practice first with a visualized image of a "neutral" person in your life, second with a visualized image of a "positive" person, and third with a visualized image of a "negative" person.

What is meant by a "neutral" person in this practice context is a person you do not know very well. You do not have any strong feelings one way or the other about this person. An example might be the check-out clerk in your local grocery store. What you are trying to consider is your relationship and attitude towards someone about whom you do not have attachments or aversions.

Visualizing is no different than simply bringing someone into your mind. It is like remembering what your mother looks like or what your car or house looks like. You simply remember the person you are using as your object of meditation. You may find it easier to visualize if you have your eyes closed.

The remainder of this instruction will be a guided meditation. You might want to ask someone else to read it for you. Another approach would be to read and record the instruction on a tape or iPOD. You can then play it while you do the practice. The best approach, however, is to memorize the steps of the practice so you can proceed through them at your own pace and without assistance.

Begin with an aspiration to cultivate impartial loving kindness and compassion. Spend the first five or ten minutes of your practice session in tranquility or mindfulness meditation (Following the Breath, Counting the Breath, or Resting your Mind on an Object). Once your mind is reasonably settled, visualize a person you are somewhat familiar with, but who is neutral in the sense that you have no strong feelings about this person one way or the other. Visualize this person standing or sitting in front of you. Try to get a reasonably clear picture of the person in your mind.

First, when you have the visualization clear in your mind, open your heart to this person. As you breathe in and out, feel your heart opening to this person. Open your heart to working with this person. If you are having difficulty understanding what is meant by opening your heart, think briefly about someone you care very much about. Then generate the same open heart for the neutral person you have visualized. Continue to open your heart as you breathe in and out.

Second, once you feel yourself open to working with this person, recognize that this person wants to be happy. Use your imagination to think about what this person's life must be like based on what you know about this person. Recognize that this person wants to be happy. Remember that you want to be happy as well. On that basis, see that there is no difference between you and this person. You both want to experience happiness and freedom from suffering.

Consider the attachments and aversions that this person is likely to have considering what you know about him or her. See that this person's attachments and aversions prevent him or her from being happy. Think about how your own attachments and aversions prevent you from being happy. See that in this regard there is no difference between you and this person.

Third, generate a desire for this person to be happy. Generate a heart-felt aspiration for this person to experience happiness and freedom from suffering. Then generate an aspiration to help this person achieve happiness. Generate an aspiration to help this person if you are able to do so. Generate a commitment or determination to help this person be happy if the opportunity presents itself.

Your determination to help this person be happy may simply be a commitment to smile and acknowledge this individual whenever you encounter him or her. Alternatively, your aspiration and determination can be to work with your own confusion so that you don't contribute to this persons suffering.

Fourth, as you breath in, imagine that you are taking in on your breath the attachments and aversions that cause this person to suffer. Imagine that you are taking in the hatred and obsessive clinging that cause this person to suffer. As you exhale imagine that you have transformed the confusions you took in and are now sending this person impartiality, equanimity, and the resulting happiness and freedom from suffering. As you exhale see this person becoming calm, content, non-judgmental, and happy. This is what is referred to as sending and taking practice. Continue breathing in and out and visualizing for several minutes.

If you wish, you can add a visualized image to the "sending and taking" aspect of this practice. Visualize a ball of light in your heart. When you breathe in, visualize the attachments and aversions of the object of your meditation (in this case the visualized neutral person) coming in on your breath as a cloud of black smoke. Visualize impartiality and the resulting happiness and freedom from suffering as white light traveling out to the other person on your out breath. Think of the ball of light in your heart as having the power to transform the other person's attachments and aversions and resulting suffering into impartiality and the resulting happiness.

End this practice session by letting go of the visualization and returning to tranquility or mindfulness meditation for a few minutes. Finally, dedicate this practice session to cultivating genuine empathy.

Do this practice in the same way on the second day. After you have done this practice once or twice, read the Impartiality Practice Comments that appear after this section of instructions.

Visualizing a "Positive" Person

When you do this practice on the third and fourth days, visualize someone who is positive in your life. Positive means someone for whom you care deeply. The practice is the same in all other respects.

Visualizing a "Negative" Person

On the fifth and sixth days, repeat this practice with a negative person. Negative means someone who causes you difficulty in your life, someone who causes you harm or makes you feel angry or hurts your feelings. Because our relationships with people who are very close to us tend to have positive and negative aspects, you may find that the same person comes up as both positive and negative for you. This is not a problem. Consider the attachments and aversions that this person is likely to have considering what you know about him or her.

Comparing "Positive" & "Negative"

Finally, on the seventh day, begin the practice with a positive person. After you have engaged in the sending and taking portion of the practice for a little while, switch the focus of your meditation to a negative individual. In other words, change your visualization to a negative person in the middle of the sending and taking practice. The point here is to compare your feelings towards the positive person and the negative person.

Impartiality Practice – Comments

Many people encounter difficulties doing this practice. Often people prefer the calm and peace of tranquility meditation. Even if you are having difficulty with the sending and taking practice, I encourage you to try it for several weeks before giving up. This practice can be very inspiring. This also is a practice that develops insight. It requires some work and commitment on our part. You will find it easier to face the challenges of this practice if you remind yourself of the reasons for doing this practice. If you have trouble giving rise to compassion for the person you have chosen as your object of meditation, simply go as far as you are able to go. Maybe you can let go of some of your antipathy. Maybe you can begin to understand the difficulties this person encounters in life. Be gentle with yourself.

One of the difficult aspects of this practice for many people is the idea of defining some people as neutral, some as positive, and others as negative. People often recognize that their relationship with everyone is mixed. This is an important insight. When we are angry with someone, we tend to see them as "all bad." It is helpful to recognize that everyone has positive and negative characteristics. It is helpful to recognize that our difficulty with others is about something they said or did, not about the whole person.

In order to do this practice, simply select the most neutral, most beneficial, and most negative individuals to work with. Alternatively, you can work with the same person in his or her different manifestations (positive and negative).

Other people have trouble understanding what it means to be neutral, negative, or positive. It is important to remember that the individuals we are considering are not inherently neutral, positive, or negative. What makes them fit these descriptions is our *own reaction* to them. These labels are all in our own minds. What we are doing in this practice is identifying individuals who we *experience and label* as neutral, positive, or negative. A significant insight that this practice promotes is noticing that we impose these labels on other people. Nobody is inherently neutral, positive, or negative. Everyone presents themselves to us as a mixture based on our perception of their speech and conduct.

Another difficulty some people encounter is that they lack confidence in their own wisdom and compassion. They view themselves with self doubt or self loathing and therefore, have difficulty visualizing sending positive qualities to someone else. If you encounter this difficulty, please read the section on *Cultivating Loving Kindness and Compassion for Yourself* which can be found at the end of Chapter 10.

> "I did the impartiality practice on my own during my vacation. For the focus of the practice I chose a former friend who causes a great amount of difficulty for me. Over the past few years, I developed a very strong and overwhelming aversion to her and for this reason was no longer able to be her friend. She is a very aggressive and competitive individual who has a hard time accepting care and concern from others and instead manages

to push people away. Since this time she had a terrible tragedy happen to her. In light of the tragedy, I have tried to conjure up new compassion for her. It has been nearly impossible for me (which is depressing and makes me feel like a bad person). As a result of this tragedy, she received help from her father, brother, and best friend. Unable to accept their help graciously, she has successfully pushed all of them away and alienated herself from everyone close to her. It is very, very ironic that I chose her to be the subject of this exercise because at the beginning of the semester, she was one of the people I identified as someone I was unable to work with.

The impartiality practice was a good first step for me to try and develop a new empathy and compassion for her. Rather than making a commitment to help her achieve happiness, however, I made my aspiration for this exercise to identify the source of my aversion and begin to generate empathy. Upon reflection, I realized that my aversion to her comes from a place of deep and insurmountable pity for her. Her inability to relate to others positively and to allow others to develop positive relationships with her and her habit of pushing loving people away makes me very, very sad. I guess this pity comes from a feeling of hopelessness for her. Do you have any comments on this?

(Participant, Contemplative Lawyering 2006)

I responded to this question as follows:

"It is wonderful that you used this practice to work on your difficult relationship with a former friend. It was very wise of you to dedicate the practice to sorting out the source of your aversion. It is interesting that you found your own sadness is the basis for your aversion. Perhaps your pity for her makes you very sad because you feel there is nothing you (or anyone) can do to help. I have seen this happen when someone experiences a terrible loss (the death of a spouse or child for example). Often other people feel uncomfortable being around someone like this because they feel there is nothing they can say or do to help.

In terms of how you can work with this, I suggest that you use your recognition of her confusion and the needless suffering she experiences as a basis for generating compassion for her and an aspiration for her to relate to the world in a different way. In order to transform your pity into genuine empathy, try to recognize her positive qualities and potential for transformation. With respect to your sadness, recognize that you can do something positive with this situation even if you don't have the skill to bring her out of her difficult place. You already have done something positive with this situation by recognizing the reason for your aversion. You have learned that you are uncomfortable with situations that make you feel sad and helpless. While this doesn't directly help her, you can mentally dedicate what you have learned to the benefit of your former friend. As you said, this is an excellent step in the direction of generating genuine empathy and compassion for her."

CULTIVATING GENUINE EMPATHY FOR "NEGATIVE" INDIVIDUALS

Perhaps the most difficult aspect of this practice for most people is working with negative individuals. Even within the context of this visualization practice, people find that they have a hard time generating a wish for such individuals to be happy.

The important thing to remember is that this practice is about changing our viewpoint about others. Second, we need to understand that aspiring for another person's happiness does not mean wishing for them to get what they want even if it is negative. We are aspiring for this person to let go of the attachments, aversions, and confusions that cause this individual to harm others. We are aspiring for this individual to attain the happiness that comes from relating to the world in a more positive way—without hatred and obsessive clinging. We are aspiring for this person to be calm and content rather than angry and judgmental.

If you are having difficulty generating a positive aspiration for the negative person you have chosen, try simply to soften your view towards this individual somewhat, perhaps by considering possible understandable explanations for this individual's behavior. Alternatively try switching to someone who is not as difficult for you—someone who causes you just a little bit of distress.

If you wish, there is a verse you can say to remind you that the point of this practice is not to wish for mundane happiness for others, but rather to wish for them to attain happiness based on wisdom. This verse, known as *The Four Immeasurables*, was taught by the Buddha to his son Rahula:[64]

> May all beings have happiness and the cause of happiness.
> May they be free from suffering and the cause of suffering.
> May they never be separated from the highest bliss which
> is without suffering.
> May they come to rest in the great impartiality which is
> free from attachment and aversion to those near and far.

---

64 Thich Nhat Hanh, *Old Path, White Clouds: Walking in the Footsteps of the Buddha* 321 (Parallax Press, 1991). This verse has been translated in a variety of forms. Thich Nhat Hanh's translation is found in this book and he also identifies the Buddha as the original source of the verse.

The question is not whether negative individuals *deserve* happiness on the basis of their negative conduct. Rather, the practice asks you to understand that *their conduct is based on confusion* and is *causing them to suffer*. Your aspiration is for them to gain wisdom and on that basis to begin to act in positive ways which will bring them lasting happiness.

Another aspect of working with negative individuals is recognizing that they have a positive potential. Even hardened criminals and really angry and hurtful people have the potential for positive conduct. Consider, for example, a story I heard about a Christian minister who walked out of her church into the parking lot one night and encountered a man who pointed a gun at her face and asked her for money. She handed over everything she had and then looked directly into the young man's eyes and said, "I love you." A few years later, a well dressed young man came up to this minister after a church service and told her that he was the person who had robbed her at gunpoint and that her response to him changed his life. He had abandoned his criminal behavior and was now working to find ways to contribute to society. If you think about people you have known or stories you have heard in the news, I am sure you can remember similar situations where someone who was noted for their negative outlook experienced a transformation in their attitude and conduct. What is important to understand from stories like this is that the positive potential is there.

Finally, you should consider the reasons for training in genuine empathy for negative individuals. As a lawyer you will often find yourself in the position of representing or working with individuals who are difficult. Some clients are angry, judgmental individuals. Some of our legal colleagues and supervisors are full of pride and arrogance which causes them to relate to us in unskillful ways.

There are many reasons why it is important to learn how to work with such individuals. First, they make it difficult for us to work because they cause us deep distress. Second, unless we develop skillful ways of interacting with these individuals, we may respond with anger. Third, if we do not like someone, we are unlikely to be motivated to do good work for them or if we do the work it will come from a place of fear rather than from a genuine wish to be helpful. Finally, if we are skillful in our dealings with difficult individuals, they will become less difficult. The most effective way to help an angry, arrogant, and judgmental person see that there are more skillful ways of operating is by acting skillfully ourselves. Therefore, there is much to be gained from learning to have genuine empathy for individuals who are difficult.

> "Although I understand the reasons why it would be beneficial to wish happiness on someone who is very difficult for me, I have found it easier to engage in empathy or compassion practice with respect to negative persons by visualizing people who I feel less negative about. When we first started this practice I would typically choose one person who I felt somewhat strongly about. I would typically not make it very far in the practice before I would lose my focus as I struggled with thinking about this person. More recently I have selecting people who I do not feel as negatively about. Similar to the building up aspect of going from a positive, to a neutral, to a negative person, I have found that using a person I do not feel as strongly about in a negative way has made it easier for me to maintain my focus on that person and engage more fully in the practice."
>
> *(Participant, Contemplative Lawyering 2006)*

THE IMPORTANCE OF DEVELOPING DISCERNMENT OR INSIGHT

Some people see their own personal confusion as overwhelming and conclude, therefore, that they cannot possibly help anyone else. This makes it difficult for them to engage in the practice.

But, what does it mean to aspire to help others? The most profound way to help others is by working with our own confusion. We cause others to suffer when we act unskillfully. By aspiring to develop our own clarity, wisdom, and compassion, we are aspiring to help others. Not only will this aspiration result in our causing less distress in others, it will also help others because our skillful conduct will provide an example for them to follow.

When we recognize our inability to work skillfully with others this is a sign of wisdom. We are recognizing the importance of developing insight or discernment before engaging in actual activities designed to help others. At the same time, it is important to have confidence in our ability to reach a place where we will be capable of helping others.

Simply by engaging in tranquility meditation, we are helping others. It is not necessary to actually *do* anything in order to be helpful. Tranquility practice pacifies our uncontrolled minds and diminishes our distractions. If we develop mindfulness to the point where we can respond to others in a peaceful and undistracted way, that is a beneficial action in itself.

IMPARTIALITY – POST MEDITATION PRACTICE

While you are engaging in the impartiality practice during formal meditation sessions, I suggest that you try the following practice during the rest of the day: whenever you encounter another person, watch your mind for judgments. Do you perceive this person as neutral, positive, or negative? Why?

PRACTICE SCHEDULE

It takes many sessions to become familiar with the practice and work through the many stages of the practice. I suggest that you engage in this practice for at least seven formal meditation sessions. This will take you more than seven days if you are unable to do the practice every day. Throughout the period of time when you are working with this formal practice (even on the days when you don't actually do the practice), use the people you encounter throughout the day as a mindfulness reminder. Whenever you encounter someone, consider whether you perceive this person as neutral, positive, or negative? Ask yourself, "Why?"

> "The impartiality practice, and its interplay with self-judging and the Slow Reversal process, has been useful, challenging and surprisingly self-revealing for me. After partaking in the practice for a bit, it is clear that the key to true empathy and the ability to feel compassion is the ability to be impartial. I think this practice (in some ways more so even than effective listening) can play a crucial role in my ability to represent clients and do so fully in their best interests. In fact, I already can see it coming in to play in this context.

For example, today I had a phone interview with a prisoner. Before speaking with him, I tried very hard not to have any preconceived notions about him, particularly as they might relate to his conviction. I reminded myself of the importance of generating true empathy for him so I could efficiently and effectively advocate on his behalf. When he was describing his disability and the assistance he required for it, I tried to put myself into his position, to exchange myself for him, without judging him as a "criminal." (I shuddered a little bit to think of being in his position actually . . .) Nevertheless, I think it worked."

(Participant, Contemplative Lawyering 2006)

CHAPTER 9:

SEEING, APPRECIATING & REPAYING KINDNESS

INTRODUCTION

This practice is the second stage of a multi-stage practice designed to generate pure loving kindness and compassion. This practice and its' associated post-meditation practice may be the most powerful practice taught in this book in terms of its ability to improve your life at work, at home, and beyond.

Unfortunately one of the habitual patterns many of us possess is that we notice negative behavior, but we neither see nor acknowledge positive behavior. One of the participants in my Contemplative Lawyering course put it this way:

> "You are on the road driving for an hour. You get home and you say to your loved one, 'Three idiots cut me off on the way home.' You continue on with more negative remarks. . . No one comes home and says, 'I drove by 1997 people who drove well on the road today.'"

> *(Participant, Contemplative Lawyering 2005)*

It is the same way when we go to a restaurant. We notice and remember when the service is sub-standard. We take it for granted when the service is excellent. This tendency is most pronounced in spousal and other close family relationships. We marry someone because we are impressed by his or her positive qualities. We come to expect the high level of courtesy and kindness we experience from this individual. We notice and complain when this person falls short of those high expectations. The one time the dishes aren't done right away or the garbage doesn't go out, we see and remark on it. Every time this person who we love dearly falls short we point it out. But we ignore the endless acts of kindness. Dishes are washed, food is purchased, the bills are paid, the lawn is mowed, errands are run, and the children are fed, clothed and so on. We take for granted all the sweet things our spouse does. The same is true for parents and children.

Outside of home we experience the kind assistance of secretaries, snow plow operators, maintenance workers, store clerks, automobile mechanics, bankers, real estate agents, and so many others, but we rarely notice or remark on it. If we consider these people and what they do for us at all, we are likely to think that they are just doing their jobs. They are paid to serve others. But consider the times when a paid worker does a poor job or is unpleasant. Being paid does not force workers to do a good job. There is more to it than that. In addition, many of these workers are not paid very much for what they do and yet they work to make our lives more pleasant day after day, week after week. We are the recipients of uncountable acts of kindness.

This practice is about recognizing and acknowledging that kindness. This practice is about seeing that the basic heart of kindness exists in every sentient being. There exists a basic tenderness and gentleness deep in the essence of mind.

Like the previous practice, this practice is a visualization practice which involves working with positive, neutral, and negative individuals. In this practice we are looking for the kindness in each of these types of individuals.

As with the previous practice, people sometimes have difficulty working with negative individuals. How is it possible to find kindness in negative individuals? Consider even the most ferocious beings such as tigers. Even tigers extend a heart of kindness to their young. No matter how ferocious or aggressive creatures are, they exhibit kindness towards some beings. The same is true of human beings. Some human beings are angry and destructive. Even beings like that have a spot of kindness deep in their hearts. Nobody is simply bad, cruel, and unkind. Somewhere in their heart there is genuine kindness. It is important to see that kindness.

Seeing someone as totally destructive is a biased view that sees only one side of the story. Recognizing the basic heart of kindness in generally negative individuals provides a more balanced view.

SEEING & APPRECIATING KINDNESS—
PRACTICE INSTRUCTION

Begin by generating an aspiration to see and appreciate the kindness in others. Then sit in tranquility meditation until your mind settles.

Start the main practice by thinking of the most positive, kindest person you have ever known. Remember that person and visualize that person. See that person clearly in front of you. Contemplate his or her kindness. Feel and experience the kindness of this person. Feel deep gratitude and warmth in your heart as a result of the kindness of this person. Feel deep appreciation for the kindness you have received from this person. Then generate an aspiration for this person to be happy and free from suffering. Open your heart to this person.

As you breathe in and out, experience the ultimate space beyond fear. As you breathe in and out open our heart to this person. Feel the texture of your breath, rest your mind on your breath. Touch your breath and be with your breath.

Then, as you breathe in feel that you are receiving all the pain and suffering of this person. You are receiving all the direct suffering this person experiences such as poverty, illness, and pain. You are also receiving all the disturbing emotions, ignorance, and confusion of this person which are the indirect cause of this person's suffering.

As you breathe out, send this person the bright clear light of joy, happiness, and openness. Send this person contentment, compassion, wisdom, clarity, and an open heart.

Then think that this person is now free from pain and has received the gift of joy and enriched experience. Feel joy that this person is happy and free from suffering.

At the end of the practice, dissolve the visualization and engage in tranquility meditation for a few minutes. End with an aspiration to see and appreciate the kindness in all beings.

Repeat this practice on the second day.

On the third and fourth days, repeat this practice with neutral individuals as the object of your practice. See and appreciate the kindness of the neutral individuals in your life. Remember the cashiers, gas station attendants, stock boys, secretaries, computer technicians, farmers, snow plow operators, building maintenance crews, and landscapers—all the seen and unseen, known and unknown legions of individuals who make our lives comfortable. For this part of the practice you can visualize one "neutral" individual. Alternatively you can visualize groups of related individuals (retail clerks for example) or visualize many different types of individuals who you do not know personally but who make your world a better place.

On the fifth and sixth days repeat this practice again with the object of meditation being a negative person. You may find it helpful to read the comments below about the kindness of negative individuals *before* doing this practice.

On the seventh day, begin this practice by visualizing a very positive, kind person. After you have practiced for a while, breathing in this person's confusion and suffering and sending this person happiness and freedom from suffering, switch the object of your meditation to a negative person and continue to practice sending and taking. Look at your mind. Does your mind change when you switch your focus to the negative person? Why?

Seeing & Appreciating Kindness—Comments

Sending and taking meditation cultivates loving kindness and compassion, but it also cultivates fearlessness. It is not easy to open our hearts to invite pain. To overcome fear and pain, we need to look at it and transform it through our aspiration to give joy. Sending and taking starts with courage. It takes courage to look at pain. It takes courage to be open and take on pain. The key point is your aspiration. If your courage is shaken by fear, overcome that fear with the power of aspiration.

The main point of this practice is to remember the kindness of others.

If you experience a great deal of pain and fear, do the sending and taking practice for yourself first. As you breath in remember your fear and pain. As you breathe out, think of yourself as free from pain and fear. Think that you have let go of pain and fear and enrich your heart with joy and happiness. This practice is described more extensively at the end of Chapter 10 in the section, *Cultivating Loving Kindness and Compassion for Yourself.*

Seeing and Appreciating Kindness— "Negative" Individuals

When you do the sending and taking practice with a negative individual as the object of your meditation, start by making a genuine effort to see that this negative individual has demonstrated kindness in some way. Perhaps an angry and judgmental supervisor has nonetheless taken the time to write a positive evaluation of your work or remembers to ask you about your family. Even if you are unable to think of ways in which this negative person has been kind to you, perhaps you can think of how this person has been kind to his or her family. Perhaps he visits his aging mother in a nursing home. Perhaps she coaches her son's soccer team.

It is nearly always possible to find some evidence of kindness in the conduct and speech of even the most angry and difficult individuals. It is good to think that you are transforming this person's heart of aggression. Think that you are growing this person's heart of kindness and transforming his or her aggression, anger, and hatred.

Even if you are unable to see the kindness in a difficult individual because all you have personally experienced is negative speech and conduct from that person, it is still possible to appreciate that person because we can appreciate the opportunities individuals like this provide for us to practice patience, kindness, and generosity. Individuals who are predominantly negative and unskillful are confused and suffering. They are suffering. As a result of their suffering, you are getting the opportunity to learn patience and compassion. How can you practice patience if there is nobody in your world who is angry? How can you practice compassion if there is nobody in your world who is in need?

For example, in my Contemplative Lawyering classes we often discuss road rage. Many of the participants find they learn a great deal about their own anger and confusion by looking at their minds when they became angry at other drivers. This is an excellent example of how difficult individuals (in this case bad drivers) can be appreciated because they provide us with an opportunity to see our own confusion and practice patience.

Therefore there are two methods available for working with negative individuals. First, we an actually look to see (or imagine) the ways in which they are kind, perhaps with their families. Second, if we are unable to see or imagine *any* kindness in a difficult individual, we can appreciate the learning opportunity they provide.

If you find that you are unable either to see this negative individual's kindness or appreciate the learning opportunity this person provides, a third approach to this exercise is to generate an aspiration to be *able* to work with negative individuals like this in the future.

If you have chosen a negative person to work with in this practice and you find that this individual is so negative for you that you cannot see their kindness, try to simply soften your view towards this person somewhat, perhaps by considering possible understandable reasons for their difficult behavior. Alternatively, you may find it helpful to select another difficult individual to work with. Try considering someone who you perceive as possessing both negative and positive characteristics. Use this practice to see and appreciate the kindness of that person.

THE STORY OF BRIAN NICHOLS

In the spring of 2005, Brian Nichols escaped from custody in the Atlanta, Georgia Courthouse. During the escape, he shot and killed several courthouse personnel and the owner of a truck that he stole for transportation.

At 2:00 a.m. the next morning, a young mother, Ashley Smith, left her apartment to go to the store. As she drove out, she noticed a blue truck pulling into the parking lot. When she returned from the store, the truck was still there. As she walked toward her apartment, a man got out of the truck, came up behind her and put a gun to her side. The man was Brian Nichols. He told her, "I'm not going to hurt you if you do just what I say." After they were in the apartment, Nichols told Smith, "I don't want to hurt you. I don't want to hurt anybody else, so please don't do anything that's going to hurt you." He continued, "You know, somebody could have heard your scream already and if they did, the police are on the way and I'm going to have to hold you hostage and I'm going to have to kill you and probably myself and lots of other people. I don't want that."

After exploring the apartment, Nichols told Smith he was uncomfortable with her. He tied up her hands and feet with masking tape and an extension cord and sat her on a stool in the bathroom with a towel over her head while he took a shower. After the shower, Nichols dressed himself in some clean clothes from Smith's apartment and then untied her.

At this point, Ashley Smith engaged Brian Nichols in conversation. She told him about her little girl. She told him that her husband died four years before and that if Brian hurt her, her little girl would be without both a mommy and a daddy. She told him her daughter was expecting her to pick her up the next morning at 10:00 a.m. and that her daughter would be very upset if Ashley didn't show up.

Brian continued to insist that he was not going to let her go, but Ashley Smith sensed some softening in his attitude towards her. She asked him if she could read and he agreed to let her read. She retrieved a book called *The Purpose Driven Life*[65] from her room and began to read to him. After she read the first paragraph, he said, "Stop. Will you read that again?" She read the paragraph again. It mentioned something about considering your purpose in life. It asked you to consider the talents you were given and asked, "What gifts were you given to use?"

Brian responded to this question by identifying Ashley's purpose,

---

65   Rick Warren, *The Purpose Driven Life* (Zondervan, 2002).

talents and gifts as talking to people and telling them about herself. At this point she talked extensively with him and tried to continue to gain his trust. She told him again about wanting to leave to see her daughter and that she did not want him to hurt anyone else. She reminded him that he said he did not want to hurt anyone else. He said he just wanted to relax, watch TV, and eat some real food. She talked about her family. She asked him about his family. After they talked together for a while, he told her that he thought she was an angel sent from God and that he was lost and God lead him to her to tell him that he had already hurt a lot of people and to let him know how they felt because she had been through it herself. Ashley Smith's husband had died from a knife wound. Brian told Ashley that he had not wanted to hurt the agent that died and that he did not shoot the deputy. He only hit her and hoped that she lived. Ashley explained to him that the agent he killed was a 40-year-old man who was probably a father, a husband, and a friend. She showed him pictures of her family.

Nichols asked Smith what he should do. She encouraged him to turn himself in because if he did not do that, more people would get hurt and he would probably be killed. He told her he was already dead and she said that wasn't true and that it was his choice whether to die or not. After further conversation he talked about his family and told her he would let her go to see her daughter in the morning. They talked about religion quite a bit and when he got hungry, she cooked breakfast for him. He was overwhelmed by her kindness.

She said, "Do you believe in miracles? You are here for a reason. You're here in my apartment for some reason. You got out of that courthouse with police everywhere, and you don't think that's a miracle? You don't think you're supposed to be sitting right in front of me listening to me tell you your reason to be here? Your miracle could be that you need to be caught for this. You need to go back to prison and you need to share the word of God with them, with all the prisoners there."

Shortly after this, it came time for her to leave to pick up her daughter. Brian let her go. She called 911 and the police came. Brian Nichols surrendered without a fight. Nobody else was hurt.[66]

THE STORY OF BRIAN NICHOLS — COMMENTS

There are many lessons from this story of kindness and compassion.

First, it is clear that even violent individuals like Brian Nichols have a heart of kindness. He regretted the pain and suffering he caused and did not want anyone else to get hurt. He allowed Ashley Smith to leave to pick up her daughter, undoubtedly knowing that she would turn him in. When the police came, he surrendered himself into their custody knowing that he would be convicted of murder and returned to prison for the remainder of his life or perhaps even put to death.

Second, it is clear that we can have a profound impact on even the most negative individuals by recognizing their capacity for kindness. Brian Nichols did what he did because Ashley Smith saw his potential for kindness. She saw that he regretted the harm he had done. She awakened his compassion for the victims of his violent rampage. She spoke to him mindfully, compassionately, and skillfully. She attempted to awaken a positive motivation in him to go back to prison and help other prisoners understand their potential for kindness and compassion.

---

66   CNN Justice, *Ex-hostage: 'I wanted to gain his trust.'* (March 14, 2005), available at http://articles.cnn.com/2005-03-14/justice/smith.transcript_1_parking-lot-parking-space-hostage?_s=PM:LAW.

The interchange between Ashley Smith and Brian Nichols centered on their belief in God. That clearly was a helpful element of this interaction because of their shared knowledge of the Christian religion. It may not, however, have been an essential element of this positive interaction. The first words Brian Nichols spoke to Ashley Smith indicated that he did not wish to hurt anyone else. The first signs of softness Brian Nichols showed came as a result of Ashley Smith talking about her little girl and the fact that her little girl's father had died. Ashley Smith was willing to look for positive qualities in this person who had killed others and who frightened her so much. She saw these signs of Brian Nichol's kindness and encouraged them to grow. Ashley Smith saw that Brian Nichols was not a uniformly bad person, but that he had the potential for kindness.

> "Using a negative person as the object of meditation is extremely difficult. Unfortunately, I picked someone who I believe has no redeeming qualities. In working with this person, I have learned that he is arrogant, selfish, inconsiderate, sloppy, and rude. Above all, he cannot be trusted. In trying to think of something nice about him, all I could think of was that he always says hello to everyone in the office when he comes in. I guess I can consider that a small act of kindness. But in my meditation practice, I only got as far as my aspiration that I wished he would become a better person. It is possible that the person I see is simply an end-product of bad life experiences. He must have gone through something bad that would enable him to develop such a "me-first" mentality. I will continue using this person as my object of meditation. Maybe this will make him a little bit easier to work with."
>
> *(Participant, Contemplative Lawyering 2006)*

SEEING & APPRECIATING KINDNESS—POST-MEDITATION PRACTICE

While you are engaging in this practice as your formal meditation you will find it helpful if you dedicate your post-meditation time to seeing and appreciating the kindness of people you encounter during your everyday activities. Notice and appreciate when people hold the door for you or give you directions or allow you to change lanes on the highway. Notice and appreciate when your spouse buys and fixes the food you like or your colleague at work offers to take on a difficult assignment. If you look for kindness, you will find it everywhere. If you can adopt this habit as a regular way of viewing the world you will find that the world is a much more friendly and hospitable place than you thought.

If you are always looking for negative behavior you will find it and your world will seem dark and unfriendly. Simply by seeing and appreciating the kindness around us we can transform our world.

> "I am finding the practice of taking notice of people's kindness towards me very powerful. Whenever I recognize someone's kindness, it immediately improves my outlook and mood. I become happier. It was amazing how instantaneous this was. It also is amazing to me how simple it is to recognize when someone is kind to you, but at the same time how seldom I do this. I have thought about the reasons for this. First, I think most of the time I am rushing to and from meetings or to the library. When I am working I am so focused on what I am doing or everything I have to do that I don't allow myself that small moment to fully notice and appreciate someone's kind action. I am not fully present in my interactions with others. I am reminded here of the mindfulness exercises of previous classes.

For example, practicing mindfulness and taking note and appreciating the beauty of the surrounding environment as well as the practice of being mindful in daily tasks ("washing the dishes to wash the dishes").

(Participant, Contemplative Lawyering 2006)

"I've really enjoyed the practice for this past week. From the man who serves me coffee, to the marshals at the court house, to my family members who drive me insane, finding kindness in others is quite a mood-booster. I found one easy way to find kindness in others is to envision that person with their family or spouse. Thinking of a neutral person as a mother or husband or sister makes me think of the person as a whole person instead of just considering them in the context where I encounter them. When I think of someone as a whole person, it reminds me that we are all here, trying to find happiness and avoid suffering. I think this is helpful to remember when someone is rude or inconsiderate. When I remember that I have something in common with all these people, it makes me think maybe they are just having a bad day or reacting to some negative event they've had earlier in their day.

This practice also was powerful because when I was able to see and appreciate the positive interactions I have with people, it made me want to treat them and others positively as well. Positive interactions that I was able to appreciate this week included: people letting me cross the street when I was running, smiles at the grocery store, encouragement from a colleague, and smiles from other neutral people. I think it's true that emotions or moods can be contagious. I find my days much more enjoyable and positive when I can get someone to smile back at me.

Another way I've come to appreciate kindness in the world is by viewing interactions other people have in their lives. I live in a residential neighborhood and do most of my work at home by the window. I see couples walking by lovingly. I see parents out playing with their kids and enjoying their families. I see owners walking their dogs, just enjoying the fresh air. All these encounters make me realize that these people are expressing kindness for others and there really is a lot of good in our world. Also, I was at the mall this week and enjoyed watching groups of kids out together just laughing and enjoying each other's company. Seeing people interact playfully and happily with others helps me embrace the idea that people do want to be happy. It helps me see them more as whole individuals instead of just in the context I encounter them."

(Participant, Contemplative Lawyering 2006)

"Last week, I visited a friend in another state. While he was working I sat in a café nearby and did some work. I did a lot of "people-watching" while I was there and was truly shocked at the number of frowns or furrowed brows I saw. This led me to really focus on incorporating a smile into my daily routine, which I immediately found to have a truly positive influence on my mood. I also noticed that when I approached people with a smile (say the lady behind the counter), she also responded with a smile. I thought it was neat to see that by approaching someone with a smile, you can easily get a smile back. It's also nice to live in a world where people smile at you and have positive interactions. It made me feel that there is a lot of good in people if you just approach them in the right way. It also made me realize that people do want to be happy. Sometimes they just need to be reminded and seeing a smile may be all it takes. Anyway, I really enjoyed my secret experiment."

(Participant, Contemplative Lawyering 2006)

SEEING & APPRECIATING KINDNESS—
PRACTICE SCHEDULE

Because this practice is complex and has many stages (positive, negative, neutral, comparing), you will find it most useful if you engage in this practice in formal meditation for seven days. Again, you may not be able to schedule consecutive days of practice. However, try to create the opportunity to engage in this practice seven times. During the period of time when you are working with this practice, whether it is a week or longer, it will be very beneficial if you work with the post meditation practice, bringing your formal practice aspiration into your interactions with others in your world.

"I think it is important to acknowledge people's kindness even when you feel they are simply doing their duty. For instance, some people think that as a cashier and a service provider a person is obligated to smile as they ring you up or wish you a "good day" when they have completed the transaction. The reality is that this person doesn't have to do anything like that. Therefore, I think it is very important to acknowledge people's politeness and praise people who do their jobs well. For instance just the other day a Dunkin' Donuts cashier asked me if I would like my coffee with extra milk after I asked for skim milk in my coffee. Her question surprised me. I didn't think she cared what I meant when I said, "Medium coffee with skim milk, please." She didn't have to ask me that, but she wanted to make sure my cup of coffee was right for me and not just technically right. I told her I appreciated her asking me that question, that the coffee was perfect and that her sunny disposition made my day. It might seem like my response was excessive, but I have received so many crappy cups of coffee that her small gesture meant the world to me and I had to let her know. I wanted someone else to benefit from her attention to customer service. I wanted her to continue to care. Too often warm and friendly people become cold and jaded because their small efforts to be pleasant and attentive go unnoticed. I don't want to be the reason why the next person in the Dunkin' Donuts line doesn't get the cup of coffee they want and need that morning.

(Participant, Contemplative Lawyering 2006)

"I've thought a lot about my expectations of others in relation to recognizing kindness. I've realized that when someone is always kind to me I take their kindness for granted and I don't acknowledge their kindness. For example, my mother is probably the kindest person to me of anyone I know. She is always there to help me when I need it and to listen. Since I've realized the extent of her kindness more fully, I've tried to be more appreciative. I've also tried to be more kind in return. For example, I've tried to be more patient and more available to listen to her.

Conversely, I've noticed that with my close friends and family I hold certain expectations of them. I expect them to be available and to help me when I need it. I think this expectation comes from feeling that I would be available to help them. When they fulfill my expectations, I'm not sure I express to them sufficiently my appreciation. However, when they don't, I become hurt and angry. I take their not helping me as a sign of weakness in our relationship and wonder if I should count on this person. This leads to conflict in the relationship. I think my expectations come from a too narrow and ego-centered place. I am thinking too much of my own needs and not considering the other person's needs and perspective. At play here is a tendency to notice when people let me down but not fully appreciate their acts of kindness. Perhaps if I remembered just as many instances of when my friends and family are kind, this would balance out the effect of someone not helping me. Since realizing this, I've tried to take notice when my friends and family are helpful to me, reflect on that and express to them how much I appreciate their help."

(Participant, Contemplative Lawyering 2006)

REPAYING KINDNESS—PRACTICE INSTRUCTION

This practice is exactly like the previous practice except that after you see and appreciate the kindness of the object of your meditation (positive, neutral, and negative), you generate an aspiration to repay that kindness. This aspiration to repay kindness can take many forms. You can simply aspire to avoid unskillful speech and conduct that will cause pain and distress to this person. You can aspire to acknowledge kindness whenever it is shown to you or you can aspire to be kind to this person. Another approach you can take is to aspire to be patient when this person is not kind. There are many forms your aspiration can take. This practice provides you with an opportunity to think about how you can repay the kindness that is shown to you by others.

REPAYING KINDNESS—
POST-MEDITATION PRACTICE

You can carry this practice into the rest of your day by making an effort to put your aspiration into practice. For example, if you have generated an aspiration to acknowledge the kindness of others, try to do that during post meditation. If you have generated an aspiration to be kind to others in return, try to do that during post meditation. Whatever aspiration you have generated, try to put it into practice during post meditation. For this practice, it is important to set a realistic aspiration so that you can carry through with it in post meditation. Even if you find that you cannot carry through with your aspiration it is important to be kind to yourself. Simply having the aspiration is wonderful and beneficial in itself.

REPAYING KINDNESS—PRACTICE SCHEDULE

Because this practice is complex and has many stages (positive, negative, neutral, comparing), you will find it most useful if you engage in this practice in formal meditation for seven days. Again, you may not be able to schedule consecutive days of practice. However, try to create the opportunity to engage in this practice seven times. During the period of time when you are working with this practice, whether it is a week or longer, it will be very beneficial if you work with the post meditation practice, bringing your formal practice aspiration into your interactions with others in your world.

OBSTACLES TO THE SENDING & TAKING PRACTICES

In my comments on the sending and taking practices we have done so far, I have addressed some of the obstacles that people experience when they do these practices. In this section, I will discuss some additional obstacles that you might encounter when you engage in these practices.

First, you may find that you are not sufficiently settled in your meditation to stay focused. Tranquility meditation is a necessary foundation for complex visualization practices. All meditation practices are either tranquility practice or insight practice or both. These practices have a tranquility aspect to them. The object of your tranquility meditation in these practices is the visualization as well as the contemplation that you engage in. If you are easily distracted, it will be difficult to maintain your focus on the visualization and the contemplation. One remedy is to engage in a longer tranquility meditation session prior to starting the sending and taking practice.

Alternatively your difficulty with maintaining focus may relate to forgetting the instruction or not understanding or believing that the practice is beneficial. If you find that you are forgetting the instruction, the remedy is simply to study and memorize the instruction before you begin.

These practices will be difficult for you if you feel that they are not useful. If you are having difficulty seeing the benefit of these practices you may find it helpful to go back and read the introductory materials about the practices to make sure you understand what the practices are designed to accomplish. It may also be helpful to read some books about the attributes of effective lawyering. You will not be motivated to do these practices if you do not believe that genuine empathy is an important characteristic of good lawyering. You also will not be able to engage in these practices if you do not believe they will help you cultivate genuine empathy. This problem may be solved by reading the scientific studies that have concluded that compassion practices are effective.

Another difficulty you may encounter with these practices is resistance based on misunderstanding the instructions. For example, if you think that compassion means approval of negative speech and conduct, you may resist the practice. You need to understand the practices correctly in order to believe that they will be beneficial. Compassion does not mean approving negative conduct. Rather, compassion means understanding that negative conduct results from hurt and confusion. Compassion means aspiring for individuals who engage in negative conduct to be free from hurt and confusion.

Another obstacle to performing the sending and taking practice is simply being in a bad mood. It is very difficult to generate loving kindness and compassion for others if you are distressed about something yourself. If this happens, you can try practicing tranquility meditation or do the sending and taking practice for yourself. This practice is described in the section on *Cultivating Loving Kindness and Compassion for Yourself* at the end of Chapter 10. This practice also is useful if you feel that you are working with too many of your own confusions to think about helping anyone else.

Another obstacle you may experience is that you may have selected a negative person who you are unable to work with. Keep in mind that there may be people in your life who create such significant difficulty for you that you are unable to use the formal and post meditation practices to work productively with the situation. If you are encountering this kind of situation in your life, please read the entry about "*Bad Friends*" in Chapter 15 (this is not what it sounds like).

CHAPTER 10:

CULTIVATING LOVING KINDNESS & COMPASSION

CULTIVATING LOVING KINDNESS

Loving kindness means desiring joy and happiness for others. Loving kindness is open, gentle understanding. The joy and happiness we aspire for others to have is not the mundane happiness that results from satisfying our material desires or experiencing a perfect, but temporary holiday. What we usually refer to as happiness is getting what we want and avoiding what we do not want. In other words we desire pleasant relationships, a good job, and a lovely place to live. We define happiness in terms of acquiring these things. We also define happiness in terms of avoiding conditions and situations that we have an aversion for. For example, it makes us happy if we are not sick and do not experience bad weather. In other words, our happiness is conditional. It is conditioned on having the right circumstances—getting what we want and avoiding what we do not want.

Because this form of happiness is conditional, any happiness we gain this way is temporary and tinged with suffering. Whenever we manage to attain the circumstances we desire, we immediately begin to experience fear that we will lose these circumstances and fear that we will be plagued with the circumstances we do not want. For example, when we get a good job, we are happy for a little while, but then we worry that we will lose the job or we become dissatisfied and want a better job. If we are healthy, we worry about getting sick. If we are rich, we worry about losing our wealth.

Unfortunately, everything we are hoping to have and keep is impermanent. It is not possible to hang on to things. At the same time, it is not possible to avoid unfortunate circumstances. Fortunes are won and lost. Possessions come and go. People get sick and die. All of this is unavoidable. But we think if we do everything correctly, we will acquire and hang on to happiness. This is a myth and as a result we are disappointed. We live in constant fear—fear of not getting what we want, fear of losing what we have, fear of getting what we do not want, and fear of not being able to escape from what we do not want.

With loving kindness, the joy and happiness we aspire for others to have is the joy of freedom from hopes and fears, the joy of freedom from attachments and aversions. This joy is possible. It is based on being content with the present moment. We get a taste of this joy every time we settle into meditation and dismiss distractions as they arise. Meditation is about resting in the present without hope and fear. We experience a taste of this joy every time we engage in an act of pure generosity—not clinging to what we are giving and not needing our gift to be appreciated.

Loving kindness is understanding how people try to attain happi-

ness and understanding how they make mistakes. Loving kindness is aspiring for others to generate the *true* causes of happiness.
We can demonstrate loving kindness through our thoughts, words,
and deeds. For example, we can generate the thought that we want
others to be happy. We can speak the words of aspiration for the
happiness of others. We can express loving kindness in our actions
by being gentle, kind, and open. We can engage in gentle looks,
gentle words, and gentle actions. We can avoid harsh criticism.

CULTIVATING LOVING KINDNESS —
PRACTICE INSTRUCTION

Begin with an aspiration to generate loving kindness for all beings.
Settle your mind with tranquility meditation for several minutes.

This sending and taking practice begins by visualizing a positive
person, a person who is very dear to you. Consider this person
in a positive situation such as a wedding, a new job, the birth of
a child, etc. Understand that this new situation could go well or
not. Generate an aspiration for this person to experience genuine
happiness whether this positive situation goes well or not.

Sending and Taking: As you breathe in, think that you are taking
in on your breath all of this person's hopes and fears. Take in all
this person's anxieties about the coming event. Take away this
person's obsessive clinging to everything going perfectly. As you
breathe out, extend loving kindness to this person. Open you heart
to this person and send gentle thoughts and aspirations. Wish for
everything to go perfectly for this person. Wish for this person
to experience happiness and joy even if everything does not go
perfectly. Wish for this person to experience the joy and happiness

that is free from fear, attachments, and aversions.

After you have engaged in sending and taking for some time, dissolve the visualization and sit in tranquility meditation. End the practice session by dedicating this practice session to cultivating loving kindness for all beings.

On the second day, repeat this practice. On the third and fourth days, repeat this practice with a neutral person as the focus of your meditation. On the fifth and sixth days, repeat this practice with a negative person as the focus of your meditation.

On the seventh day, begin again by visualizing a positive person in your life who is experiencing a positive situation such as a wedding, a new job, the birth of a child, etc. As you practice sending and taking, gradually extend your aspiration for happiness to all beings (positive, neutral and negative) who are experiencing the same positive situation. This is immeasurable loving kindness without barriers, loving kindness for all sentient beings.

Cultivating Loving Kindness – Comments

Take this practice as far as you are able. If you have difficulty extending loving kindness to negative individuals, simply extend your loving kindness as far as you are able. If you can generate an aspiration to cultivate loving kindness for all beings, that would be a beneficial thing to do. If you find you cannot generate that aspiration, generate whatever aspiration for loving kindness you are able to honestly experience.

CULTIVATING LOVING KINDNESS —
POST-MEDITATION PRACTICE

During the seven days that you are engaging in this formal sending and taking practice, try to cultivate an aspiration for the happiness of all beings you encounter during the day.

Remember that the happiness you are aspiring for is not mundane happiness. You are not wishing for everyone to get what they want. Rather you are wishing for them to be content with what they have. You are wishing for them to let go of their fears, attachments, and aversions. You are aspiring for them to let go of their anger, hatred, pride, greed, ignorance, and jealousy. You are aspiring for them to acquire pure selfless joy and happiness.

CULTIVATING KINDNESS IN MARITAL
(& OTHER CLOSE) RELATIONSHIPS —
THE BEST STRAWBERRY

The practices we have been working with can be a powerful basis for a wonderful marital relationship or any close personal relationship. You can use your spouse, family member, or friend as your mindfulness reminder and by doing so, ensure that whenever you are with this person you will be fully present and listen deeply and with genuine interest to whatever he or she has to say. I can assure you that this will be appreciated. When you find yourself annoyed or angry at your loved one, you can practice Slow Reversal, stop and look at your mind and apply an antidote that can prevent you from lashing out and causing great harm. We will be discussing additional practices for working with anger later in the book.

In the context of the current practice, cultivating loving kindness, you can take that practice from aspiration to action by practicing generosity. If you practice generosity in the context of your marital (or other close) relationship, you will enhance the depth and quality of your relationship immeasurably. I call it "The Best Strawberry" practice. What this means is that every time you sit down to have a meal with your loved one, you have an opportunity to practice generosity. Instead of taking the best strawberry or the largest cookie or the most perfectly barbecued chicken breast, you can offer these items to your loved one. This can be a beautiful practice of pure kindness and generosity.

Of course there are confusions that can undermine the purity of this practice. If your motivation for offering the best strawberry is to gain favor, then your motivation is ego centered rather than a pure intention to benefit. It is important to watch your mind to see what your intentions might be.

Offering the best strawberry should not be a practice that is based on fear. In some relationships, one individual is very controlling and angry in their treatment of the other. In that context, the best strawberry might be offered out of fear. This is not a positive situation. It is important to watch your mind and notice your motivation. If you are acting out of fear, think about whether you are able to work with this relationship. While it is possible to practice compassion and generosity when you live with a psychologically abusive individual, this is very difficult. If you are unable to work productively with an abusive relationship, then it may be best to leave. I will talk more in the final chapters of this book about what it means to work skillfully in an abusive situation. See *Working With Difficult Individuals—Bad Friends* in Chapter 15.

Another way the purity of this practice can be undermined is if offering the best strawberry is motivated by feelings of lack of self worth. This is not healthy for you. "All sentient beings" includes you. In this context, the better approach might be to practice taking the best strawberry for you. Giving to others should not be based on feeling that you are undeserving. You should give because you genuinely want your loved one to be happy.

The bottom line here is that every thought, word, and action in a marital or other close relationship can be a powerful context for applying all of the practices I am offering in this book.

CULTIVATING LOVING KINDNESS— PRACTICE SCHEDULE

I recommend that you engage in the practice of cultivating loving kindness for at least seven formal practice sessions. Again, they may not be on consecutive days because of your scheduling difficulties. Throughout the period of time when you are engaging in this formal practice, use your encounters with other people as your mindfulness reminder. Whenever you encounter others, try to generate an aspiration for their happiness.

> "I think simple gestures such as holding the door open for people, something I tend to do frequently, are motivated by an unconscious desire to make another person happy even if it's for just those 5 seconds that the gesture lasts. Even simple eye contact with a slight smile to acknowledge the other person in passing can make some kind of impact. I remember one time an older female co-worker was walking past me when all of a sudden she randomly stopped, smiled and hugged me. I couldn't

stop smiling for the next five minutes and was amazed at how much that affected me. I can't remember if maybe I was having a bad day and that showed on my face, but I do know that her kindness took me away from my thoughts and brought me to the present, where it is much nicer to be."

(Participant, Contemplative Lawyering 2006)

"Over the past few weeks, I have been using the same negative person as my object of meditation during post meditation practice. In my efforts to wish that he become a better person, I noticed a change in *me*. Initially, when I would say hello to this person at work it was because I wanted to get it out of the way; it was simply a formality I needed to get through so I could get on with my work and ignore him for the rest of the day. However, now when I say "Hello, how are you?" I actually wait for an answer and I even smile!

That is when I remember Thich Nhat Hanh's book, *The Miracle of Mindfulness*. He says that we should be mindful while we are washing dishes. We should wash dishes simply to wash the dishes. He says we should not wash dishes just to get them clean so we can move on to the next task in our lives. Rather, we should wash dishes for the sake of washing the dishes. The first time I read that I laughed because I really didn't understand what he meant. But after my experience with this negative person, I was able to apply that principle. In the beginning, I would say hello to him just so I could get on with the rest of my day. But now, when I say hello, I actually stop and listen for his response. This is the difference. It is amazing how something so small can lead to a change in someone's attitude and behavior.

I used to find him so irritating and it seems that now he does not get to me as much. I no longer view him as the mosquito that I would try to swat away from me when I was trying to get to sleep on a hot summer night. In sum, what I have noticed is that our words have creative power. In my thoughts and aspirations for him to become a better person, I have been able to show him an act of love (well, at least compassion), and this has resulted in me being better able to deal with him. I am almost positive that he has noticed the change in my attitude towards him as well.

(Participant, Contemplative Lawyering 2006)

GENERATING COMPASSION

Compassion is the wish for another being to be free from suffering. Compassion includes the wish for others to be free of mundane suffering. Therefore compassion means wishing for sick people to be well and hungry people to be fed and wishing for beings to be free from the mental suffering associated with physical suffering. Compassion means aspiring for beings to experience equanimity even when things do not go well for them. Compassion includes wishing for others to be free of the suffering that results from clinging to attachments and aversions.

GENERATING COMPASSION—
PRACTICE INSTRUCTION

Begin with an aspiration to generate compassion for all beings. Settle your mind with tranquility meditation for several minutes.

This sending and taking practice begins by visualizing a person who is very dear to you who you know is experiencing suffering.

For example, consider someone who is experiencing a very difficult situation such as sickness, loss of a job, loss of property, or loss
of a loved one. Generate an aspiration for this person to be free
from suffering. This aspiration can include a wish for the negative
situation to improve as well as an aspiration for this person not to
experience mental suffering even if the negative situation does not
improve.

Taking and Sending: As you breath, take in on your breath all of
this person's pain, suffering, hope, and fear. Take in all this person's
anxiety, grief, and distress about the difficult situation. Take away
this person's clinging to the hope that circumstances will improve.
As you breathe out, extend compassion to this person. Open
your heart to this person and send gentle thoughts and aspirations. Wish for this person to be free from suffering. Wish for this
person's mundane suffering to end. Wish for this person not to
suffer even if everything does not go well. Wish for this person to
be free from the suffering of physical pain and mental fear, grief,
and anguish.

After you have practiced sending and taking for some time, dissolve
the visualization and sit in tranquility meditation. End the practice
session by dedicating this practice session to cultivating compassion for all beings.

On the second day, repeat this practice. On the third and fourth
days, repeat this practice with a neutral person as the focus of your
meditation. On the fifth and sixth days, repeat this practice with a
negative person as the focus of your meditation.

On the seventh day, begin again with someone you love who is
experiencing a difficult situation that involves suffering. As you

practice, gradually extend your compassion to all people (positive, neutral and negative) who are experiencing the same difficult situation that your loved one is experiencing. This is immeasurable compassion without barriers, compassion for all sentient beings.

> "Right before Tuesday's class I talked with my grandmother who I am very close to. She has two herniated disks and is in a lot of pain and discomfort and feels helpless and frustrated. In short she is suffering a lot of physical pain and mental anguish. My meditation was so focused. I think I turned it into a hybrid of prayer for her and an aspiration for her pain and mental anguish to subside. It was amazing. I really felt like I was sending her that energy—everything that was positive in me."
>
> *(Participant, Contemplative Lawyering 2006)*

"For the sending and taking exercise, I chose first to focus on my sister. I love my sister unconditionally. I only want good things for her in life and I am willing to do anything to lessen her suffering. Accordingly, it was easy to generate love, kindness, and compassion for my sister during meditation. I was able to stay focused on the exercise, to follow the instruction, and to make a genuine effort to transfer positive thoughts to her. I did not feel pity (i.e. "I'm glad that's not me") for my sister when I thought of her suffering. If anything, I felt genuine empathy for her—a true desire for that suffering to be alleviated.

For the second exercise, I chose to focus on the bank teller who usually helps me. I do not know anything about this person. My feelings towards him are entirely neutral. From the outset, I had trouble staying present. My mind kept wandering and I could not focus on the instructions. I think this was because I am not interested in the bank teller. I decided to create a story line for the bank teller. I decided the bank teller was trying to save money in order to buy his first home for his family. I probably chose this because lately I have been pre-occupied with trying to purchase a condominium. One would think the storyline that I selected would help me see myself and this person as the same, with the same struggles, desires, fears, and sufferings. Nevertheless, I did not really see myself as the same. If anything, I found myself feeling pity for the bank teller because I saw that his financial struggles would be more difficult than mine.

I found the following paragraph in *The Tibetan Book of Living and Dying*[67] compelling:

> Compassion is a far greater and nobler thing than pity. Pity has its roots in fear and a sense of arrogance and condescension, sometimes even a smug feeling of "I'm glad it's not me."

I really like how the author distinguishes compassion from pity. I think of myself as a compassionate person, but I am starting to think that any compassion I feel for others might be blended with pity. During this exercise, I came to appreciate that most of us reserve genuine feelings of love, compassion, and kindness for an intimate, exclusive group of people. This feels sad and pathetic. However, I am not entirely sure where to go from here. Is it a long process to develop true compassion for others?"
(Participant, Contemplative Lawyering)

It appears that this person came away from this practice session feeling that the session had been ineffective because she was unable to generate genuine compassion for a neutral individual.

---

67   Sogyal Rinpoche, *Tibetan Book of Living and Dying* 199 (Harper 1994).

Actually, this person had two significant insights during this practice session. Simply seeing the limited nature of our habitual way of thinking is significant. Most of us save our feelings of love and compassion for close family and friends without ever realizing that it would be beneficial to extend that love and compassion to a broader group. The participant also clearly saw the difference between genuine compassion and ego-driven compassion. This is a subtle distinction. Most of us generate feelings of "compassion" and "empathy" without realizing how much ego is involved in our feelings.

This individual asked where she should go from here and whether it is a long process to develop true compassion for others. The insight she gained from this practice session is a substantial step in the direction of developing true compassion. The aspiration she has expressed to cultivate genuine compassion ensures that genuine compassion will arise in her heart.

> "The first time I engaged in the practice of transferring an open heart from a positive to a difficult person and then to a neutral person, I had a powerful experience. For the positive person, I chose my grandmother. After I opened my heart to her, I was able to see her clearly, to see her confusion and suffering, and to generate a wish that she be free from suffering. As soon as I shifted the focus from my grandmother to my mother (my negative person), I saw all of my mother's suffering and confusion very clearly. I had the insight that in actuality, my mother and my grandmother are one and the same; that regardless of the source of their suffering, they both suffer just the same. The only difference is that my grandmother does not dump her suffering on others, while my mother often unloads her suffering onto those around her. Nonetheless, seeing their suffering as one and the

same made it easier not to take what my mother does personally. In short, I was able to see her negative actions for what they are, the result of her own suffering and confusion. I was able to have an open heart and a certain amount of compassion for her. The feeling of that realization—that they are actually the same— lasted only briefly. Nonetheless, it was a profound experience because I clearly saw that it is in fact possible to view everyone with equanimity and loving kindness."

(Participant, Contemplative Lawyering 2005)

Generating Compassion – Comments

Take this practice as far as you are able to take it. If you have difficulty generating compassion for negative individuals, try to extend your compassion as far as you are able. If you can generate an aspiration to cultivate compassion for all beings, that would be a beneficial thing to do. If you cannot generate that aspiration, generate whatever aspiration for compassion you are able to honestly experience.

Compassion as an Antidote for Anger

Compassion is a powerful antidote for anger. It is primarily for this reason that I have put these materials on cultivating loving kindness and compassion at this location in the book. Following these practices, we will return to working with strong emotions, including anger. It is not possible to remain angry with someone if you have generated loving kindness and compassion for that individual. The practices presented in the next chapters will be much more beneficial to you now that you have been introduced to impartiality, loving kindness, and compassion.

The individual who wrote the following entry was suffering from a chest cold. She became angry when a waitress in a coffee bar gave her unwanted and arrogant advice on what she should drink to avoid dehydration.

> "I was so angry. I couldn't understand why this person was trying to force her "knowledge" down the throat of a paying customer. I was so sick. Couldn't she see that I didn't have the emotional capacity to deal with my illness and her arrogance at the same time? I didn't go back to that restaurant for a week and a half. How could this have gone better? I think now, in hindsight, that I should have tried the "impartiality" practice on the spot to recognize that I am not the only one allowed to have "off" days."

A few weeks later, this student wrote the following journal entry:

> "I went to the coffee bar for the first time in a few weeks and as I walked out the girl (from my previous journal entry) apologized for hurting my feelings the other day. She told me that she was feeling off that day and she shouldn't have projected her anger on me. I thought this was particularly amazing because I had recently come to understand that our altercation was more about me and my inability to be sane during my illness. I would really like this woman to be happy, not because she made up with me, but because I see the way her happiness would affect the people around her. With us both being "off" the other day, we were both able to spread our negativity and that probably affected many more people than just each other."
>
> *(Participant, Contemplative Lawyering 2005)*

GENERATING COMPASSION –
POST-MEDITATION PRACTICE

While you are engaging in this practice during formal meditation, try to generate compassion for all beings you encounter during the day including people and animals. As you encounter beings, generate a wish for them to be free from suffering. Wish for them to be free from the physical sufferings associated with sickness and poverty. Also wish for them to be free from the mental suffering of grief, anxiety, fear, anger, hatred, jealousy, desire, and greed.

GENERATING COMPASSION—
PRACTICE SCHEDULE

In order to work through the multiple stages of this practice it will be helpful to work with this practice for seven days. During the period of time when you are working with this practice in formal meditation, use the people (and animals) you encounter throughout the day as your mindfulness reminder. Whenever you encounter someone, try to generate an aspiration for that person or animal to be free from suffering.

> "I've been able to understand difficult individuals in a better way and have compassion for them by recognizing that their negative behavior stems from suffering or insecurity or confusion. Recognizing the source of their negative behavior doesn't mean that I approve or validate that behavior, but it may help me deal with them in a more constructive way. For example, my father is a diabetic. When his sugar gets low he starts to act in an irrational way and is short-tempered. Because this behavior stems from an illness and because he is my father it is easier

for me to generate loving kindness and compassion towards him rather than towards a colleague who is simply rude and arrogant. Nevertheless, understanding the source of his negative behavior allows me to let it go for the moment and then come back and talk with him skillfully when he has stabilized his sugar. With others, realizing that their negative behavior is a product of suffering or confusion allows me to be somewhat more patient with them and enables me to work with them in a more skillful way whereas before I simply tried to shut them out and not deal with them. This is a good thing since in many cases I have to work with these individuals and avoiding dealing with them is not productive."

(Participant, Contemplative Lawyering 2006)

CULTIVATING LOVING KINDNESS & COMPASSION FOR YOURSELF

"I have found the impartiality practice to be both eye-opening and challenging. It has been eye-opening in the sense that it brought to my attention the fact that I am much more judgmental about myself than I am about others. I am most critical of myself and this is a source of a lot of negativity in my life."

(Participant, Contemplative Lawyering 2006)

Quite a few of the individuals who have participated in the Contemplative Lawyering course have reported to me that they experience strong self-criticism, self-doubt, and self-loathing. This makes it extremely difficult to engage in these sending and taking practices. It is difficult to generate loving kindness and compassion for others if we are filled with hatred for ourselves.

These feelings of self-hatred can be worked with in much the same way that we have been generating loving kindness and compassion for others. **First**, it is important to recognize that, just like everyone else, we are simply trying to achieve happiness even if our efforts to do so are confused and ineffective. **Second**, it is very important to see and appreciate our own positive attributes. Just like seeing the kindness in others, we can cultivate a habit of seeing and appreciating our own acts of kindness towards others. **Finally**, we can work with this issue by recognizing that any negative behavior we engage in is the result of confusion, not the result of basic negativity. From a practice perspective, it can be helpful to engage in all of the sending and taking practices we have learned to do for others, but change the focus to work with our view of ourselves.

In order to do sending and taking practices with yourself as the focus of the meditation, begin with an aspiration to cultivate love and compassion for yourself or an aspiration to see and appreciate your own kindness. Then engage in tranquility meditation until your mind settles.

For the main practice, visualize yourself sitting in front of you and looking back at you. Then perform the practices using this visualized version of "you" as your focus. Alternatively, you can look at your self from the perspective of the visualized "you" that is sitting in front of you.

This practice requires a little bit of mental gymnastics, but it can be very powerful. In a sense, you are viewing your confused self from the perspective of your wise and compassionate self. If you simply generate that visualization, it will be powerful for you because generating this visualization requires you to recognize that you are inherently wise and compassionate even though you see yourself manifesting as confused and suffering.

Another practice you can do to work with self-hatred is to visualize in front of you all the people in your life who view you in a positive way and for whom you have respect. In your visualization, imagine all of these individuals recognizing and appreciating your positive qualities and sending you love and compassion.

Another practice you can do is to simply write down all of your positive qualities. It is best to do this when you are feeling in a positive mood. Keep your list with you and look at it any time you find yourself falling into self-critical judgments and self-hatred.

> "Practicing this giving and receiving practice on ourselves in class was huge. I can't imagine what reading all our journals must be like but I am sure that there is a lot of self-loathing or self-doubt and/or lack of self-compassion. And it makes more sense to me now why I am having such a hard time opening up for others. It is probably because I am lacking a good foundation. If I don't have compassion for myself, what am I supposed to draw from to give to others?"
>
> *(Participant, Contemplative Lawyering 2006)*

CHAPTER 11:

CULTIVATING LOVING KINDNESS & COMPASSION FOR INDIVIDUALS WHO INTENTIONALLY HARM OTHERS

When someone's negative behavior extends to conduct that intentionally harms another person, it seems impossible that the victim of that harm could actually generate loving kindness and compassion for this person. This is, however, possible. I feel very fortunate to be able to offer you the transcript of a talk a young woman presented at my one of my Contemplative Lawyering classes. She had been kidnapped and physically abused by a disturbed young man. She talked about the process of generating compassion for her attacker. This is what she said:

> "About five years ago when I was living in California, I was introduced to a young man. We went on a date - to a movie. I liked him, so we went on a second date and that went well. However, on our third date he said some things about his past relationships (including an ex wife) that raised red flags for me. I really felt like there was something not quite right about him. I told him that night that I didn't feel like it was going to work

out for us. We could stay friends. We could see each other again, but that it really wasn't going to work out for us.

He seemed to be fine with what I said, but he knew where I lived. He had picked me up there. Also, on a previous date I had talked about my daughter and that school was about to be out and that my daughter would go and visit her father during the summer. I had talked about how she was going away and that it was really hard for me because my life revolved around her.

After that third date, he started to stalk me. He watched me coming and going. He watched my daughter leave to go stay with her dad for the summer. He saw me leave and take her to the airport with her bags. About four days later I went out with some friends. When I came back that evening he was hiding in the bushes. As I went into my house he attacked me and came into my house. He proceeded to hold me hostage in my house for about two weeks. I couldn't use the phone. I tried to get away but it was not possible. He did many awful things to me. He carved "slave" in my arm. He beat me. He held knives to me. I was tied up. I felt like I couldn't get away. He kept saying he wasn't going to let me go. He said that if somehow the cops came he was going to kill me.

I tried to reason with him. I tried everything from talking to him to trying to fight back. At one point I was trying to get away. I had made it out into the garage and he caught me and grabbed my face. He squeezed my face hard and slammed my head into concrete and shattered two teeth on each side of my mouth.

The way I got away is that I played a mind game with him.

I managed to get him to trust me and let me do more things around the house. I got him to let me take the garbage out and then I ran and flagged down a car, went to the hospital and called the police. He followed me to the hospital. The police arrested him outside the hospital.

In California they are really good about pressing charges in "domestic" disputes. Because of OJ California is one of the best States to be in and have something like this happen. They have laws that make it possible to press charges without actually having to confront your attacker. I would have pressed charges anyway, but I didn't have to go to court or see him or anything like that. They charged him with felony assault. He was sentenced to two years, but after serving two months, they released him on probation.

Even though I had a restraining order against him, he wrote letters to me while he was in jail. I knew I could call the court and stop him from writing me letters, but that process was complicated and at the same time I didn't want him to get angry. He knew where I lived. Even with the restraining order I thought that when he got out he is just going to come get me. He would be angry with me. What would stop him?

I decided the best thing for me was to leave California. I moved back to Connecticut with my daughter. After we moved, Victim's Services helped me track him. They gave me updates. He was from Oregon. He moved back there. He ended up going back to jail for almost two years because he did the same thing to another girl in Oregon, but this time he made the mistake of using a gun. That is pretty much what happened.

Once I got back to Connecticut, it took me two years and lots of money just to take care of my teeth. And that was just my teeth—just a physical thing.

Obviously a number of years have gone by and I think what I really had going for me is that I had already spent a lot of time previously working through difficult situations having to do with compassion and forgiveness.

I have learned that there are three mindsets that can help you deal with a situation like this—any situation where somebody harms you. The first is not feeling sorry for your self, not thinking, "Why did this happen to me?" The second is generating forgiveness. The third is actually generating compassion for the person who harmed you.

With respect to the first mindset, I was very sick for a long time. When this kidnapping and attack happened to me I was recovering from an arthritis condition that previously made it so I could not walk for weeks at a time - a reactive arthritic condition. I was twenty-five years old and not able to walk. There were times when every inch of my body hurt. While I was sick, I would go to the doctor and see that everyone else in the Rheumatologist's office was eighty years old and I was only twenty-five. It is easy for me to think, "How and why is this happening to me? I have already had other things happen. What is this about? What is this not walking thing about?" At the same time, taking a step back I could look at all the old people there and see that there were also people even younger than me. There are many children who have juvenile rheumatoid diseases and who can't walk or use their hands. It is not just arthritis conditions. It is seeing someone in a wheelchair, seeing someone who broke their leg, seeing and realizing that you have a connection to all those people. People have migraine headaches. People have asthma. They are all people who have some kind of disorder that gives them a hard time. Having that arthritis condition really helped me feel a connection to everyone around me.

That is the first thing. Not feeling sorry for myself for having this happen. I saw that being intentionally harmed like this was a way for me to have even more of a connection to other people. There are so many people who have things happen to them. They have car accidents or someone beats them, hurts them or rapes them or hurts someone they love. I realized that this situation was just another thing that I could even be thankful for because it helped me to grow as a person and helped me to be more connected with others. That is the first point.

The second point is about forgiveness. When I was much younger my father was killed in a car accident. Although it was an accident, I had a great deal of anger towards the man who killed my Dad. It took me many years to work through generating forgiveness for him. Since I had already worked through this forgiveness issue in the context of losing my father, applying that lesson to an intentionally harmful act wasn't really that hard. It was not doing anything for me to hold onto some sort of anger or not be able to really forgive him for what he did.

In order to generate forgiveness it is helpful to understand that for somebody to do something that hurtful to another person they must be in an extreme state of inner turmoil. He might not ever work through the issues that are going on with him, but all I can do is forgive him and hope that my forgiveness and my compassion for him will possibly help someday for him to become a better person. My heart goes out to this girl that he did this to again. He has continued to be in this situation. I am hoping maybe he will someday come to a place where he can work through whatever issues he has that make him do these things.

It is also helpful for generating forgiveness if we can realize that we all do things that are wrong. Nobody is perfect. As much as I like to think I am a good person it doesn't mean that I have never lied to someone or hurt someone or let them down or done something that just wasn't right. Realizing that I am so not perfect helps me understand his confusion even though it is greater in magnitude. When I think about how awful I feel about the things that I have done, that helps me to see that he must be in an even a worse place. And if he is repressing that awareness, not even in touch with and aware of the damage he has caused that is really sad. That means he is not seeing the humanity of his victims. That is even worse than if he is suffering for the things he has done. Either way, I can't imagine being in the situation of actually hurting someone to that degree. I would so much rather be on my side, where he hurt me, than be on his side and actually cause that much hurt to someone else.

All of this helped me realize that, not only could I forgive him, I also could feel compassion for him and really hope that he's a better person. For a period of time before I started back to school all I had was time on my hands. I had been sick for many years. I moved back here. I was concentrating on my physical and mental health, getting my teeth together, and getting my life in order. I was able to spend a long period of time just sending positive vibes in his direction and praying for him and for his family—all the people who stepped forward to try to help him. I spent a lot of time sending prayers and positive thoughts in their direction. At this point it's not something that I do regularly but I cannot say that I do not think about him on occasion. I definitely think about him. I hope that he is okay. I hope his family is okay. It is important for me to do that.

The greatest lesson I can take from this experience is that in my everyday life, in my interactions with people if somebody has something that is going seriously wrong with them, it is something I can directly relate to. For example, even if I have not directly experienced losing someone who had cancer I can say that I have been sick, my father died, I have had these things happen to me that make it possible for me to relate and feel compassion towards other people who are suffering."

The following are some questions and answers that followed her talk:

Question: How long did it take for you to get to this place— mentally? How long did it take before you could generate compassion for this person? What process did you use to get there?

Answer: This didn't take as long as you might think mostly because of what had happened with my father. I *did not* work through his death in a short period of time. It took me a long time, maybe eight years, to get to a better place with my dad's death. This situation happened very shortly after that. The insights I gained as a result of my father's death and my illness made dealing with this easier. However, it was still hard. It still took me a few years. As far as the process I used, I use prayer—I am orthodox Christian.

Question: How did you work through having various emotions, maybe combined with emotions you really do not know are there—maybe anger, maybe fear? Even though you generated compassion and feel settled. Do you still feel those tinges of something every once in a while and how do you work through that?

Answer: Yes I do. It is easy to be in this good positive place but at the same time not really putting myself out there to meet other people. That was the hardest part—the fear. I didn't have any friends. It was easy to just be with family. My whole family is here. I could seem like I was outgoing. I wasn't becoming a hermit, but in reality I wasn't really trying to meet anyone. After a pretty short period of time I recognized I was doing that and made a concerted effort to go places and meet people and go on dates. I do sometimes get scared. I'll have a fear issue. I will be in my house and get scared. I cannot really say this is any different than what anyone feels—being a woman home alone. But in my mind I will have a direct correlation with this situation—I'll think, "Maybe he got out. Maybe I didn't get a phone call. Maybe he is right outside my house." I feel like that could happen. I could walk outside my house any day and he could just be there. But I cannot let that stop me from leaving my house. I make a concerted effort to manage my emotions and feelings when they come up—be aware. It is easy to go through life and when some sort of feeling comes up just push it aside and keep going forward. For me if something comes up, I definitely look at it. I look directly at it right then and say, "Oh, what is that?" Otherwise it is going to still be there.

Question: What happened has such magnitude and what you learned are such huge lessons, but can you take those lessons and incorporate them into your everyday life and just deal with the deadlines and everything we all go through or is it very separate—

big lesson, I dealt with it, but it doesn't filter down to the small stuff.

Answer: It definitely filters down. It filters down in that I really try to be a compassionate and kind person. I try to live that on a daily basis. The one thing I try to do every single day that I walk out of my door is to be as helpful to others as I can and shine light on as many people as possible. With respect to deadlines—I am not as stressed as I would be if I hadn't had these experiences. I have a different outlook on life. Because of those bigger things I am able to not stress as much about the little things.

COMMENTS

Together with the class, I was deeply impressed with this woman's wisdom and with the skillful way she explained the process of working with and recovering from being the victim of an intentional physical and mental attack.

I have shared the transcript of this woman's talk because what she said can be helpful to anyone who has experienced intentional harm by another. The woman who gave this talk has gone on to pursue a profession. In that context she has encountered individuals who have been the victims of some form of intentional harm. She has shared the recording of the talk that appears in this Chapter with many of these individuals, some of whom have been able to use what they learned from her talk to help them work towards healing their suffering.

As lawyers we are in the position to do the same thing. While our training is in legal representation, of necessity we frequently find ourselves working with individuals who have been harmed by others. We may represent an abused spouse seeking a divorce or the victim of intentional or accidental physical or psychological harm seeking damages or injunctive relief in a tort lawsuit. Often plaintiffs in lawsuits alleging discrimination have experienced trauma—for example, victims of discriminatory harassment or discriminatory firing experience significant psychic pain resulting from the intention acts of others.

One way we can help clients who have experienced trauma is to have available a list of professional counselors to refer our clients to. At the same time, if we have resources, such as this talk, that we can provide to our clients, this can be helpful as well.

Also, if you or someone close to you has been the victim of an intentional attack, you may find it distressing to represent victims of intentional harm. You may be distracted by your own distress. It can be helpful to use this material to bring yourself to a place of forgiveness and compassion for the perpetrator of that intentional attack. If you are able to do this, not only will it become easier for you to remain present and non-distracted when you are meeting with your suffering client, you also may be able to share your insight directly with victims of intentional harm to help them come to a place of forgiveness and compassion.

As lawyers we may also find ourselves representing clients who have intentionally caused harm to others. This could be a spouse in a divorce action or perhaps a defendant in a criminal case charged with intentionally harming someone in an assault, rape, or murder. It is important to be a zealous advocate. If we are having difficulty advocating on behalf of a client who has intentionally perpetrated harm we can use the methods presented in this Chapter to generate forgiveness and compassion for this client. If we can see clients like this as confused rather than evil and if we can see that clients like this have the potential for wisdom and compassion, it will be easier to accept the role of zealous advocate. It may also become possible to help the client see his or her positive potential. It may be possible to help the client recognize that this experience with the legal system can be a healing experience.

CHAPTER 12:

LOVING KINDNESS & COMPASSION IN THE CONTEXT OF LEGAL PRACTICE

Before we leave the topic of loving kindness and compassion, it is important to consider the relationship between these practices and law practice. Lawyers often tell me that the world of lawyering is characterized by greedy clients, aggressive opposing lawyers, and a general lack of concern for fairness. Where does loving kindness and compassion fit in this world?

First, as legal practitioners we have multiple relationships, not only with clients, but also with colleagues, secretaries, cleaning staff, administrators, and others in the law office. Some of these individuals approach the world with anger, jealousy, or greed. Some of these individuals are suffering from personal losses. All of these individuals want to be happy and would like to be treated with respect. Having a positive relationship with our co-workers and staff is not specific to law offices. Nonetheless this is an important part of our world as legal practitioners. We can make our immediate world a much better place by seeing the kindness around us, by having aspirations for everyone to be happy, by generating compassion when approached by an angry or grieving co-worker.

Second, most of the work we do with clients is not in the context of mediation, negotiation, or litigation. Before any of these typical lawyering encounters take place, we may spend countless hours gathering information from clients and other parties relevant to a dispute. All of these encounters, whether in person, through email or on the phone, provide opportunities to listen mindfully and interact skillfully. Clients frequently come to us because they are suffering from some form of loss. This situation provides the opportunity to listen and to generate compassion. For clients who have experienced intentional harm by others, we may be able to help them work with their anger and suffering by sharing with them the talk presented in Chapter 11.

Third, when we reach the stage of counseling clients on the options available to resolve their dispute we need to be clear about the appropriate role that compassion and loving kindness plays. Once we have investigated the facts of a dispute, we may conclude that our client was actually the guilty party in the dispute. We may feel compassion for the party on the other side of this dispute.

What is the skillful way to approach a client in this situation? This situation may be particularly difficult for us to face if our client has been charged with an intentional crime that has caused significant physical or psychological harm to a victim.

As a lawyer, our obligation to our client is to inform him or her that this claim (or defense) may be difficult to win because the facts are not in the client's favor. At the same time, even though we have concluded that our client was at fault, we are obligated to provide the best arguments available under the circumstances. We need to counsel the client on the likelihood of success or failure and provide advice on the alternative approaches that are available, including dropping a claim or defense, settling a claim, or pleading guilty to a charge. In addition, we may even propose the option of apologizing to the other side. However, *it is up to the client* to decide whether to drop the case, settle, enter a guilty plea, or continue pressing forward with a charge or defense. We cannot impose on the client *our* idea of how this case should be handled. We can explain that dropping the claim or defense is an option, but in the end it is up to the client. It is up to us as counsel to do the best that we can to pursue the client's chosen approach (assuming there are legally relevant arguments to be presented that are supported by facts and do not involve perjury).

What role have our practices of loving kindness and compassion played in this situation? Loving kindness and compassion has made it possible for us to see the weaknesses in our client's case and to counsel our client accordingly. We have been able to see the arguments on the other side clearly rather than simply demonize the other side. Our compassion for the opponent in the case has provided us with some alternative approaches we can present to our client. If the client accepts responsibility for harm he or she has caused and chooses to apologize or plead guilty or engage the other side in productive dialog, we have helped the client learn from this situation and perhaps transform a relationship. This is wonderful. However, if our client chooses another approach, our obligation is to respect the client's right to make that choice and help the client in any way we can.

"Attorneys have to be very careful and not fall into idiot compassion. Separate the compassion and generosity that you think your client should feel from that of your own."

(Attorney Carmen Rumbaut, Madison, Wisconsin)

When we investigate our client's claim we may discover that our client clearly has been wronged. This makes our legal job easy from the perspective of proving our client's claim. What role does compassion play in this situation? Having worked with compassion practices we may find that we have compassion for the individual who has wronged our client. Having generated that compassion, we may be able to use what we understand about the opponent's situation to help our client work with feelings of hurt and distress. As mentioned earlier, if the client has suffered intentional harm at the hands of another, it may be possible to help our client work with this situation by encouraging the client to forgive and generate compassion. If we do not feel competent to help our client work with hurt, fear, or anger, we can at least recognize the importance of working with these feelings and recommend to our client that he or she seek counseling to work through these feelings.

However, even if our client is able to generate forgiveness and compassion for the perpetrator of harm this does not necessarily mean dropping charges.

Continuing forward with a tort claim or criminal complaint can be beneficial from many perspectives. No matter how much compassion we feel for the intentional wrong doer, that person needs to understand that what he or she has done is harmful. It may be that generating forgiveness and compassion will help our client work with his or her suffering in a more effective way than simply by bringing the legal claim. However, bringing the legal claim may benefit our client in other ways. Winning this claim may provide compensation to pay for losses incurred. Winning this claim puts the client in control of a scary situation and lets the client know that society cares.

When we finally reach the actual negotiation, litigation, or mediation, what role does compassion and loving kindness play?

Compassion does not mean giving in to the other side. Even if we feel compassion for the opponent in a dispute, we should not let our client down by failing to effectively present the case he or she has asked us to present. Compassion also does not mean being a doormat for other individuals who are angry and aggressive. At the same time, compassion may be what we need to help us avoid responding to an opposing lawyer's anger with anger. Compassion may be what helps us maintain our equanimity. From that space we will be in a much better position to present our case effectively.

Reconsider Susan Busby's comments about how she uses mindfulness and compassion to work with opposing attorney's in domestic disputes who not only insult her, but also insult her client.[68]

---

68   See Introduction, How Meditation Helps Lawyers Practice Skillfully.

PART III

WORKING WITH EMOTIONS
& CONFLICT

CHAPTER 13:

PATIENCE IN SMALL MATTERS

The practice in this Chapter is similar to the practice of Recognizing Kindness in the sense that this one practice can bring you tremendous benefit both in your work life and in your life outside of work.[69] We waste an enormous amount of energy fretting about small annoyances in life. For many of us, they are the source of great suffering because everyone is constantly assaulted with small difficulties one after the other. If we respond with anger to insignificant difficulties, we will carry anger around with us all day. This practice helps us let go of our anger at small matters.

This practice, like Slow Reversal, is aimed primarily at depriving anger of its force by seeing its negative attributes, giving it space, not feeding it, and applying antidotes in order to let it go. These two practices are designed to help us avoid engaging in unskillful speech and action.

---

69   The post-meditation practice presenting in this Chapter (Patience in Small Matters) is based on a portion of a teaching on anger presented by Bardor Tulku Rinpoche at Hartford Karma Thegsum Choling in Hartford, Connecticut in 2003. CD's of *Transforming Anger* are available from Vajra Echoes Dharma Recordings (www.vajraechoes.com).

During the seven days that you are working with the post-meditation practice of Patience in Small Matters, I suggest that you use your formal meditation period to contemplate the negative aspects of strong emotions.

THE NEGATIVE ATTRIBUTES OF ANGER

Patience can be cultivated as an antidote to anger. Consider what happens when we get angry. Anger is a state of aversion. It involves not liking something. Usually anger is directed at another being. We identify the other being as an enemy and feel adverse to him or her. Anger causes irritation to the mind. It is not pleasant. When you are experiencing anger, it is not possible to achieve true tranquility. Genuine meditation is not possible with anger.

We already have seen that every being wants to be happy and that every action we engage in is for the purpose of achieving happiness and avoiding suffering. It is amazing, therefore, to realize that we get angry even though it is not possible to be happy when we are full of anger.

If you are in a position of responsibility, employing or supervising others, if you are chronically angry, your employees will not like you. They will not like you even if you pay them well. Imagine you are the named partner of a small law firm and that you are extremely generous to your associate lawyers and staff. You lavish them with excellent pay, generous benefits, and a comfortable work environment. Even with all this kindness, your employees will not appreciate you if you are abusive. Even someone who, in all other ways, is wonderful will not be appreciated for all of their virtues if they are prone to anger. Therefore, if you are simply average in terms of your qualities and you are an angry person, all that people will remember about you is your anger.

Consider the impact of anger. Anger often leads to speaking harshly or even physical violence. Anger causes sadness and suffering for everyone around the angry person, including those who love him or her. Friends, family, and colleagues all suffer immeasurably from constant assaults of harsh criticism and anger. Eventually such a perpetually angry person will be abandoned. People can only take so much. Even if an angry person is generous in a material sense, he or she will constantly lose staff, employees, and family and then will need to find replacements.

If you are constantly angry and mean, you are not going to be happy and your environment will not support you. There is nobody who is angry who is happy. Therefore, it is worth putting some effort into transforming your anger.

> "I no longer express my anger in outward physical ways (well sometimes I yell, but it is completely different from the hysteria of my younger days). However, my anger still affects me in a physical way and to me this is the most negative aspect of anger. When I become angry, whether it is at another driver or a family member or whomever, I feel the physical effects—a knot in my stomach, sweating, my blood pressure going up, and tension in my whole body. These effects are exacerbated by the fact that, once I get angry about something, I tend to stay that way. The anger does not diminish but actually festers and multiplies the more I think about the thing I am angry about—probably because I have not addressed the root of the anger. There have been times when I have been physically and mentally consumed with anger for days about some small event. I recognize my anger

as a negative thing. It prevents me from being happy, keeps me living in the past instead of the present, detracts from my relationships with others, and makes me feel physically ill.

This week's discussions have helped me think a lot about my anger and how I could handle it using the patience practice. When something happens that makes me feel anger and the other physical responses I have mentioned, I first think about whether that thing is a big deal or a small matter. In the huge majority of instances it is a small matter—someone has cut me off or failed to signal, my boyfriend is late coming home from work or has left his clothes on the floor. Then I think about whether this thing that happened is worth getting worked up over and whether it will or should matter to me tomorrow. The obvious answer in pretty much every case is no. Just taking a moment to consider these questions has been really helpful in giving me patience for these small things."

(Participant, Contemplative Lawyering 2006)

THE BENEFITS OF PATIENCE

A patient person will be happy in this life. A patient person will be appreciated by everyone around him or her. A patient person will be happy as a result of being patient.

SOURCES OF ANGER

We become angry when something we do not want to occur happens. For example, we become angry when we perceive opposition to ourselves or to people we care about. This could be family, friends, colleagues, clients, political allies, or even sports teams. Opposition means something we perceive as impeding or preventing what we want or what the people we care about want. We do not like this situation and our mind becomes full of aversion or dislike. This mental pain becomes anger.

FEEDING ANGER

Once we become angry, we feed our anger by running a story line through our head that justifies our feeling of having been mistreated. When we feed our anger, it grows. When it grows it becomes more and more powerful. When it becomes powerful, it completely obscures and impedes our positive qualities.

ANGER IS NOT BENEFICIAL

You may think that if you maintain composure in the face of difficulties, this will put you at risk of harm. This is not true. You are actually more at risk when you lose your composure and become agitated than when you approach a dangerous situation with clarity and calmness. Responding with anger tends to escalate dangerous situations while remaining calm may diffuse the situation. This is easy to see in law practice. When our client is on the receiving end of nasty allegations by the other side during a mediation, responding with anger escalates the situation while remaining calm can diffuse the agitation. Further, agitation and anger does not accomplish anything. It doesn't harm the person who has harmed you. It simply destroys your well being. Anger rarely gives you what you want and nearly always makes things worse.

WORKING WITH ANGER

There are two situations that make us angry: difficult situations that cannot be changed and difficult situations that can be changed. One way to work with anger is to recognize that if a difficult situation can be changed, then it would be good to do whatever is needed to change it. But, that has nothing to do with being angry. Being angry does not help you fix the situation.

On the other hand, if the difficult situation you encounter cannot be changed or fixed, then becoming angry does not help. If it cannot be fixed, anger only makes you feel miserable.

There is no point in getting angry at situations that can be changed. Simply work to change them. There is no point in getting angry at situations that cannot be changed because anger will not accomplish anything.

As lawyers we are often asked to evaluate the merits of a claim. Once we have investigated, if we see that the facts do not support a claim, there is no point in getting angry. The best thing to do at that point is to recognize the futility of pursuing the claim. On the other hand, if we find that there is a basis for a claim, there is no point in getting angry. At that point the most helpful thing we can do is generate the factual and legal arguments necessary to prevail in court.

STARVING ANGER

You can starve anger to death by not giving it the food it needs, which is agitation or lack of ease in our minds. If you do not become agitated or disturbed when you do not get what you want, then there will be no anger. Anger is not possible without disturbance or agitation. To prevent anger, simply deprive it of its necessary nourishment. How do you do this? Remember the harm that anger causes. Anger causes disaster and unhappiness. Disturbance feeds anger. Therefore, generate an aspiration not to allow disturbance to arise.

"On Monday I worked at a Co-Op where all afternoon people threw money at me, forgot to ask for things nicely, and made a mess at the counter. I wasn't angered by their actions. I wasn't even annoyed or frustrated. In fact, the entire time I just starved my anger. I didn't get wrapped up in what other people were about. When you observe an act in its purest form without guessing as to its motivation, most things are insignificant and meaningless. The girl who threw the coins at me wasn't doing it because she dislikes me. In fact I think she was focused on getting change out of her small change purse. The man who barely acknowledged my presence behind the counter was just wrapped up in thought. I have done something similar in the past and meant nothing of it. Why can't someone else do the same thing? It must be said that I usually ignore people's rudeness and don't let it get to me in a significant way. However, in the past ignoring the act would be accompanied by a spike of anger and then pride. I would first become angry by the act because I read too much into it. Then I would ignore it and then I would pat myself on the back for being so composed and letting it go. My pride would leave me with a sense of unfounded superiority. Monday I was able to starve my anger and not buy into negative pride. I acknowledged and let go of the small things without judgment."

(Participant, Contemplative Lawyering 2006)

CULTIVATING PATIENCE IN SMALL MATTERS

Is it possible to put up with the kind of suffering that causes us to be angry? People put up with unnecessary suffering that they cause themselves all the time. For example, people go to the beach and sit in the hot sun and get burned. They choose to engage in this activity. Other people go to the mountains in the winter to ski. They expose themselves to bitter cold and wind way above tree line. They willingly choose to suffer in order to experience the thrill of skiing down the mountainside. Other people go to concerts in hot, stifling venues where people are smoking and drinking, causing the air to smell bad and become difficult to breath. Again, people willingly expose themselves to this uncomfortable situation.

If we can put up with unnecessary suffering, certainly we can put up with suffering we cannot avoid. It is good to start with small matters such as the physical discomfort of insect bites, hunger, thirst, or a small itch. Other examples of small matters you can begin with in your patience practice are lost glasses and significant others who forget to do the dishes after a meal. In the context of law practice, small matters might include being interrupted by a phone call or being late for a meeting.

This practice can be combined with the Slow Reversal practice. Patience in Small Matters is one of the approaches that can be employed when we see anger arising. This practice uses Slow Reversal in the context of working with small matters. It is easier to generate patience about matters that are small. After a while we begin to see that many of the matters we thought were significant actually are small. We tend to make a bigger deal about difficult circumstances than they deserve. The result is suffering for our selves and our coworkers, family, and friends.

In this practice, we can employ all of the antidotes that we used in the context of Slow Reversal. For example, look for misperceptions that may be the basis of anger or generate compassion for people who have caused you to be angry.

The small sufferings that are the focus of this post-meditation practice do not have great significance in themselves. You can deal with them. They are not sufferings that are really intolerable. These are situations that just happen and are not too hard to endure. Start with these. Do not try to create situations. Just take advantage of what comes up naturally. In this practice we are using small annoyances in life as our mindfulness reminder.

These situations may be small and insignificant, but the patience you develop through cultivating patience with them is not insignificant. Begin with small matters like getting wet in the rain, experiencing a minor illness or injury, or finding that nobody prepared hot water for coffee in the office kitchen. In law practice, other small sources of annoyance include slow computers, misfiled information, or unproductive work meetings. Then gradually try to increase the intensity of what you can have patience with. Begin with situations that obviously do not require anger. Then work on unavoidable situations that would normally cause you to be angry. This way, you can gradually cultivate patience.

This is a practice of insight. When you look at your response to small matters and understand that anger is not helpful, you cultivate wisdom that applies to larger matters as well. This is also a practice of familiarization or habit. Good habits, like bad habits, become natural and effortless the more you practice them. In this way, patience in small matters cultivates patience in more difficult matters.

Consider people you know. Some get very distressed at small matters. Others maintain calmness through very difficult circumstances. From this observation you can see that a given situation does not necessarily require you to become distressed. People who remain calm during difficult circumstances are no different than you. We can all learn to respond to situations in the same way, with calmness. Mental stability allows us to maintain composure during difficult circumstances. It eventually becomes natural—easy and effortless.

> "I tried to practice patience and was successful in the driving context. Being settled behind a slow person driving in front of you really does not need to have a negative impact on your entire day! You pretty much get where you need to be in the same amount of time and you are more composed when you get there."
>
> *(Participant, Contemplative Lawyering 2006)*

"My computer crashed last week and I lost everything on my hard drive. This happened suddenly and unexpectedly despite the virus software installed on my computer which I update weekly. Needless to say, this was a source of anger and frustration for me. It was interesting however to find that my immediate reaction was to look for someone to blame. First I blamed my father because he's always sending me e-mails with attachments to internet jokes; I thought that was where I picked up the virus. Next I blamed my friend who downloaded my virus software, thinking that he downloaded it incorrectly. Next I blamed the makers of my computer and finally I blamed the virus software.

It wasn't until after about six hours of placing blame that I realized the loss of data is my own stupid fault for not backing up my documents like I know I should. It wasn't until I finally settled down and looked at what really happened that I was able to put this incident in context and realize that this wasn't such a huge deal. Luckily I have only two situations where I take notes on my computer. I can get those notes from my colleagues. Once I was able to take a couple of deep breaths and realize that what happened actually wasn't going to ruin my life, I was able to move forward with the issue and work on repairing my computer."

(Participant, Contemplative Lawyering 2006)

INWARDLY-DIRECTED ANGER

Working with anger that is directed inwardly relies on the same practices we have learned to use when we experience anger that is directed outside. You can use Slow Reversal and all of the antidotes for anger that were listed in the Slow Reversal instructions.

First, ask yourself how important the issue you are angry about is. If it is a small matter, simply let it go on this basis. This is the practice of patience with small matters. As with external objects of anger, if we begin by developing patience with the small mistakes we make, we can gradually work up to having patience with larger shortcomings that we perceive in ourselves.

Second, when you are critical of something you have done, consider whether this is something that you could change or not. If you can change it, simply generate an aspiration to do better next time. If it is something you cannot change, then why be angry with yourself about it?

Third, a powerful antidote for self-directed anger is compassion. Try to generate compassion for yourself. Remember that we all make mistakes. Remember that your unskillful actions result from ignorance and confusion. We all have ignorance and confusion. Working with negativities is a long process. Have patience with yourself. Do not expect perfection right away. Remember that everyone makes mistakes. For several practices related to working with self-hatred, see *Cultivating Loving Kindness and Compassion for Yourself* at the end of Chapter 10.

Fourth, consider whether the anger you are directing at yourself is based on some misperception. Often we blame ourselves when there really is no blame. If someone else judges you negatively, reconsider the issue from an objective perspective. Do not assume the other person is right. This is particularly important to do when you are criticized by a spouse or close family member. Because those relationships are so driven by need, it may be that you actually did nothing wrong. It may be that the criticism comes from the other person's confusion and need. Try to generate compassion for yourself and also for the other person.

> "Since my last journal entry, I have attempted to work with the emotion of anger. I normally have a friendly and amicable disposition. When I do become angry, my emotion is directed inwardly. By far, the most recurring instance that causes me to become angry is my performance on exams or other law school related assignments. . . .

Graduating first in my class in college is one of the proudest moments in my life. It was the culmination of four years of blood, sweat and tears as well as many sacrificed nights with my friends for the purpose of studying. At the same time, graduating from college in this manner has become burdensome for me and a source of anger. This is due to the fact that I now expect to be the best in all things academic. On numerous occasions in law school, I have become upset because I did not get one of the five "A" grades given by the professor. Rather than being content with how I performed, I became angry at how I did not perform. I set expectations so high as a result of my performance in college.

In addition to my anger with myself, my obsession with grades has caused me to start projecting my anger onto external sources, in particular the professors of those classes in which I did not get a grade I was accustomed to. I would internally say things such as, "The exam was unfair." Or "The professor doesn't know how to teach." I would have these reactions without even considering what I may have done or not done on an exam or in preparation for an exam to warrant the grade I received. Finally, I often became angry at and jealous of my peers.

Using the post meditation exercise, I attempted to make grades a small matter. I did this by putting law school grades in their proper context. I did this by contemplating how important grades are in the grand scheme of life. As a result, I realized and accepted the fact that grades do not make one a better person. Grades cannot and should not define who I am as an individual. I became better able to accept my performance in law school because I realized that I have done everything in my power to prepare for examinations. In turn, this caused me to realize that it is absolutely impossible to be the best at everything in life. Trying to be perfect will only lead to further anger and alienation.

The most dramatic effect the post meditation exercise had on me was the sense of accomplishment it instilled within me. The exercise caused me to reflect upon how I have actually done thus far in law school. While the tone of this journal entry may make it seem that I am barely passing, I have been successful academically in law school. I am ranked in the top quintile and have accepted a position at a distinguished law firm upon graduation. Because of my anger, I have been unable over the course of the past three years to truly reflect upon and enjoy the successes that I have experienced. Rather, my anger has always had me focused on what I could do better to become perfect. In so doing, I have failed to live in the present. As a corollary to the renewed sense of appreciation I have developed for my accomplishments in law school, I have also developed a sense of confidence in my legal skills.

In conclusion, the post meditation practice has helped turn my anger into contentment. I expect to be able to enjoy and properly appreciate my accomplishments throughout my remaining months in law school as well as beyond my graduation from this institution."

(Participant, Contemplative Lawyering 2006)

THE DANGERS OF CONSUMING ANGER

When we read newspaper articles and watch television programs that glorify anger and frustration, we contribute to our own habitual patterns of engaging in anger. We are encouraged by what we are seeing and hearing to participate in the emotion of anger. We take the anger that we see and hear into our minds and express it later.

When you listen to the news or read the paper or discuss difficult situations with others, watch your mind. If you approach these programs and articles with mindfulness they can be a basis for generating patience and compassion. Approaching them with mindfulness means observing and listening without getting caught up in the emotions being depicted or discussed. Approached in this way, these experiences provide a powerful opportunity to see the suffering that results from anger.

If you find that you engage in angry thoughts and speech as a result of what you are reading, watching, or listening to, it might be best to refrain from watching and listening to that kind of material. The same is true of conversations with friends. When friends become angry and invite you to join in their anger, this can be an opportunity to practice patience and compassion or you can get drawn into their anger. For example, consider what happens to you when a friend is gossiping or bad mouthing a colleague or a judge. Your friend may be angry because of how a judge ruled on a motion and become upset, speaking ill of the judge. She wants you to join in on the ridicule session. Perhaps you actually hold no ill-will towards this judge but feel compelled to sustain the fervor of the conversation. If you are unable to remain calm in these circumstances, you may be better off avoiding them.

USING SMALL MATTERS TO WORK WITH JEALOUSY

As we discussed earlier, jealousy has many negative attributes and causes a great deal of suffering. Jealousy is grounded in feelings of inadequacy. It is a form of poverty mentality. Jealousy often causes negative behavior, including retaliation and theft. Jealousy contributes to wars motivated by wanting someone else's oil fields, mineral deposits, farmland, or other form of wealth. Jealousy sometimes results in murder—for example, when someone is jilted by a lover. In the law firm context, jealousy over salaries, good assignments, and partnership can cause an enormous amount of suffering. This suffering can undermine trust and good working relationships.

Working first with small matters is a practice that can be applied to jealousy in the same way that it is applied to anger. Generate an aspiration to transform jealousy. Then begin by working with small situations, like somebody else having the biggest cookie or somebody else having a nice shirt we would like to have. Start small and work up to more difficult situations.

Patience, which is primarily an antidote for anger, also applies to jealousy. Another powerful antidote for jealousy is to rejoice in the good fortune of others. When another person has the best cookie, try to be happy for that person. When another person has a nice shirt, be happy that person looks handsome in that shirt. Rejoice in that person's good fortune.

The most fundamental antidote for jealousy is to recognize your own fundamental self worth. You do not need the biggest cookie in order to be worth something. You are a wonderful person even if you don't have the nicest shirt.

Practicing with small matters provides the foundation for working with jealousy resulting from larger issues such as salaries and promotions.

USING SMALL MATTERS TO WORK WITH OBSESSIVE DESIRE

Here again, it is good to start with small matters. When you have a desire to get up from your computer and go to the kitchen to have a snack, work with that desire. When you pass a window in a shop and see a pretty dress, work with that desire. The practice is to start with small matters and work to larger matters. How important is it that you have this small item?

The antidotes we discussed with Slow Reversal continue to be relevant here. Start by contemplating the suffering that comes from desire. How often have you purchased some cute little item at a store, brought it home and realized that you really have no place for it. Try to remember all the small gifts you have received and items you have purchased that you ultimately gave away to Salvation Army. Remember the suffering involved in caring for, cleaning and storing all the items you buy. How often have you bought something to wear on an impulse only to realize later that you really do not look very good in that outfit?

Another example of a small matter relating to desire is the suffering associated with creating a vacation. Going online to cash in frequent flyer miles or to find the best price on an airline ticket involves desire. We want to get the best deal and the ticket prices keep going up or the seats that were available yesterday are now gone. The same is true of looking for the right accommodations.

These are examples of small matters that we can work with. Look at your mind. Ask yourself, "how important is this really?"

Contemplating impermanence is an excellent antidote for desire. Whenever you desire something, try to remember that it will not last. This is particularly true of items that age quickly like computers or video equipment. Again, start with small matters. When you encounter a small desire, consider the impermanence of the item you desire.

A powerful antidote for desire is to cultivate generosity. When you want the last cookie on the plate, consider that someone else may want it as well. The more you focus on benefiting others, the less you will desire for yourself.

Finally, meditation is an antidote for desire because it cultivates contentment. Use small desires as your mindfulness reminder. When a small desire arises, stop and rest on your breath before acting on the desire. When you rest in meditation, you may find that the desire simply dissolves.

Obsessive desire drives many difficulties that arise in law practice. The desire for respect or money can lead to misreporting hours. The desire to win a case can lead to fabricating evidence. The examples are endless. Working with desire in the context of small matters can help us begin to deal more skillfully with the larger issues.

USING SMALL MATTERS TO WORK WITH PRIDE

Again, it is good to begin with an aspiration to transform your pride. This aspiration can be fueled by contemplating the negative attributes of pride. As mentioned earlier, pride tends to be a cover for deep insecurity. It is a cause of suffering in others because it makes them feel uncomfortable. If we have pride, we suffer because we fail to see the positive qualities of others and therefore are not able to benefit from those qualities.

When you apply the small matters practice to working with pride, begin with small situations in which pride comes up. For example, you may feel pride when you don't order dessert while others indulge. You may feel pride when you get up to exercise in the morning while others sleep. You may feel pride when you know a shortcut that others are unaware of. Start working with pride by watching your mind and seeing all the little instances of arrogant thought. Then apply antidotes specific to pride.

Begin by remembering that whatever you have accomplished in life has an enormous element of good fortune to it. For example, you are fortunate to understand the negative impact of eating dessert and the positive impact of exercising in the morning. Remember that many people have confusions or maybe health problems that prevent them from taking the same positive actions that you are taking. You are fortunate to know the shortcut. Someone taught it to you or you were born with the innate intelligence and blessed with the education and knowledge required to read maps and find the shortcut. People who do not know the short cut may not know how to read a map or they may be operating from fear that prevents them from trying a different route. Whenever you feel pride and arrogance about small matters, consider whether it makes any sense to feel superior to others who are less fortunate than you.

Another approach you can take is to see and appreciate what is good about others. Alternatively, you can consider the ways in which others are superior to you. For example, although you got up and exercised in the morning, you didn't get up and practice music in the morning. You also did not get up and write a book in the morning. You are feeling prideful about what you have done without considering that others may be engaging in activities that are equally or maybe even more beneficial than running. You are, therefore, superior in one way, but inferior in other ways.

The most powerful antidote for pride is recognizing our own self worth and understanding that recognizing our own value does not require putting others down. You are a worthy person whether or not you eat the dessert, get up and exercise, or know the shortcut. You do not need those "superior qualities" in order to be a worthwhile person. You do not need to put others down in order to recognize that you have value.

In legal practice it is easy to get in the habit of comparing ourselves to others, feeling superior about the number of cases we have tried and won or the size of the judgment our client was awarded. Bragging about these accomplishments may dissuade others from wanting to work with you or send you referrals. Your colleagues who respect and trust your work, who know and appreciate your accomplishments, will want to work with you and refer clients on the basis of recognizing that your work is good, not because you are arrogant and prideful about your work.

When we work on a case with a group of lawyers, viewing ourselves as superior to others can prevent us from benefitting from their knowledge. Feeling superior to clients and other lawyers on the basis of our legal knowledge can contribute to a condescending attitude towards others which will make them uncomfortable.

If we begin by using this practice to work with small matters we will gradually be able to use the same antidotes to work with larger issues such as pride based on earnings, education, or winning cases.

CHAPTER 14:

SITTING WITH EMOTION

Sitting with Emotion is a powerful approach to working with anger. To get the full benefit out of this chapter and the following two chapters, I suggest that you purchase and read *Anger*, by Thich Nhat Hanh.[70] *Anger* is readily available at many bookstores and at online bookstores as well. The entire book is useful, but for this chapter and the following chapter I particularly recommend pages 23-107.

In Chapter 6, we used mindfulness to see anger and other negative emotions arising. In the space created by mindfulness, we were able to consider how to respond skillfully to the situation that gave rise to anger. In Chapter 13, we used mindfulness again to notice and dismiss anger precipitated by small matters. Both of these practices are post-meditation practices. These practices relate to the practice of Sitting with Emotion because all three of these practices are helpful for working with anger and other strong emotions.

In Chapters 7–10, we engaged in formal "sending and taking" practices in order to cultivate impartiality, recognize kindness in

---

70   (Riverhead Press, N.Y. 2001).

others, and generate loving kindness and compassion. Those practices relate to Sitting with Anger because we are again using a formal practice to generate compassion for ourselves and for other people who are difficult in our lives.

Sitting with Emotion, when applied to working with anger, is a practice that brings together everything we have learned up to this point in order to help us work with our most difficult interactions with others. You will find the practice in this Chapter most useful if you use it to transform your negative interactions with individuals about whom you care a great deal, but with whom you have some degree of conflict.

When we are dealing with small annoyances in life, it is possible to simply let go of our anger over these situations once we recognize the harm and futility of anger. However, when anger arises because of a hurtful remark by someone we depend on or need, even if we manage to use mindfulness to back away from the situation and avoid regrettable words or actions, we are likely to revisit the hurt and refuel our angry response over and over again. In such circumstances, it is difficult simply to let go of the hurt and anger.

When we are unable to let go of hurt, we may use the hurt to re-fuel anger. Anger is a way of avoiding acknowledging or experiencing the hurt. At the other extreme, we may turn the anger inward, blaming ourselves for the situation. This may result in feelings of guilt. If the hurt is simply too much to face, we may repress both hurt and anger. Sitting with Anger provides us with a way to actually work with anger and transform it rather than refuel it, turn it inward, or repress it.

Sitting with emotion is a practice that is designed to work with these deeply hurtful situations. It can be used in less hurtful contexts, but it is particularly effective when applied to negative interactions with people we care about. I suggest that you do this practice for at least two weeks.

SITTING WITH ANGER— PRACTICE INSTRUCTION

Unlike Slow Reversal and Patience in Small Matters, Sitting with Emotion is a formal meditation practice.

Begin this practice by generating an aspiration to transform your anger. Beginning with an aspiration will increase the power of the meditation session and help you focus on the practice. The aspiration reminds you why you are doing the practice. When you find yourself distracted, the fact that you have identified and expressed a reason for doing the practice will make it easier to let go of the distraction and return to the practice. Beginning with an aspiration is particularly helpful for this practice because it requires you to intentionally bring to mind difficult circumstances that have made you angry or hurt. It is helpful, therefore, to begin by reminding yourself why you are engaging in this practice.

After generating your aspiration, sit in Tranquility Meditation (following your breath, counting your breath or meditating on an object) for five or ten minutes.

Once your mind is reasonably settled, recall a recent interaction with another person that made you very angry or deeply hurt. Run this scenario through your mind so that you begin to experience the same hurt and anger that you felt during the original incident. Bring the feeling up so that you truly experience it, but do not allow it to get out of control. Use your mindfulness meditation skills to keep this strong feeling just under control. Whenever you find yourself getting engaged in the anger, let go of the thoughts that are fueling the emotion and return to your breath. Once you have settled your mind, return to your thoughts in order to bring up the anger so you can experience it, but not get lost in it, not engage it.

Look at your hurt and anger. Look at your experience of hurt and anger and notice which thoughts cause it to well up in you. The point is *not* to justify your anger. The point is *not* to place blame on the other person. This is the way we usually work with anger. Rather, the point is to see and experience your anger in order to come to some understanding about what is causing you to feel so hurt and angry.

When you look in this way, you are likely to find that underlying your anger is a deep feeling of hurt or fear. You may be hurt because someone said something that you believe means they do not care about you. You may be hurt because the words someone said suggest to you that they perceive you as lacking in positive qualities. You may be hurt because you believe someone has seriously misjudged you. You may be hurt because someone spoke harshly to you or insulted you. You may be afraid because you think someone threatened you. There are many reasons why you might feel hurt, but if you look you are likely to find that your hurt is based on your attachment to being perceived in a certain way and your belief that someone has failed to see you clearly. There are many reasons why you might feel fear, but if you look you are likely to find that your fear is based on attachment.

During this process, if you find yourself distracted or find yourself losing control of your strong feelings, simply return to resting on your breath. Calm the hurt and anger by letting go of the story line and returning your attention to your breath.

Be gentle with yourself throughout this process. This is not a blame game. You are not looking to blame yourself or to blame the other party. You are hurt and you are looking at the hurt, embracing the hurt, experiencing the hurt, and learning from the hurt. Look deeply into the hurt and anger in order to learn how it came about. Was your hurt (and anger) really caused by the speech and actions of another person, or is it the result of your own needs and attachments? Is your hurt (and anger) based on what this person said or did, or are you responding instead to something that you are reminded of, something that happened far in your past? Are you mistaking this person for someone else who hurt you in the past? Are you hurt and angry because you are feeling physically exhausted or suffering from an illness?

In this practice, look at your actual experience and see it clearly. This is not a conceptually-based contemplation. Nonetheless, it may help you in this process of looking at your anger to remember that the typical roots of anger include misunderstanding, ignorance, wrong perceptions, lack of compassion, and in some cases, clear seeing.

This last category (clear seeing) recognizes that often the driving force behind anger is wisdom. For example, when we become angry because we see someone engaging in hurtful behavior with others, such as intentional discrimination or physical assault, our anger is based on recognizing that what is going on is harmful. The victims of this conduct are suffering physical or psychological harm and the perpetrator's mind is ignorant, unsettled, and distressed. Recognizing this reality is clear seeing. However, becoming engaged in the emotion of anger and acting out on that basis is not helpful even when the foundation for anger is clear seeing. If we witness a physical assault, we are much more likely to deal skillfully with the situation if we act with a cool head rather than lashing out in anger. Anger escalates an already confrontational situation. Similarly, when we witness discrimination we will be most effective if we can calmly interact with the discriminating individual. He or she will not listen to an angry attack.

Once you have identified the nature of your hurt and anger and developed some insight about where it comes from, you will begin to feel much better. But have you considered the other party in this dispute? He or she is still suffering. At this point in the practice, consider deeply the person whose speech or actions precipitated your anger. Remember your love for this person. Remember the kindness this person has shown to you at other times. Are you sure this person intended to hurt you? Consider why this person may have spoken or acted as he or she did. Did you do something or say something that may have hurt this person? Is she or he sick or injured or experiencing some kind of stress? Bring your understanding of your own anger and hurt to your mind as you seek an answer to these questions.

Consider the ways in which this other person suffers. Try to see the ways in which this person is similar to you. Consider how you can help this person. Remember how much you care for him or her and generate an aspiration to help in any way you can. Realize that what you have already done is deeply beneficial. You have transformed your anger and hurt into compassion. This alone is helpful. As a result of your practice of Sitting with Emotion, you are unlikely to engage in harsh words and conduct with this person in response to the incident that initially gave rise to your hurt and anger.

When you have finished Sitting with Emotion, return to tranquility meditation for a few moments. End your practice with an aspiration to transform your anger.

Sitting with Anger—Comments

There are many examples that I could give about how the Sitting with Anger practice works. I will provide you here with just a few examples. You will have your own experiences as you engage in this practice.

One situation I have faced is what I call "free floating anger" on my "Uzi days." This happened many times while I was going through menopause. I would find myself experiencing anger and start looking around for something to attach that anger to, something to explain it. I would eye my husband suspiciously, trying to find something he was doing to set me off. By Sitting with Anger I was able to see that there was no outside trigger for this anger. It was a product of the hormonal imbalance in my body. I was simply angry without any actual reason for being angry. Knowing this, I was able to laugh at myself and see that the people in my environment (primarily my husband) were not doing anything at all to cause my anger.

Another situation involved a close friend of mine who became angry with me because I was late for a meeting. Her anger made me angry because she did not seem to understand how busy I was and how hard I had tried to get there on time. After I returned home, I sat with my anger. I brought up the interaction with my friend and looked at my anger. I saw that what made me so angry was that my friend did not appreciate my good qualities and intentions. I felt devalued because all she saw was that I was late. I realized that my anger was really grounded in hurt and that this hurt was based in part in my memory of having been treated in the same way by my mother and by my first husband. It was not my friend's anger that made me angry. It was my need to be appreciated for my other qualities and for my good intentions.

Once I came to this understanding, I realized that my friend's anger at me was no different than my anger at her. She was angry because she perceived my lateness as evidence that I did not value her. If I valued her, I would have put her first and therefore would have arrived on time. Because I understood the underlying basis for my own anger, I was able to see and understand her anger. We both wanted the same thing—to be loved.

> "I had a bit of an emotional epiphany this week. I think all of our class dissection of emotions has led me to believe that our emotions are not the result of what is outside of us; rather they are part of us. Our emotions are something we create.   .   . Although our emotions are triggered by stimuli on the outside, they are really nothing more than the reactions we give to these stimuli."
>
> *(Participant, Contemplative Lawyering, 2005)*

"When we first began discussing these practices [about emotions], I was a little bit skeptical because I had never really thought about emotions and where they came from other than focusing on the impetus that led to them. Gradually over the course of this week, however, I began to see that many emotions, particularly anger and jealousy, developed in me because of much greater issues in my life than what was specifically going on at the time that I experienced the emotion. I am intrigued by the idea of exploring my emotions more thoroughly in the future and to not necessarily accept them as resulting from other's actions when in fact many of them may stem from my own emotional issues."

(Participant, Contemplative Lawyering, 2005)

"Throughout this year, I have had an acrimonious relationship with a person I work with. For most of the year, I thought the source of the problem was this other person. I believed that this person was being deliberately difficult for some reason. After most encounters I was consumed with anger and completely annoyed that this person had generated all this negativity.

In the last few weeks, I started to think about my own responsibility in the situation. I have a tendency to be insecure. I am prone to thinking that everyone is smarter or more informed about things. When this person would nitpick everything I said or did, I felt defensive and would retaliate. I wanted to prove that I was smart or that I knew what I was talking about. I was trying to somehow "win" every exchange. And to be honest, I think he was too.

By practicing mindful listening and generating an aspiration to restrain myself, I think I have started to correct this. When I practice mindfulness, I am less likely to lash out from a place of ego. Instead, I am more likely to see that if my comments are motivated by anger, I am only going to cause more damage to the relationship and cause both myself and this other person more suffering. Lashing out in anger is never going to fix my own insecurities.

I have also made an effort to change my frame of reference. Instead of looking at our exchanges and our working relationship as difficult and annoying, I try to see it as an opportunity to develop patience and self-restraint. This sounds bizarre, but I have started to feel thankful for this challenging relationship. I have learned so much about myself and about other people. I think it will only benefit me in the future."

(Participant, Contemplative Lawyering 2006)

"This week I had a chance to work with anger in the context of someone actually yelling at me. It happened with my boss. He yelled at me for something that I really had nothing to do with. I made a snide comment back to him. . . .

When I got home, I sat and thought about what had happened. I thought about how I had let my relationship with my boss get to the point where I was ready to snap at him. I also thought about why he acted the way he did, and realized he's pretty unhappy with his life right now and was displacing some of his dissatisfaction on me. I made an aspiration to not allow my relationships with others develop the way this one had. I want to have healthy, open, helpful relationships with those I work with. I think those relationships are imperative to fostering a productive, respectful work environment.

After I thought this through I felt a lot better about what had happened. Later the same day I thought about the incident again and I really didn't feel angry any more. I couldn't even conjure up the anger I felt. It was the first time I'd ever noticed this phenomenon, but I thought maybe because I had really addressed it, the anger just truly wasn't with me anymore. It was quite a learning experience and now I'm kind of glad it happened because I got a lot out of it."

(Participant, Contemplative Lawyering 2006)

MINDFUL SPEAKING REVISITED

Reconsider the practice of Mindful Speaking. We learned that speaking mindfully means not being motivated by egocentric needs. Mindful speech is motivated by an aspiration to benefit others. Remember also that speaking mindfully includes beginning with a positive statement. Mindful speech is very important in the context of resolving deep conflict. When you and someone you love have made each other angry, compassion together with mindful speaking can help you work your way out of your conflict. When you are angry and hurt, when you have had a deep disagreement, it is as though a wall has come up between you. You cannot look at each other. You cannot touch each other. There is a wall that seems impenetrable. Once you have practiced Sitting with Emotion, understood the source of your anger, and generated feelings of compassion for your friend or family member with whom you were angry, this is the time to use Mindful Speaking.

Mindful speech, even in difficult circumstances, begins by saying something positive. Contemplate what you can say at this moment that will be positive and genuine. Do not make something up. Generate a genuinely positive thought. Perhaps you can express regret that you are having difficulties with each other. Perhaps you can acknowledge your role in precipitating the dispute. Perhaps you can simply say that you are hurt and that you need help working with your tendency to be hurt easily. Perhaps you can ask if there is anything you can do to make the other person feel better.

If you have not been able to understand and work with your anger, you may need to communicate that you are still hurt and angry. This can be done with mindfulness as well. It is possible to communicate that you are hurt and angry without blaming the other person or using harsh language. You can speak with a gentle and kind voice and explain that you are hurt and angry, but that you do not want your anger to hurt others. You can say that you need help understanding your anger.

You may think that the other person will not listen to you. You may think that it is not possible to break through the wall of distrust that has built up as a result of your dispute. This is not so. If you approach the other person with loving kindness and a genuine motivation to help, it is quite likely that he or she will hear you and soften. Even if you are still hurt and angry, if you can remain calm and mindful rather than engaging your anger and acting on it, you will be able to communicate skillfully.

MINDFUL LISTENING REVISITED

A very powerful way to work with situations of deep conflict is to engage in Mindful Listening which can also be referred to as Listening without Judgment. Often individuals who speak in angry harsh language are simply trying very hard to be heard. Something is bothering them on a very deep level and they feel like nobody listens to them. This is readily seen with small children who have not yet developed speaking skills. They will cry and cry because they cannot express the source of their discomfort. Adults will sometimes engage in similar conduct. They see clearly that something is not right and that it is causing them distress. When they perceive that they are not being listened to, they get angry and shout in an attempt to be heard.

If you are on the receiving end of that angry tirade, it is very hard to stand your ground without either trying to escape or fighting back. It is really hard to listen deeply and with an open heart when someone is shouting at you. Shouting makes us defensive. We want to say something to defend ourselves. Or the shouting is so hurtful and uncomfortable that we want to either shout back to protect ourselves or run away. The usual response to shouting is to judge. When someone is angry, our immediate response is to go on the defensive and try to prove that the angry person is wrong. We can do a great service for an angry person by simply listening without judgment. Try to be fully present with the angry person. Try to listen calmly, without distraction and without judgment. When you do that you may find that you finally hear what the person is trying to say. At that point you can reframe what the person has said in order to demonstrate to him or her that you have heard correctly. It is often helpful to reframe what has been said in a way that does not blame anyone. Instead, say something that affirms the hurt feelings that are being expressed.

When you encounter a difficult person in your life, try this prac-tice-- listen deeply without judgment. You may be surprised at what happens. You may find out that the person is willing to calm down once he or she feels truly heard.

> "By listening in mindfulness to others, I am able to better hear the inner dynamics expressed in other's speech. By not being occupied with my own thoughts while others are talking I am better able to sense the balance of confusion and peacefulness in people's voices. I am able to extend more compassion to people when I understand that they too are coming from a place of confusion."
>
> *(Participant, Contemplative Lawyering 2005)*

"I would like to share with you how I think I was able to make some progress towards my overall aspiration to manage my emotions better and to do so by using my watchfulness and the Slow Reversal practice. This situation concerned the person in my life with whom I have the most difficulty, my dad. While visiting my parents, an incident occurred that sent my dad into one of his verbal tirades, a big part of which was directed at me. I did NOT react like I normally do by yelling back at him. (I think this course really has had an effect on me, because for the first time ever, I actually did not feel the same level of anger that I usually do when he starts to yell and I was able to generate calmness in myself . . . it was kind of strange actually. I did not recognize myself for a second. Because his yelling spells are typical, I think I was prepared for this to come up . . .).

Instead, I was able to sit back and not react and just take it all in. It was an important moment of self-reflection. I waited for him to finish and then I asked him what my mom and I could do to avoid upsetting him so much next time. He calmed down much faster than he normally does and was all apologies for overreacting."

(Participant, Contemplative Lawyering 2006)

POST MEDITATION EXERCISE – "SELECTIVE WATERING"

Thich Nhat Han teaches a very powerful practice in his book, *Anger*.[71] He calls this practice "selective watering". Doing this practice is like watering beautiful flowers to help them grow. When you interact with others, you can encourage their positive qualities of wisdom, loving kindness, and compassion or you can encourage their anger and other destructive emotions. If you are judgmental and critical, constantly commenting on the shortcomings of others at your job and in your home, your harsh speech will encourage fear, hurt, and negative interactions. Consider how you feel and react when others are critical and judgmental about your work, appearance, and conduct.

On the other hand, if you look for the kindness and positive qualities in others and acknowledge and encourage those qualities, your relationships with people will gradually soften and improve. If you approach people with harsh words and anger, they will respond in kind. If you approach them with a smile and words of encouragement, they will respond in the same way. This is the process of selective watering. If you reconsider the story of Brian Nichols in Chapter 9, you will recognize that Ashley Smith practiced "selective watering" with Brian Nichols.

The post-meditation practice for this week is to find ways to acknowledge and encourage positive qualities in individuals with whom you have difficult relationships. This could be people at home, at work, or in any part of your life.

"There was a small way in which I saw the benefits of this prac-

---

71 *Anger*, 74-76.

tice this week. It involved an interaction with someone who had previously done something to me that made me angry. Since then, I have avoided dealing with this person and have had a negative view of her. This week she entered into a conversation I was having with another friend and actually provided some helpful advice. This small encounter helped me change my view of her slightly. I didn't outwardly express my appreciation to her, but we both engaged in a friendly and helpful conversation. After that encounter, I passed her and we exchanged a friendly hello whereas previously we probably would have simply walked by without comment. It was very informative to see how allowing yourself to be open to another person's positive qualities, even when the person can be difficult for you to work with, helps to improve your overall interactions with the person."

(Participant, Contemplative Lawyering 2006)

SITTING WITH ANGER & SELECTIVE WATERING – RELATIONSHIP TO LAW PRACTICE

Although these practices are extremely effective when applied to relationships with close family and friends, they are applicable in the context of law practice as well. Remember what Attorney Susan Busby said about working with clients who are experiencing hurt and anger in the context of a divorce. Because she had used contemplative practices to understand and work with her own emotions, she was able to help her clients deal skillfully with their hurt, anxiety, and anger.

Much of law practice is about resolving conflicts between individuals. This means that lawyers are constantly working with individuals who are suffering from hurt and anger and who are attempting to resolve disputes with other people. Even in the context of litigation there are opportunities to help clients recognize their role in causing a dispute and encourage clients to take ownership of their contribution to the problem. Also in the context of litigation, there are significant opportunities to speak mindfully. Remember again Susan Busby's advice about responding skillfully to malicious and hurtful letters from the other party in a dispute.

Developing skills of conflict resolution in your own life through the practices of sitting with anger and selective watering can result in acquiring skills and understanding that enable you to help others engage in skillful conflict resolution. This is particularly true in the context of mediation. In mediation one is regularly called on to reframe issues and help people see their role in the dispute as well as develop some recognition of the needs of the other party. Bringing this transformative approach to mediation is the subject of Robert A. Baruch Bush and Joseph F. Folger's book, *The Promise of Mediation*.[72] Even if you have no intention of taking on the formal role of a mediator, I recommend that you buy and read this book. It can be extremely helpful for any lawyer because lawyers frequently are in the position of working to resolve conflicts. One could say that resolving conflicts defines the role of a lawyer. The ideas and skills presented in *The Promise of Mediation* can be used in settlement conferences and in any situation where you or your client must communicate with the other party to a dispute. These are contexts where strong emotions tend to arise and find expression.

A further way in which these practices are helpful for law practice is to improve your relationship with other lawyers in your office, whether supervisory or collegial. Whenever multiple people are

---

72   (Jossey-Bass Publishers, 1994).

required to work together, there is room for misunderstanding, hurt, and anger.

Learning to deal skillfully with contentious situations is essential in lawyering contexts that include a great deal of litigation. Kris Shaw, a criminal defense attorney in Seattle, put it this way:

> "Meditation helps me deal with the stress and incredible suffering implicit in criminal public defense work. Meditation has helped me not "other-ise" the opposition so I don't worry too much about them changing their view, or liking me. Nor do I spend energy disliking them or thinking they should be different. As I always say: 'the definition of insanity is yelling at a green banana that it should be yellow.':)"

When you encounter a situation at work that causes you to become angry, you can engage in Slow Reversal or Patience in Small Matters to avoid speaking or acting unskillfully. If the hurt and anger stays with you, you can take it back to your meditation cushion and work with it there using the practice of Sitting with Emotion. In addition, when you encounter supervisors or colleagues at work who engage in unskillful behavior and harsh words, you can search for instances of positive behavior on their part to acknowledge and encourage. You can do the same with your colleagues and with lawyers who you supervise.

Even for individuals who are not difficult to work with, it is always helpful to approach people with a smile and words of praise and encouragement. You can improve the relationships and atmosphere in your law office if you behave in this way. You can also engage in Selective Watering with secretaries, paralegals, and other individuals who work for you at the law office.

Practice Schedule

This is a practice that is most useful if you can remember to use it any time you find yourself in a very conflicted relationship. It can also be helpful to engage in this practice in a formal setting two or three times during a two week period. For these sessions you will need to bring to mind conflict situations you have experienced in the past if you do not have a live conflict situation in your life at this time. During these two weeks you can engage in Selective Watering as a post-meditation practice, acknowledging positive conduct whenever it arises.

The primary practice in this section is Sitting with Anger. If, however, you find that you experience pride, jealousy, desire, sadness, or fear, you may wish to substitute the following practices for Sitting with Anger.

SITTING WITH PRIDE, JEALOUSY & OBSESSIVE DESIRE

Applying this practice to the other negative emotions is reasonably straight forward. In each case begin by generating an aspiration to understand and transform the emotion. In each case practice tranquility meditation and then generate the story line needed to bring up the negative emotion. Experience and look at the emotion to learn its source and develop a skillful way of working with it.

Working with either pride or jealousy can help you see the positive qualities of other individuals. Working with obsessive desire can help you see the suffering that you bring on yourself as a result of your desire. It may also help you let go of neurotic attachments and cultivate generosity.

SITTING WITH SADNESS

> "I am feeling unresolved sadness. What can I do with this? I would
> welcome any suggestions you might have on how to understand or
> process these feelings through meditation practice."
> *(Participant, Contemplative Lawyering 2006)*

Many individuals who have participated in my Contemplative
Lawyering courses have told me that they experience deep sadness.
In some cases this sadness has been exacerbated by engaging in the
practices that I have suggested. For example, some students found
that when they tried to do the Sending and Taking compassion
practices, they could easily see the sufferings of others, but were
unable to believe that they could help in any way. This resulted in
feelings of sadness.

Other students became sad when they tried the practices associated
with strong emotions. They became sad because they felt they were
not making sufficient progress and could see themselves engaging
in harsh speech and unskillful conduct. I have already talked about
working with these feelings of guilt by transforming guilt into
an aspiration to do better on the next day. See *Dealing with Guilt
by Using the Four Powers* in Chapter 6. I have also explained that
working with our minds can be a slow process and that it is best to
be gentle with ourselves when we see that we make mistakes.

Another source of sadness that results from working with strong
emotions is the sadness that individuals often identify as the
underlying reason for anger.

With respect to sadness that results from recognizing suffering
in the world, it is important to understand that while we cannot

actually solve the problems of the world, we can create tremendous benefit by working skillfully in our corner of the world, starting with working to transform our own confusion. It can be helpful to think that your positive actions are like a stone thrown into a lake. When you throw a stone into a lake, it creates waves that spread outward from where the stone drops. Our effort to work with our own confusion is like that. The more skillful we become in our dealings with others, the more we help others learn to be skillful by seeing our example. Then they help others and on and on. Every person who takes responsibility for his or her own mind, speech, and conduct creates enormous benefit in the world. Nonetheless, it is hard to put yourself in touch with all the suffering in the world and it is not always easy to see that we can help by working with our own minds.

Seeing the suffering in the world as well as our own suffering is a form of insight. Sadness is uncomfortable, but it is not a negative emotion like anger. Unlike anger, sadness doesn't cause negative behavior unless sadness develops into anger. Sadness is simply a form of suffering.

There are several contemplative practices one can do to work with sadness. The primary practice is to simply sit with sadness in the same way we sit with anger. Of course, sadness like any emotion can be dealt with by sitting in tranquility meditation. When a thought of sadness comes up, acknowledge it and return to following your breath. However, the practice instruction in this chapter takes a different approach. This instruction teaches you how to develop insight by looking straight at your sadness.

SITTING WITH SADNESS – PRACTICE INSTRUCTION

Begin your session of meditation with an aspiration to understand your sadness and use that understanding as the basis for developing compassion and wisdom. Then sit for a while in tranquility meditation. Once your mind is reasonably settled, generate a story line that makes you sad. Allow yourself to experience the sadness clearly, but do not allow it to build to the point where it is out of your control. If you become overwhelmed by it, let go of the thoughts that created the sadness and return to resting on your breath. Once you are settled again, bring the sadness back up. Try to maintain a level of sadness that you can experience and look at without feeling overwhelmed.

Look at the sadness and the thoughts that create sadness. Try to understand the source of your sadness. Is it based on a feeling that you are not competent or have limited or no positive qualities? Is it based on a feeling of helplessness in the face of tremendous world-wide suffering? Is it based on feeling overwhelmed and stressed by your responsibilities? Are you sad because someone you love very much is sick or has died? It is helpful to identify the source of our sadness in order to work skillfully with it.

"I have been giving a lot of thought to the source of my sadness. I discovered that the source of my sadness is not the hurtful comment made by my friend. The comment triggered a memory of how this friend completely rejected another person for no reason. I recognized that she was treating me the same way that she treated this other person . . . I feel so much better now. I couldn't get beyond my sadness before because I kept misunderstanding the source of my sadness. But now that I see

the situation for what it really was, I have a certain level of peace."
(Participant, Contemplative Lawyering 2006)

Working with Sadness About Suffering

If the source of your sadness is the suffering of others, whether your family and friends or people and animals around the world, it is important to fully connect with that suffering, be willing to sit with it, and be comfortable experiencing it. If you can do this, it will be extremely beneficial for many reasons.

First, fully connecting with your own suffering provides the basis for generating compassion for others. Second, being comfortable sitting with suffering is an essential prerequisite to being helpful to others who are suffering. If you are uncomfortable with suffering, you will not be able to sit and listen to a person who is suffering. It is a great gift to simply be capable of listening deeply to another person who is suffering. If you are uncomfortable with suffering, you will not be able to be present with someone who is sick, grieving, or dying. If you are uncomfortable with suffering, you will find it difficult to provide helpful advice to someone who is suffering. You will be intent on fixing the situation so that you no longer feel uncomfortable. When you listen to or are present with someone who is suffering, they do not necessarily want you to fix the problem. They just want you to be there with them.

For all these reasons, it is helpful to do the practice of sitting with suffering. Sadness is not inherently an uncomfortable feeling. If you look at it deeply, you will find that it is quite rich and beautiful. Sadness connects us with other beings. Sadness connects us with compassion. Sadness has a rich and beautiful texture to it.

Working with Grief

If the source of your sadness is grief over the loss of a loved one, it is again important to become comfortable with that sadness. Grief is not a negative emotion because it does not necessarily result in unskillful speech and conduct. Grief is simply a form of suffering. Let yourself experience your grief. If you repress it, the grief will stay with you for many years, perhaps for your entire lifetime. If you repress it, grief can cause you to be physically sick. It is important to let yourself experience it. Do not expect grief to go away quickly. It can take a very long time to heal after the death of a loved one. Try to give your grief some space. Try not to allow it to get solid and substantial. If you look directly at it, you will see that it is just a very large and powerful thought. It is not anything solid or substantial. Try to let go of your fear of the sadness. It will not harm you. Grief that is based on the strong connection you have with a loved one is quite beautiful. Allow yourself to experience this beauty.

If your grief is complicated by guilt relating to the death of your loved one or your relationship with your loved one before he or she died, transform that guilt into an aspiration not to repeat the unskillful speech or conduct that you feel guilty about. Dedicating this aspiration to your loved one's memory can make the aspiration very powerful and may make you feel much better.

Another way to make your grief beneficial is to use it as the basis for cultivating compassion for other people who are grieving over the death of a loved one.

If your grief is complicated by anger at your deceased loved one or at others who may have contributed to the death of your loved one, it can be helpful to do the practice of Sitting with Anger or perhaps the practice of Sending and Taking—generating compassion for whoever you are angry at.

With respect to guilt and anger relating to your deceased loved one, try to generate some faith that this person still knows what you are thinking or saying. It can be helpful to apologize to your loved one or communicate with your loved one about your anger just as you would with a living person —Speaking with Mindfulness.

Working with Sadness Related to Self-Hatred

If the source of your sadness is self-hatred, then the approach to working with this sadness is the same in some ways, but there are additional practices you can do.

First, as with other sadness, you can use your sadness as the basis for generating compassion for other individuals who are experiencing self-hatred.

Second, it is important to look at the basis for your self-hatred and see that it is mistaken. If your self-hatred is based on feeling that you have made mistakes, it is likely that you will find that you are correct. We all make mistakes. And you could, of course, be better looking, smarter, more diligent in your work, etc. None of us are perfect or even close to perfect in terms of possessing positive qualities. What you need to see is that you are mistaken in judging yourself as lacking in worth simply because you are not perfect. Nobody is perfect. All of us are struggling. Look around and see all the confusion around you and recognize that you are no more confused than anyone else.

You can work with self-hatred by doing the formal sending and taking practice using yourself as the focus of the practice. This practice was described earlier at the end of Chapter 10.

A second practice that you can use to work with self-hatred was actually developed by one of my students in Contemplative Lawyering. The practice, which I mentioned briefly in Chapter 10, is to visualize in front of you all of the people who respect and love you and who see you as having many positive qualities. Imagine these people in front of you and imagine that they are sending you positive energy and love and recognition in the form of white light. The white light comes from their hearts and flows into your heart. Allow yourself to feel their love deeply and clearly.

Working with Sadness — Meditation versus Medicine

It is important to understand that while meditation practices can be helpful for working with sadness and other difficulties in life, we sometimes experience problems that should also be addressed by a competent psychiatric professional. If you find that in spite of your best efforts to meditate regularly and engage in the post meditation exercises, you continue to experience severe anxiety or depression, you should consider seeing a skilled counselor. It can be helpful to work with your problems using both approaches simultaneously.

WORKING WITH SADNESS — THE RELATIONSHIP TO LAW PRACTICE

These practices may make you feel better which is wonderful in itself. However, these practices also can make you a better lawyer.

As lawyers we often encounter people who are suffering. We can be most helpful to suffering individuals if we are comfortable with suffering and sadness. A lawyer who is not distressed by working with people who are extremely sad will be a much more effective counselor than someone who is uncomfortable with suffering.

These practices also can assist your practice of law if you use them as the basis for generating genuine empathy for others, including your clients.

Finally, a lawyer who is suffering from overwhelming sadness and depression often has a hard time functioning effectively. Many lawyers experience debilitating depression. Insofar as the practices in this book bring new meaning and efficiency to legal work, that may be enough in itself to reduce feelings of depression. In addition, these practices relating to sadness provide a means of directly alleviating depression. Again, however, anyone who is suffering from debilitating depression should consider consulting with a qualified psychiatrist in addition to working with the problem through meditation practices.

SITTING WITH FEAR

Many lawyers encounter anxiety and fear in the course of practicing law. Most of these fears are associated with an attachment to performing well. A lawyer may feel anxious about his or her ability to write a good brief or make a good oral argument. A lawyer may experience anxiety when meeting with clients--fear of not being able to answer questions. In addition, lawyers face the fear of being denied partnership.

These fears all result from attachment to performing well. Lawyers are individuals who have succeeded in law school and in the professional world because of strong motivations to work hard and perform well. Unfortunately, we tend to confuse our aspiration to perform well and the resulting hard work with an attachment to the result. What we do is solidify our expectations. Instead of simply aspiring to do well, we set up a solidified goal or expectation that requires us to perform at a certain level in order to be happy. When we set up a solidified goal like this, it becomes a distraction from working hard because it gives rise to anxieties and fears.

In addition, solidified goals ensure that we will suffer. It is not possible for everyone to be the very best at everything they do. The odds are dramatically against our being the very best at anything, much less everything. In addition, circumstances beyond our control frequently step in and make it impossible for us to realize the solidified goals we have set. We can be most effective and efficient and free from anxiety if we generate an aspiration to perform well, but avoid solidifying that aspiration into a goal with our happiness dependant on achieving it.

Many of us believe that we cannot work hard without that ego-driven attachment to the result. The reality is that ego gratification is not a necessary prerequisite to hard work. We can be motivated by a desire to benefit our clients and others. We can be motivated simply by recognizing that we are paid for our work and owe our employers and our clients the best that we have to offer in order to earn our compensation. We do not need to turn our performance into our identity in order to work hard and perform well. In fact, when we set up solidified goals that define our self worth, the fears and anxieties that result can interfere with our ability to perform well.

Finally, setting expectations and goals for ourselves can result in failing to recognize our positive qualities. We are so distressed at not meeting our solidified goals that we fail to see what we actually have accomplished.

This is all a repeat of what was said in earlier chapters about using tranquility meditation to calm fears and anxieties. This chapter is about focusing on fears and anxieties from a different perspective. Rather than simply acknowledging them and letting them go, as we do in tranquility meditation, here we are looking straight at our fears in order to develop insight.

> "Today you said 'Fear like sadness is a form of suffering.' I couldn't agree more with this statement. My own day-to-day fear of failure has been a crippling force for most of my life. I have to work against it almost every day. I am unsure where it comes from, but I know it is there. I am working against it all the time. Is there a type of meditation that would be particularly helpful to combat fear?"
>
> *(Participant, Contemplative Lawyering 2006)*

SITTING WITH FEAR – PRACTICE INSTRUCTION

The practice of sitting with fear is like the other Sitting with Emotions practices. Begin by generating an aspiration to develop insight based on your fear and to transform your fear. Then sit in tranquility meditation until you are reasonably settled. Once your mind is reasonably settled, generate the story line that brings up your fear and anxiety. Bring it up so that you can look at it and learn from it, but not so that you are overwhelmed by it. If you become overwhelmed, stop the story line and return to following the breath until you calm down.

Once you have brought up your fear, look straight at your experience of that fear. What is it based on? What are you afraid of? Fear is not a negative emotion because it does not give rise to negative speech and actions unless fear transforms into anger, which it can do. Fear, itself, is simply a form of suffering based on attachment. What is it that you want and are afraid you will not get? What is it that you do not want that you are afraid will happen? Once you have identified what you are afraid of, then it is possible to work with your fear.

As with sadness and any other emotion it is possible to use our fear as a basis for generating compassion for others who experience the same kind of fear. Beyond that, however, identifying the source of our fear can be very enlightening.

I can give two examples of the results of this practice from my own experience. At one point, I realized that I was experiencing a great deal of fear about being around and talking with a certain teacher. When I sat with the emotion and looked at it, I realized that I was afraid the teacher would tell me that something I believed as true was actually incorrect. I was afraid of being wrong. I was attached to what I thought was right and did not want to be embarrassed by being wrong.

Once I identified this source of fear, I immediately realized that it made no sense. If he could tell me that something I believed was actually wrong, I should be deeply grateful. Why would I want to walk around with incorrect thoughts in my head when this teacher could help me by setting me straight? As soon as I let go of my attachment to being right, I was able to let go of my fear.

Another example concerns fear of heights. I went on a bike ride with my husband on a bike path constructed on an old railroad bed. The path ended just before a river. The railroad bridge over the river had not yet been converted into a paved bike path. The bridge was about one hundred yards long and about seventy feet above the river. The bridge was constructed out of railroad ties and train rails. It was wide and the space between the railroad ties was about four inches. Some of the railroad ties were rotting, but it was quite possible to walk around those places.

My husband got off his bicycle and walked right out to the middle of the bridge. I stopped after going out about ten feet because I was terrified of the height. I could see down to the river between the railroad ties as I stepped from one railroad tie to the next. There was nothing to be afraid of because it was not possible to fall down between the ties. In addition, even if I tripped, it was a long way from the middle of the bridge to the edge. Falling off was highly unlikely. Nonetheless, I was frozen with fear and practically crawled back to the beginning of the bridge.

Between this visit to the bridge and my next visit to the bridge, I engaged in the practice of sitting with fear. I brought my fear up, looked at it, and recognized that it made no logical sense. I visualized walking out on the bridge without fear. In my mind, I walked out there several times. The next time I visited the bridge I was able to walk out on the bridge. I was still afraid, but I was no longer paralyzed by my fear.

From these experiences I realized that it is possible to learn something about your fear and perhaps overcome it if you can sit with it and clearly identify what you are afraid of.

WORKING WITH FEAR BY SEEING THE BENEFIT OF NOT GETTING WHAT YOU WANT

Another way to work with fear is particularly effective when you are working on some project that you are hoping will succeed. This could be a trial that you are working on (and hoping to win) or perhaps you are up for partnership or have applied for a new job that you really want. In these situations, it can be helpful to say the following verse to yourself:

> If it will be beneficial for me to (win this trial, make partnership, get this job, etc) let it happen.
> If it will not be beneficial for me to (win this trial, make partner ship, get this job, etc) let it not happen.[73]

These two short lines, repeated with conviction, can be very effective in calming hopes and fears. I would guess that if you think back on your life, you can remember times when you did not get what you thought you wanted or something happened that you did not want and it turned out that it really was better than what you initially hoped for. It may have been better in a material sense or perhaps it was better because you learned and grew from the experience. Or it could be that it was better in terms of being more beneficial in some way—immediately helping others or making it possible for you to help others.

This verse relates to that understanding. If you clearly see that getting what you are hoping for is not always the best result and that getting what you fear could be positive, then you will be able

---

73   I learned this verse from Dzogchen Ponlop Rinpoche many years ago. I am quite certain that he is not the original source, but I know that this verse is typically taught as an antidote for attachment. I have used this verse myself many times and found it to be very helpful.

to say this verse with genuine conviction.

Further, if you understand that not getting what you want or getting what you do not want can be beneficial to others and you are strongly motivated to benefit others, you will be able to say this verse with an even stronger conviction. I have found that saying this verse helps me recognize how it could be beneficial not to get what I am hoping for—I could learn from the failure or perhaps something else will happen that is even better. As soon as I realize that not getting what I am hoping for could be beneficial, then I can genuinely let go of my hopes and fears.

CHAPTER 15:

CONTEMPLATING THE INSUBSTANTIAL NATURE OF EMOTIONS

In Chapter 14, the practice was to sit with anger and other emotions with an aspiration to learn something from the experience. In this chapter, we will again sit with emotions, but with a different intention. Begin this practice by generating an aspiration to recognize the insubstantiality of emotions. After settling your mind with tranquility meditation, generate a story line that will bring up a strong emotion, such as anger or a strong form of suffering such as sadness or fear.

Sit with that emotion and experience it. Then, look at the emotion and ask yourself where it came from and where it goes when you stop running the story line that feeds this emotion and keeps it alive. Ask yourself whether this emotion has a color or a shape. Consider whether this emotion has a size or any other identifiable characteristics. You can do this practice with any emotion.

INSUBSTANTIALITY OF EMOTIONS – COMMENTS

Emotions are simply very loud and strong thoughts. Emotions begin with a small thought and grow when we feed them. If you look at an emotion, you cannot find that it has any substantial characteristics. The question then becomes, why are emotions so powerful? Why is it that they cause us so much distress?

My most powerful teaching on this came in the context of working with grief. My first husband of twenty five years died suddenly in an automobile accident. I suffered from deep and lengthy grief as a result of his death. After several years, I asked one of my meditation teachers for advice on dealing with my grief. He told me that I was holding onto grief because of some unresolved issue, but that I should not try to figure out what that issue might be. He advised me to simply let it go. In addition, he advised me to try dedicating my experience of letting go of grief to the benefit of others who experience the same form of suffering. I contemplated this advice and decided that I was willing to try to do this practice of letting my grief go to benefit others.

As soon as I seriously considered letting the grief go, I understood why I was still holding on to it. I realized that I was holding on to it in order to prove to myself (and anyone else might be watching, including my dead husband) that I loved him. My immediate thought was, "How silly is that? I do not need to be miserable in order to prove that I loved him. Everyone knows that." At that moment, the grief, which had seemed to me like an enormous and very solid black cloud, simply broke apart and drifted away. That was the end of it. The emotion that I thought was so solid and real was gone.

Relationship to Law Practice

This practice provides another approach to working with emotions. The relationship between law practice and working with emotions was discussed extensively in Chapter 14.

Practice Schedule

I recommend that you engage in the formal practice of contemplating the insubstantiality of emotions for seven days.

WORKING WITH DIFFICULT INDIVIDUALS — SUMMARY OF PRACTICES

This book offered many different formal meditation and post-meditation methods for working with negative or difficult individuals in your life:

1. Tranquility meditation allows us to acknowledge and let go of the anger, sadness, and fear that arise when we are dealing with difficult individuals.

2. The Slow Reversal practice post-meditation practice helps us create space in which to consider skillful ways of working with difficult individuals.

3. Deep listening skills allow us to be present and listen when we encounter individuals whose suffering causes them to engage in harsh language and conduct.

4. The sending and taking practices help us see that difficult individuals are confused and suffering, rather than simply

bad. These practices also help us see the kindness in difficult individuals and generate loving kindness and compassion for difficult individuals. These practices also provide
an antidote for the anger that arises when dealing with
difficult individuals.

5. Patience in Small Matters helps us cultivate patience in
    small, annoying situations in order to gradually cultivate
    the patience necessary to work with larger and more diffi-
    cult situations, including difficult individuals

6. Mindful Speech helps us communicate skillfully even in
    the context of conflict with difficult individuals.

7. The formal practice of Sitting with Anger helps us trans-
    form anger at difficult individuals into compassion.

8. The formal practices of Sitting with Sadness and Sitting
    with Fear provide methods for working productively with
    the sadness and fear that can result from difficult relation-
    ships.

9. Finally, the Insubstantiality of Emotions practice helps us
    avoid solidifying difficult emotions.

Even with all these practices available to work with difficult individuals, you may find that you are unable to make much progress.

> "I must admit that since we've been doing the impartiality prac-
> tices, I have found that it's really hard for me to wish happi-
> ness for people I dislike. The image of a person will pop into my
> head and my mind immediately lets out a sigh of disgust and
> the image disappears before I can even try doing anything. It's

horrible. Not only do I not accomplish anything with the practice for that person, I find myself recounting what the person has done or said to hurt or annoy me and then proceed to call them names or just think angry thoughts. I feel like I have a Rolodex of people in my head that I can't do this practice with. That might be an exaggeration but I think what I am saying is that I'd rather keep those cards bound together in that stack than start acknowledging them one by one. Hopefully this will change with time!"

(Participant, Contemplative Lawyering 2006)

"One problem I had with the practice this week was with one lady I work with in my externship. She is the secretary for the office and is SO SO SO negative!!! She is always complaining about how her life is miserable (hates her commute, job, family, house, etc.) and how she's uncomfortable (arthritis, overweight, trouble breathing—smoker). Dealing with her on a day-to-day basis is very trying and I'm finding that I'm looking for ways to avoid her. She is, however, never mean to me; she's just very hard to be around because she brings my mood down too. It's not that she's mean, but she is suffering and I think she's really lonely and this is her way of getting attention from others. I try to be positive and supportive around her and hope it kind of rubs off, but because she's so negative in so many realms of her life, it's hard to stick by her and take it all in. I do not think she's a bad person, but I still don't really want to be around her. I'm wondering if you have any suggestions on how to deal with this situation."

(Participant, Contemplative Lawyering 2006)

WORKING WITH DIFFICULT INDIVIDUALS — BAD FRIENDS

Unfortunately, in spite of all the available practices, you may find yourself in a relationship with a family member, friend, client, or work colleague who continues to cause you deep pain, anguish, and perhaps anger. If this is the case, my first advice is to do your best to work with the situation. Try all of the practices to see if you can make them work and improve the situation. It is especially important to use Slow Reversal to back away from negative interchanges, go back to your meditation cushion, and try to work with the relationship using Sending and Taking practices or Sitting with Emotion practices as described in this book and in Thich Nhat Han's book, *Anger.*[74]

Sometimes, despite our best aspirations and efforts, we find that we simply are unable to work productively with another person. What I mean by this is that we are unable to remain calm in the face of perceived attacks by the other person. I mean that we are unable to generate compassion for this person and regularly find ourselves embroiled in angry disputes with this individual.

Living, relating, or working with a difficult person can be a source of great learning and personal growth if we are able to let go of our feelings of hurt and use mindfulness and compassion to work with the situation. If we can do this, it may be possible to listen mindfully to the other person's complaints and speak mindfully about the difficulties we are having with the other person. In this context, even though the relationship is difficult, we can benefit from the relationship and the difficult person can benefit as well.

---

74 *Anger,* at 23-46.

However, your hurt may be so deep and unmanageable that you are not able to remain calm and you end up distressed or angry with the other person, including engaging in harsh words and unskillful conduct. If this is the situation, then the relationship is not helping you grow and learn. Instead, the relationship is causing you to engage in negative speech and behavior. This does not help you and it does not help the person you are trying to relate with. You are both suffering and neither of you is able to learn from your suffering.

When this happens, my advice is to try to leave the relationship. If it is a work relationship, you could try to find another job or seek a transfer to another department. For example, if you are working under the supervision of a partner who is very difficult you could ask to be assigned to a different case supervised by a different attorney. If this is not possible because the firm is small or your expertise makes it appropriate for you to continue with the same supervisor, then you may need to consider looking for another job. If the difficult relationship is with a client, you cannot simply abandon the client's work. You will need to find suitable alternative representation for the client and provide whatever assistance is needed by the new attorney.

If the person is a friend, it would be a good idea to end the relationship at least temporarily. If the relationship is with a spouse or family member, I suggest that you separate from this person at least temporarily.

Once you have left the relationship, you can continue to work with the relationship in formal meditation practices. When you separate from someone in this way, it will be helpful if you try not to leave with anger in your heart. You should try to recognize that the separation is for the benefit of both you and the difficult person. Try to communicate mindfully with the difficult person to explain why you are leaving. You are not leaving because you are angry. You are leaving because you are hurt and you are not able to work skillfully with that hurt. You are leaving because you do not want to hurt this person any more by responding with harsh words and unskillful actions.

This is the situation referred to as "bad friends." This does not mean that your friend, co-worker, or family member is a bad person. Rather it means that the relationship is unworkable. This is a bad friend in the sense that it is someone to whom you are so attached that you are not able to remain calm in dealing with him or her. The problem is not simply that the friend is difficult. The problem is that it takes a great deal of mindfulness, clarity, presence, wisdom, and compassion to work with an individual who is very difficult. If you have not yet developed that level of mind training, then the most beneficial thing you can do for you and for the difficult person is to separate from him or her and continue working on training your own mind and working with your own confusion. Once you have done that, it may be possible for you to work with this person skillfully. Then it may be time to return depending on the circumstances.

CHAPTER 16:

WHAT'S NEXT?

Having worked through the practices and comments in this book, I hope you have found practices and information that have been useful for you on both a personal and professional level. At this point you may be asking yourself, "Where do I go from here?" This Chapter is designed to help you with that question.

Aspirations

First, I recommend that you look back through the book and consider what you learned that was most valuable for you. Then consider how you have integrated this insight into your life or whether you have found it difficult to integrate this insight into your life. Write down what you identified as a valuable insight and then contemplate what you have learned.

Second, with respect to the valuable insight(s) you have identified, consider how you are going to take this insight with you, how you are going to make this insight part of your life. What is your aspiration for making use of the most important insight?

Third, the practices in this book may have made you aware of issues that are difficult for you to work with. You may have recognized that these issues cause problems in your life and that you want to work with them further. With respect to these issues, generate an aspiration to continue working with them.

Continuing to Practice

We all have a tendency to think that once we have had a significant personal insight or learned something we consider useful, this insight and this useful information will stay with us—we will not forget. Unfortunately, unskillful habitual patterns of approaching the world cannot be banished that easily. No matter how clearly we understand a new and more beneficial approach to the world, until we have incorporated that understanding into our way of being, we will continue to fall back into our previous habitual patterns of behavior.

In order to make the lessons learned in contemplative practices part of our habitual way of being in the world, it is important to continue to engage in these practices on a regular basis.

The most important daily practice is tranquility meditation. Having worked through this entire book, you probably have already found a way to incorporate contemplative practice into your daily life. Continuing to practice every day or nearly every day (especially in the morning) is a wonderful way to start your day and will make it more likely that you will be able to sustain what you have learned.

The formal practices associated with generating compassion (Sending and Taking) and working with strong emotions (Sitting with Emotion) can be practiced whenever we encounter difficult relationships in our lives. The trick is to remember to use these practices in appropriate circumstances.

The post-meditation practices such as Slow Reversal, Mindful Listening, Mindful Speaking, Seeing and Appreciating Kindness, Aspiring for the Happiness of Others, Selective Watering, and Patience in Small Matters can be practiced all the time in our daily lives. The trick is to find mindfulness reminders that make these practices an integral part of your daily life.

Perhaps the best way to ensure that you continue to maintain a connection with contemplative practice is to find a group to practice with and learn from.

Enhancing Your Practice

While it is possible to make a great deal of progress on your path of contemplative practice simply by following the instructions in this book, the best way to build on what you have learned is to get further instruction and engage in further practice by attending weekend or weeklong teaching and meditation retreats or by joining a group that meets and practices together regularly in your area.

Teaching and Meditation Retreats and Programs

There are a variety of organizations that offer weekend or weeklong teaching and meditation retreats and programs. I have provided contact information in the Resources Appendix. In this Chapter I simply want to describe some of the organizations and introduce you to what they offer.

In terms of working with stress reduction, there are a variety of programs and books available based on the work of Jon Kabat-Zinn, an emeritus professor at University of Massachusetts Medical Center who is also a Zen practitioner.

If you are looking for programs that are directly related to law practice, The Mindfulness in Law Program at Berkeley School of Law offers a variety of programs for lawyers, judges and law students.

Programs based on the teachings of S.N. Goenka, an Indian Vipassana meditation practitioner, are offered at centers throughout the world. There are programs offered in several areas of the United States.

The Insight Meditation Society presents programs and meditation instruction based on the Vipassana meditation tradition of Burma and Thailand. IMS has centers in Barre and Cambridge, Massachusetts; Seattle, Washington; Washington, DC; and Woodacre, California.

Entering a Path of Practice

There are significant advantages to associating yourself with a center that presents a path of meditation practice. It is said that the Buddha taught 84000 paths of practice. Anywhere in the United States you can find many different centers and traditions of practice. In a big city, you may find several centers on one city block. If you search for books on meditation practice online or at a bookstore you will find a dizzying array of offerings. We are blessed in this country with many genuine teachings and paths of practice. They have come here from all over the world. The downside of this situation for practitioners in the United States is that it can be confusing. We are left wondering which practices will be useful for us and what we should practice first. If you associate yourself with a center that teaches a path of practice, you will be provided with guidance about what to practice, how much to practice, and an order of practices to follow that will build on each other.

In the Resource Appendix I have provided you with contact information for a variety of organizations and centers. I recommend that you "shop around" at first. You can read about the different groups online to see what they offer. You can read books published by the teachers associated with different centers and organizations. This process of shopping around can help you identify a group that works for you in terms of their location, offerings, and style of presentation.

The Vipassana Meditation centers mentioned in the previous section not only offer weekend and week-long teaching and meditation programs, they offer a complete path of practice. One advantage of the programs offered by *The Insight Meditation Society* is that the teachers (including Sharon Salzberg, Joseph Goldstein, and Jack Kornfield) are Western and therefore speak English and understand Western culture.

There are a variety of centers and organizations that are based on the teachings of the many realized masters who escaped from Tibet and now teach throughout the world. Tibetan Buddhism has four lineages, Gelugpa, Sakya, Nyingma, and Kagyu. I am most familiar with teachers in the Nyingma and Kagyu traditions. All of the organizations and teachers I mention in this chapter and in the Resource Appendix are from these two traditions. Although there are excellent teachers and organizations in the Gelugpa and

Sakya traditions, they are not mentioned here because I am not familiar with them.

Organizations located in the United States that provide teachings based on the Tibetan Buddhist Nyingma and Kagyu Lineages include Karma Triyana Dharmachakra (The Seventeenth Gyalwang Karmapa, Khenpo Karthar Rinpoche), Nalandabodhi (Dzogchen Ponlop Rinpoche), Pundarika Foundation (Tsoknyi Rinpoche), Shambhala (Sakyong Mipham Rinpoche), and Tergar Meditation Community (Mingyur Rinpoche).

While some of these teachers speak only Tibetan and use translators to present teachings to a western audience, others speak English and are familiar with Western culture. All of these organizations and teachers provide complete paths of practice. The advantage of the Tibetan teachings over the Vipassana teachings is that they provide a greater variety of practices.

Another tradition of contemplative practice that is widely available in the United States is Zen. You can find listings of centers online. I am not personally familiar with any Zen Centers but I am certain that many of them provide genuine teachings and a path of contemplative practice. The one Zen teacher with whom I am familiar is Thich Nhat Han. He has published many wonderful books and teaches throughout the world. His organization is The Community of Mindful Living.

Finding a Teacher

Once you settle on a practice tradition that appeals to you, you may find it helpful to associate yourself with a particular teacher. Following many different teachers can be confusing because they each may offer a different path of practice. My recommendation is that you take your time. It is helpful to examine teachers for several years before associating yourself with one teacher to the exclusion of others. On the other hand, endlessly searching can lead to your practice not progressing. It can be very helpful to your practice to generate faith in one teacher and the path he or she is presenting. This does not mean you stop reading materials by other teachers or stop attending retreats presented by other teachers. It simply means that you follow one path in your personal practice.

I have found that many individuals are afraid to commit to one teacher. While it is important to examine teachers before committing, if you have an aspiration to move along the path of contemplative practice do not hesitate to commit to one path. Do not be afraid you will choose the wrong organization or the wrong teacher. There are many wonderful teachers and organizations.

There really are only two reasons for rejecting a teacher or organization. First, if you are told to read only teachings and books presented by one organization or teacher and to stop reading anything else, this is perhaps a sign that you should consider another organization or teacher. Second, if you see that the organization or teacher you are considering appears to be operating for their own benefit rather than for your benefit, this is also a sign that you should look elsewhere for teachings.

MY ASPIRATION

My aspiration for writing this book has been to benefit anyone who reads this book and works with these practices as well as benefit your family, friends, colleagues, clients, associates, opponents, and everyone else you encounter in your life. Everything useful and beneficial I have presented in this book has been based on the teachings and I have received from my teachers. Any mistakes are my own.

For anyone who has completed some or all of the practices presented in this book, my aspiration is that you continue to benefit from what you have learned here and that your path of practice grows and develops further. It is wonderful that you have committed your precious time to bringing the benefits of contemplative practice to yourself, to your law practice, and to everyone you encounter in life.

APPENDIX I

PRACTICE SCHEDULES

Each box in the practice schedules represents one session of formal practice. One hour is the recommended length for each practice session, but as a new practitioner, you may want to start with shorter sessions and gradually work up to one hour per session. Using check boxes like this makes it easy to keep track of what you are practicing even if you are unable to practice every day. Sometimes you may even be distracted from practice for weeks at a time. The check boxes help you pick up where you left off. The suggested post meditation practice should be continued throughout the day and night until you complete the suggested formal practice sessions. All of this is merely a suggestion. Use your experience to determine whether more (or less) time with a practice is helpful for you.

TRANQUILITY PRACTICES & ASSOCIATED POST-MEDITATION PRACTICES

Formal Practice: Following the Breath

Post Meditation: Return to your breath whenever you encounter your mindfulness reminder.

Formal Practice: Counting the Breath

Post Meditation: Whenever you encounter your mindfulness reminder look at your mind—are your thoughts in the past, present or future?

Formal Practice: Meditation on an Object

Post Meditation: Use a mindfulness reminder to be present with objects

Post Meditation: Use written materials as an object of meditation—remain present while reading and writing.

Three Weeks of Listening Exercises

Post Meditation: Listening Exercises

1ST Competing Voices	2ND Just Listen	2ND Just Listen	2ND Just Listen	3RD Suffering	3RD Suffering	4TH Preparing
4TH Preparing	4TH Preparing	5TH Speaking	5TH Speaking	5TH Speaking	Listen & Speak	Listen & Speak
Listen & Speak	Listen & Speak	Listen & Speak	Listen & Speak	Listen & Speak	Listen & Speak	Listen & Speak

Formal Practice: Tranquility Meditation (resting on the breath, counting the breath or resting on an object).

Slow Reversal

Formal Practice: Tranquility meditation

Post Meditation Practice: Work with whatever emotion is the most challenging for you. Each box represents one day of post meditation practice.

SENDING & TAKING PRACTICES FOR GENERATING COMPASSION & LOVING KINDNESS

Impartiality Practice

Formal Practice: Sending and Taking Practice (Impartiality)

Impartial	Impartial	Impartial	Impartial	Impartial	Impartial	Impartial
Neutral	Neutral	Positive	Positive	Negative	Negative	Compare

Post Meditation Exercise: Watching for judgments

Seeing and Appreciating Kindness

Formal Practice: Sending and Taking Practice (Seeing and Appreciating the Kindness of Others).

Kindness	Kindness	Kindness	Kindness	Kindness	Kindness	Kindness
Positive	Positive	Neutral	Neutral	Negative	Negative	Compare

Post Meditation Exercise: Seeing and appreciating kindness

Repaying the Kindness of Others

Formal Practice: Sending and Taking Practice (Aspiring to repay the Kindness of Others)

Repay Positive	Repay Positive	Repay Neutral	Repay Neutral	Repay Negative	Repay Negative	Repay Compare

Post Meditation Exercise: Repaying the kindness of others

Cultivating Loving Kindness

Formal Practice: Sending and Taking Practice (Cultivating Loving Kindness)

Loving Positive	Loving Positive	Loving Neutral	Loving Neutral	Loving Negative	Loving Negative	Loving All Beings

Post Meditation Exercise: Aspiring for the happiness of others

Generating Compassion

Formal Practice: Sending and Taking Practice (Generating Compassion)

Compassion Positive	Compassion Positive	Compassion Neutral	Compassion Neutral	Compassion Negative	Compassion Negative	Compassion All Beings

Post Meditation Exercise: Generating compassion for others

WORKING WITH INNER & OUTER CONFLICT (EMOTIONS)

Patience with Small Matters

Formal Practice: Contemplate the negative attributes of strong emotions

Contemplate Anger	Contemplate Anger	Contemplate Jealousy	Contemplate Jealousy	Contemplate Desire	Contemplate Desire	Contemplate Pride

Post Meditation Practice: Patience in Small Matters (work with whatever emotion is the most challenging for you; work with inwardly directed anger if that would be helpful for you.)

Sitting With Anger

Formal Practice: Sitting with Anger (or pride, jealousy, desire, sadness, or fear)

Post Meditation Exercise: Selective Watering

The Insubstantiality of Emotion

Formal Practice: Contemplate the insubstantiality of emotion

Post Meditation Exercise: Write a "Heart Sutra" letter as described in Chapter 6 of *Anger*, pp. 109-124 (Riverhead Books, 2002).

APPENDIX II

RESOURCES

MEDITATION RETREATS AND PROGRAMS

The Center for Mindfulness in Medicine, Health Care and Society

University of Massachusetts Medical School
55 Lake Avenue North
Worcester, MA 01655
Phone: 508 856 2656
Fax: 508 856 1977
Email: mindfulness@umassmed.edu
Website: http://www.umassmed.edu/content.aspx?id=41252
Includes a worldwide directory of Mindfulness Based Stress Reduction Programs.

Insight Meditation Society

1230 Pleasant Street
Barre, Massachusetts 01005
Phone: 978 355 4378 (Retreat Center)
Email: RC@dharma.org
Website: www.dharma.org
They run a variety of meditation programs, long and short. If you are interested in Insight or Vipassana meditation (which is Buddhist meditation in its most direct and uncomplicated form), I would contact them for recommendations about local centers and meditation groups. The Barre Center runs excellent programs.

Other insight meditation centers are located in California; Washington, DC; Cambridge, Massachusetts; and Seattle, Washington. Information about all of these centers and their programs can be found the website mentioned in the previous paragraph.

Vipassana Meditation Center

Dhamma Dharā
Shelburne, Massachusetts
Website: www.dhara.dhamma.org/ns/
Dhamma Dharā is one of more than 120 centers worldwide offering courses in Vipassana Meditation, as taught by S.N.Goenka and his assistant teachers in the tradition of Sayagyi U Ba Khin. Almost 2,000 students per year attend our residential 10-day meditation courses. For a general introduction to Vipassana Meditation, visit the International Vipassana Meditation website

For information about S.N. Goenka Vipassana Meditation centers and retreats worldwide, visit http://www.dhamma.org/

ENTERING THE PATH OF PRACTICE

The Insight Meditation Society mentioned in the previous section also provides a complete path of practice. Like the organizations mentioned in the previous section, the centers and teachers mentioned in this section on Entering the Path of Practice offer weekend and weeklong teaching and meditation retreats. I mention them in this section because their *central* focus is providing a path of practice.

TIBETAN PRACTICE TEACHERS AND ORGANIZATIONS

Karma Triyana Dharmachakra (KTD)

335 Meads Mountain Road
Woodstock, NY 12498
Phone: 845 679 5606
Email: office@kagyu.org
Website: kagyu.org
KTD is the North American Seat of His Holiness the 17th Karmapa who is head of the Kagyu Lineage of Tibetan Buddhism. Karmapa is based in Dharmasala, India. He sometimes travels to the United States to teach. The Abbot of KTD Monastery is Khenpo Karthar Rinpoche, who is also a wonderful teacher. KTD has associated centers around the world. These centers are listed at the KTD website.

Nalandabodhi

Nalanda West
3902 Woodland Park Ave, North
Seattle, WA 98103
Phone: 206 529 8258
Fax: 206 632 3859
Email: info@nalandawest.org
Website: nalandabodhi.org
Nalandabodhi is the organization established by Dzogchen Ponlop Rinpoche together with his teacher, Khenpo Tsultrim Gyamtso Rinpoche. Nalandabodhi has associated centers all over the world. In the United States, centers are located in Seattle, Washington; Boulder, Colorado; San Francisco, California; New York, New York; and Bloomfield, Connecticut. Contact information can be found at the Nalandbodhi website. Teaching Schedules for Dzogchen Ponlop Rinpoche can also be found at the Nalandabodhi Website. Dzochen Ponlop Rinpoche has created an extensive set of practice and study curriculum materials and is deeply committed to bringing genuine Buddhist study and practice to the West.

Pundarika Foundation

P.O. Box 57
Crestone, CO 81131
Phone: 719 256 4011
Website: pundarika.org
Pundarika is the organization established by Tsoknyi Rinpoche. Pundarika practice groups are located in San Francisco/Bay Area, California; Boulder, Colorado; and Crestone, Colorado. Tsoknyi Rinpoche teaches in a variety of locations in the United States and around the world. His teaching schedule is available at the Pundarika website.

Shambhala

1084 Tower Road
Halifax, Nova Scotia
B3H 2Y5, Canada
Phone: 902 425 4275
Fax: 902 423 2750
Website: shambhala.org

Shambhala was originally established by Chogyam Trungpa Rinpoche. The current temporal and spiritual director of Shambhala is The Sakyong Mipham Rinpoche. Shambhala has teaching and meditation practice centers located throughout the world, including many centers in the United States. You can find a listing of centers at the Shambhala.org website along with information about Shambhala and the teachings and practice opportunities available at Shambhala centers. Shambhala centers offer an extensive practice and study curriculum.

Tergar Meditation Community

Tergar International
810 S. 1st St., Suite 200
Minneapolis, MN 55343
Phone: 952 232 0633
Email: info@tergar.org
Website: tergar.org

Tergar Meditation Community is the organization established by Yongey Mingyur Rinpoche. Tergar has teaching and meditation practice centers located around the world. Tergar offers an extensive practice and study curriculum. Centers and schedules of teachings are available at the tergar website.

Zen Practice and Study

There are many Zen Centers located throughout the United States. I am not listing information here about locating a Zen center because I am not familiar with this practice and teaching tradition except for teachings by Thich Nhat Han (listed below). However, if you are drawn to Zen, I encourage you to explore Zen Centers. I am sure you can find help for your path there.

Community of Mindful Living

Website: iamhome.org

The Community of Mindful Living is Thich Nhat Han's organization. At this website you can find information about Thich Nhat Han's teaching schedule, retreat centers and practice groups. Thich Nhat Han has monasteries in the Hudson Valley in New York, in California and in Batesville, Minnesota. He also has practice groups located throughout the United States and around the world.

Yoga

Yoga can provide a wonderful context for deepening your contemplative practice. There are many Yoga centers throughout the United States. My only suggestion here is that you will benefit most from Yoga teachers who emphasize mind as well as body.

APPENDIX III

SUGGESTED BOOKS & SOURCES OF TEACHINGS

In addition to the books listed below, I encourage you to seek out other books written by the authors I have recommended.

Bringing Buddhist Teachings to the West

Rebel Buddha, Dzogchen Ponlop Rinpoche (Shambhala, 2010)

Meditation and Practice

Mahamudra: Path of Simplicity, Dzogchen Ponlop Rinpoche (August, 2005) (DVD & MP3 recordings available at www.vajraechoes.com)

The Practice of Tranquility and Insight, Khenchen Thrangu Rinpoche (Snow Lion, 1993)

The Middle–Way Meditation Instructions of Mipham Rinpoche, Thrangu Rinpoche (Namo Buddha Seminar, 2001)

Wild Awakening, Dzogchen Ponlop Rinpoche (Shambhala, 2003)

The Miracle of Mindfulness, Thich Nhat Hanh (Beacon Press, 1976)

Peace is Every Step, Thich Nhat Hanh
Stages of Meditation, The Dalai Lama

Post-Meditation and Compassion Practices

Compassion Without Limit, Dzogchen Ponlop Rinpoche
      (April, 2003) (DVD & MP3 recordings available from
      www.vajraechoes.com)
The Wisdom of No Escape, The Path of Loving–Kindness,
      Pema Chodron (Shambhala, 1991)
Start Where You Are, A Guide to Compassionate Living,
      Pema Chodron (Shambhala, 1994)
Enlightened Courage, Dilgo Kyentse Rinpoche (Snow Lion, 1993)
Loving–Kindness: The Revolutionary Art of Happiness,
      Sharon Saltzburg (Shambhala)
A Heart as Wide as the World, Stories on the Path of Loving–Kindness,
      Sharon Saltzburg (Shambhala, 1999)
The Great Path of Awakening, Jamgön Kongtrul Lodrö Thaye
      (Shambhala, 1987)
The Way of the Bodhisattva, Shantideva (Shambhala, 2003)

Working with Emotions

Anger, Thich Nhat Hanh (Riverhead Books, 2001)
Emotions, Dzogchen Ponlop Rinpoche (Sept. 2006) (DVD, MP3
      & CD recordings available at www.vajraechoes.com)
Wisdom of Emotions, Dzogchen Ponlop Rinpoche (Apr. 2008)
      (DVD, MP3 & CD recordings available at
      www.vajraechoes.com)
Vast Heart, Profound Mind, Dzogchen Ponlop Rinpoche
      (Sept. 2005) (DVD & MP3 recordings available at
      www.vajraechoes.com)

General Buddhist Teachings

Cutting Through Spiritual Materialism,
    Chögyam Trungpa Rinpoche (Shambhala, 1987)
Meditation in Action, Chögyam Trungpa Rinpoche
    (Shambhala, 1969)
The Myth of Freedom, Chögyam Trungpa Rinpoche
    (Shambhala, 1979)
The Heart Treasure of the Enlightened Ones,
    Dilgo Khyentse Rinpoche (Shambhala, 1992)
Showing the Path of Liberation, Khenchen Thrangu Rinpoche
    (Namo Buddha Publications, 2001)
The Tibetan Book of Living and Dying, Sogyal Rinpoche
    (Harper Collins, 1994)
The Garden, A Parable, Geshe Michael Roach (Doubleday, 2000)
Shenpen Ösel Magazine provides transcripts of teachings by many
    of the great Kagyu lineage masters, including Tai Situ
    Rinpoche, Kalu Rinpoche, Kenchen Thrangu Rinpoche,
    Khenpo Tsultrim Rinpoche and others. Shenpen Osel
    magazine is available by subscription or on-line at
    http://www.shenpen-osel.org/.
Wild Awakening, Dzogchen Ponlop Rinpoche (Shambhala, 2003)

Buddhist Philosophy

Progressive Stages of Meditation on Emptiness,
    Khenpo Tsultrim Gyamtso Rinpoche
    (Zhyisil Chokyi Ghatsal Publications, 2001)
The Sun of Wisdom, Khenpo Tsultrim Gyamtso Rinpoche
    (Shambhala, 2003)

Websites—Buddhist Teachings

www.rinpoche.com
> (Kenchen Thrangu Rinpoche books published by
> Namo Buddha)

www.shenpen-osel.org
> (Shenpen Ösel Magazine with teachings by Kagyu
> lineage masters)

www.namsebangdzo.com
> (Buddhist books, tapes, etc.)

www.vajraechoes.com
> (Audio and video recordings of Buddhist teachings)

www.nalandastore.com
> (Buddhist books, recordings, etc.)